INFUSING EQUITY & CULTURAL COMPETENCE

INTO TEACHER DEVELOPMENT

SECOND EDITION

Aaron Thompson

Joseph B. Cuseo

EQUALITY

EQUITY

Kendall Hunt publishing company

www.kendallhunt.com
Send all inquiries to:
4050 Westmark Drive
Dubuque, IA 52004-1840

Copyright © 2012, 2020 by Kendall Hunt Publishing Company

ISBN: 978-1-7924-2407-6

Printed in the United States of America
10   9   8   7   6   5   4   3   2   1

Brief Contents

Chapter 5: The Societal Context for Diversity Education: Family, School, and Community 89

Examines how family, school, and community exert an intersectional influence on students' academic achievement. Specific strategies are suggested for building productive partnerships with parents and for strengthening school-community relations. The chapter documents the pivotal role that teachers and school leaders play in promoting the educational achievement of diverse students. Lastly, practices are identified for creating an inclusive multicultural curriculum and a school climate conducive to culturally competent teaching and educational leadership.

Chapter 6: Student-Centered Teaching, Part I: Culturally Inclusive Strategies for Motivating and Engaging Students with the Subject Matter 117

Supplies a detailed set of student-centered, culturally inclusive teaching strategies for motivating and engaging students with the subject matter. The instructional strategies identified in this chapter elevate the academic achievement of all students but have a particularly positive impact on closing the achievement gap, and give disadvantaged students equal opportunity to participate in and benefit from the classroom learning experience.

Chapter 7: Student-Centered Teaching, Part II: Culturally Inclusive Strategies for Promoting Positive Student-Teacher and Student-Student (Peer-to-Peer) Relationships 139

Provides instructional practices for building teacher-student rapport and for developing positive relationships with students from diverse cultural backgrounds. Specific strategies are supplied for building a sense of community among classmates, designing small-group work that promotes appreciation of both cultural differences and cross-cultural commonalities, and for intentionally forming diverse learning teams to ensure that students experience multicultural perspectives and engage in intercultural teamwork.

Chapter 8: Culturally Inclusive Assessment: Evaluating Student Learning with Equity & Validity 165

Identifies a comprehensive array of practices for evaluating and grading student performance both fairly and accurately. The assessment practices discussed in this chapter also increase students' motivation to learn and strengthen the quality of feedback students receive about their academic performance, which serves to elevate the educational achievement of all students and the achievement of minority students in particular.

Contents

3: Barriers to Diversity Appreciation: Stereotypes, Prejudice, and Discrimination 39

4: Overcoming Bias, Combating Prejudice, and Developing Cultural Competence 65

5: The Societal Context for Diversity Education: Family, School, and Community 89

6: Student-Centered Teaching, Part I: Culturally Inclusive Strategies for Motivating and Engaging Students with the Subject Matter 117

7: Student-Centered Teaching, Part II: Culturally Inclusive Strategies for Promoting Positive Student-Teacher and Student-Student (Peer-to-Peer) Relationships 139

8: Culturally Inclusive Assessment: Evaluating Student Learning with Equity & Validity   165

Focus and Purpose of this Book

Infusing Equity & Cultural Competence into Teacher Development is a book designed to provide future teachers, current teachers, and educational leaders with effective, research-based strategies for delivering culturally competent, responsive, and inclusive instruction. The tools offered in this book serve to close the achievement gap while simultaneously promoting the academic achievement and personal development of all students.

Research demonstrates that one distinguishing feature of effective teachers is that they engage in a continuous process of reflecting on and improving their teaching practices (Darling-Hammond & Bransford, 2005). High-impact, action-oriented teaching practices make up the heart of this book; however, these practices are not presented in the form of a laundry list of teaching "tips." Instead, the book's recommendations are accompanied by a research-based rationale about why they are effective and worthy of implementation. If educators have a deep understanding of the underlying principle that makes a particular instructional strategy effective, they're more likely to put that instructional strategy into practice with their own students.

> "We know that professional development by bullet point does not work because it uncouples practical 'tips' from the principles that enable practitioners to make the tips work in their own setting."
>
> —Viviane Robinson, *Student-Centered Leadership*

Furthermore, when the learning principle behind an effective teaching practice is understood by practitioners, it empowers the practitioner to create additional instructional practices that are consistent with the same principle. Research indicates that instructional development programs are ineffective if teachers are just exposed to instructional tips unaccompanied by supporting empirical and theoretical principles (Robinson, 2011). Research also indicates that high-quality instructional leaders co-construct goals with their staff to provide professional development experiences in which teachers are not only equipped with high-impact practices strategies, but also with evidence that supports the effectiveness of those strategies (DeWitt, 2018; Hattie, 2012).

Because the strategies cited in this book are research-based, references are infused throughout all chapters and a sizable reference section is included at the end of each chapter. The breadth and depth of references cited underscore the fact that multicultural education is a rigorous field of study, and like any other academic discipline, it is built on a solid body of research and scholarship. The practices offered in this book are supported by multiple studies using multiple methodologies. When a variety of studies point to the effectiveness of the same practice, such convergence provides cross-validation, increasing our confidence that the practice is worthy of implementation.

The references cited in this book reflect a balanced blend of older, "classic" studies and more recent "cutting edge" research. The extensive time span of research cited, plus the wide range of fields in which the research has been conducted, suggest that the practices recommended are timeless, are transferable across the curriculum, and are applicable at different levels of education. Some practices may be more easily adopted for students at a certain level of education; however, virtually all of the book's recommendations are adaptable and can be tailored to meet the needs of students at any stage of educational development. The point of this book is not to be prescriptive and suggest that educators conform to a tightly scripted curriculum or a rigid set of pedagogical practices. Instead, the effectiveness of the book's strategies relies ultimately on the insight and diagnostic skill of effective teachers who are able to adapt the suggested strategies to the distinctive characteristics and needs of the students they serve.

Lastly, this book focuses on educational practices for addressing and advancing racial, ethnic (cultural), and socioeconomic forms of student diversity; however, these practices are applicable to other forms of student diversity as well. Teachers and educational leaders should be able to adapt the book's practices to respond effectively to particular forms of diversity found in their school's student population and its surrounding community.

Chapter Organization

Chapter Sequence

The chapters in this book are ordered in a way that asks and answers the following sequence of questions:

1. What is diversity?
2. Why is diversity important?
3. How can barriers to diversity appreciation be understood and overcome?
4. How can multicultural education be delivered to maximize the power of diversity and close the achievement gap?

The first four chapters focus on diversity per se—describing it, articulating its benefits, identifying obstacles to diversity appreciation, and supplying strategies for overcoming these obstacles. The last four chapters focus specifically on diversity education—the roles of home, community, and school, and the use of culturally inclusive teaching and assessment practices.

Process and Style of Presentation

The educational impact of any book depends both on the quality of information it contains (content) and on how that information is delivered (process). The information-delivery process in this book is infused with effective teaching-and-learning features designed to: (a) stimulate motivation to read, (b) deepen understanding of what is being read, and (c) strengthen retention (memory) of what has been read. These features are described next.

Chapter Purpose & Preview

At the start of each chapter, a short summary of the chapter's primary purpose and essential content is provided to supply readers with an overview and preview of what they are about to read. This feature provides readers with a (and motivation) to read the chapter and a sense of direction. Educational research has repeatedly shown that when learners see the reason or relevance of what they are expected to learn, their motivation to learn increases and they learn more deeply (Yeager et al., 2014).

Authors' Experiences

Relevant personal stories drawn from the authors' experiences appear throughout the book. Studies show that when concepts being taught are illustrated by storytelling, the learner's comprehension and retention of those concepts are strengthened (McDrury & Alterio, 2002). We share our stories with the intent of both personalizing the book and enabling the reader to learn from our experiences, both from our success stories and the mistakes we made.

Sidebar Quotes

In the book's side margins, quotes from researchers and practitioners appear that relate to and reinforce the ideas just discussed in the chapter. The cultural and historical diversity of the people quoted throughout the book suggests that their words of wisdom are universal and timeless, and both serve as a source of inspiration and a resource for learning.

Internet Resources

At the conclusion of each chapter, websites are recommended where additional information relating to the chapter's major ideas can be found. If the chapter ignites the reader's interest in the topic, these current online resources can be used by the reader to take a deeper dive into the chapter's content.

Reflections & Applications

Reflective exercises are included at the end of each chapter that prompt deeper thought about the chapter's key concepts and apply them to the reader's personal and professional life. Acquiring knowledge is just the first step to effective performance. Knowledge acquisition needs to be followed by knowledge *application*—taking the knowledge acquired and putting it into actual practice. When we move beyond acquiring knowledge to applying our knowledge effectively and altruistically, we exhibit *wisdom* (Staudinger, 2008).

The end-of-chapter reflective exercises also require the reader to respond in *writing* to the chapter's concepts. Writing promotes active involvement in the reading process and serves to deepen learning for and strengthen retention of what has been read (Sorcinelli & Elbow, 1997).

We sincerely hope that the ideas contained in this book, and the manner in which they are delivered, will enhance your appreciation of diversity and your ability to provide powerful multicultural educational experiences for the students you serve.

Sincerely,
Aaron Thompson & Joe Cuseo

About the Authors

Aaron Thompson, PhD is a nationally recognized leader in higher education with a focus on policy, student success, and organizational leadership and design. He currently serves as the President of the Council on Postsecondary Education in Kentucky and holds the title of Professor Emeritus in Educational Leadership and Policy Studies at Eastern Kentucky University. He has served in many faculty and higher education administrative capacities, such as Interim President of Kentucky State University, Executive Vice-President and Chief Academic Officer, Vice President of Academic Affairs, Associate VP for University Programs, Associate VP for Enrollment Management, and Executive Director of the Student Success Institute, to mention several. Many of these roles were served at Eastern Kentucky University, where he also held the position of tenured full professor.

His leadership experience spans 29 years across higher education, business, and numerous nonprofit boards. Throughout his career, Thompson has researched, taught, and consulted in areas of diversity, leadership, ethics, teacher education, educational leadership, multicultural families, race and ethnic relations, student success, first-year students, retention, cultural competence, and organizational design.

As a highly sought after national speaker, Thompson has presented more than 800 workshops, seminars, and invited lectures in areas of race and gender diversity, living an unbiased life, overcoming obstacles to gain success, creating a school environment for academic success, cultural competence, workplace interaction, leadership, organizational goal setting, building relationships, the first-year seminar, and a variety of other topics. He continues to serve as a consultant to educational institutions (elementary, secondary, and postsecondary), corporations, nonprofit organizations, police departments, and other governmental agencies. Dr. Thompson has accumulated many awards for his service, including being inducted into the Kentucky Civil Rights Hall of Fame.

Thompson has more than 30 publications and numerous research and peer-reviewed presentations. He has authored or co-authored the following books: *The Sociological Outlook, Infusing Diversity and Cultural Competence into Teacher Education,* and *Peer to Peer Leadership: Research-Based Strategies for Peer Mentors and Peer Educators.* He also co-authored *Thriving in College and Beyond: Research-Based Strategies for Academic Success, Thriving in the Community College and Beyond: Strategies for Academic Success and Personal Development, Thriving in High School & Beyond: Strategies for Academic Success and Personal Development Diversity and the College Experience, Focus on Success* and *Black Men and Divorce.*

Joe Cuseo holds a doctoral degree in Educational Psychology and Assessment from the University of Iowa and is Professor Emeritus of Psychology. For more than 25 years, he directed the first-year seminar—a core college success course required of all new students.

He's a 14-time recipient of the "faculty member of the year award" on his home campus—a student-driven award based on effective teaching and academic advising; a recipient of the "Outstanding First-Year Student Advocate Award" from the National Resource Center for The First-Year Experience and Students in Transition; and a recipient of the "Diamond Honoree Award" from the American College Personnel Association (ACPA) for contributions made to student development and the Student Affairs profession.

Most recently, Joe has served as an educational advisor and consultant for AVID—a nonprofit organization whose mission is to promote the college access and college success of underserved student populations. He has delivered hundreds of campus workshops and conference presentations across North America, as well as Europe, Asia, Australia, and the Middle East.

References

Darling-Hammond, L., & Bransford, J. (2005). *Preparing teachers for a changing world: What teachers should learn and be able to do.* San Francisco: Jossey-Bass.

DeWitt, P. M. (2018). *School climate: Leading with collective efficacy.* Thousand Oaks: Corwin.

Hattie, J. (2012). *Visible learning for teachers: Maximizing impact on learning.* London: Routledge.

McDrury, J., and Alterio, M. G. (2002). *Learning through storytelling: Using reflection and experience in higher education contexts.* Palmerston North, New Zealand: Dunmore Press.

Robinson, V. (2011). *Student-centered leadership.* San Francisco: Jossey-Bass.

Sorcinelli, M. D., & Elbow, P. (1997). *Writing to learn: Assigning and responding to learn across the curriculum.* New Directions for Teaching and Learning, No. 69. San Francisco: Jossey Bass

Staudinger, U. M. (2008). A psychology of wisdom: History and recent developments. *Research in Human Development, 5,* 107–120.

Yeager, S. S., Henderson, M. D., D'Mello, S., Paunesku, D., Walton, W. M., Spitzer, B. J., & Duckworth, A. L. (2014). *Boring but important: A self-transcendent purpose for learning fosters academic self-regulation. Journal of Personal and Social Psychology, 107*(4), 559–580.

What is Diversity?

Chapter Purpose and Preview

This chapter defines diversity, delineates its key forms or dimensions, and describes its relationship to humanity and individuality. Race, ethnicity, culture, and social class are also defined and distinguished. The chapter then documents the growing racial and ethnic diversity in America, the challenges associated with closing the achievement gap for low-income students and students of color, and the benefits of closing the gap for these students, their future families, and America's future.

Diversity: Definition and Description

Literally translated, the word *diversity* derives from the Latin *diversus*, meaning "various" or "variety." Thus, *human diversity* may be defined as the variety of differences among different groups of people that comprise humanity (the human species). The relationship between humanity and diversity may be likened to the relationship between sunlight and the variety of colors that make up the visual spectrum. Similar to how sunlight passing through a prism disperses into a variety of colors that comprise the visual spectrum, the human species residing on planet Earth disperses into different groups that comprise the human spectrum (humanity). This metaphorical relationship between diversity and humanity is illustrated in **Figure 1.1.** As depicted in the figure, human diversity manifests itself in a multiplicity of ways, including differences among human groups in terms of their national origins, cultural backgrounds, physical characteristics, sexual orientations, and sexual identities. Some dimensions of diversity are easily detectable, some are delicately subtle, and others are invisible.

Diversity is a topic that addresses issues relating to equal rights and social justice for minority groups. However, diversity is not just a political or social justice issue that pertains exclusively to certain groups of people. Diversity is also an *educational* issue—an integral element of the school experience that enhances the learning, development, and career preparation of *all* students (Banks, 2016; May, 2012). Diversity enriches the quality of students' educational experience by exposing them to multiple perspectives and different approaches to *what* is being learned (the content) and *how* it is being learned (the process).

> "We are all brothers and sisters. Each face in the rainbow of color that populates our world is precious and special. Each adds to the rich treasure of humanity."
>
> —Morris Dees, civil rights leader and co-founder of the Southern Poverty Law Center

> "Ethnic and cultural diversity is an integral, natural, and normal component of educational experiences for all students."
>
> —National Council for Social Studies

Figure 1.1

Humanity and Diversity

_____ = dimension of diversity

*This list represents some of the major dimensions of human diversity; it does not constitute a complete list of all possible forms of human diversity. Also, disagreement exists about certain dimensions of diversity (for example., whether certain groups should be considered races or ethnic groups).

© KendallHunt Publishing Company

Spectrum of Diversity

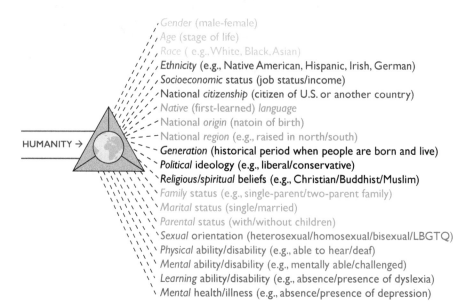

HUMANITY →

Gender (male-female)
Age (stage of life)
Race (e.g., White, Black, Asian)
Ethnicity (e.g., Native American, Hispanic, Irish, German)
Socioeconomic status (job status/income)
National citizenship (citizen of U.S. or another country)
Native (first-learned) *language*
National origin (natoin of birth)
National region (e.g., raised in north/south)
Generation (historical period when people are born and live)
Political ideology (e.g., liberal/conservative)
Religious/spiritual beliefs (e.g., Christian/Buddhist/Muslim)
Family status (e.g., single-parent/two-parent family)
Marital status (single/married)
Parental status (with/without children)
Sexual orientation (heterosexual/homosexual/bisexual/LBGTQ)
Physical ability/disability (e.g., able to hear/deaf)
Mental ability/disability (e.g., mentally able/challenged)
Learning ability/disability (e.g., absence/presence of dyslexia)
Mental health/illness (e.g., absence/presence of depression)

Consider this . . .

Diversity is a human issue that embraces and benefits all people; it's not a code word for "some" people. Although a major goal of diversity is to promote appreciation and equitable treatment of particular groups of people who have experienced and continue to experience prejudice and discrimination, it's also a learning experience that enhances all students' education, civic and career preparation, and leadership potential.
(For specific details about these benefits of diversity, see chapter 2.)

"We all live with the objective of being happy; our lives are all different and yet the same."

—Anne Frank, victim of the Holocaust and renowned author of *Anne Frank: The Diary of a Young Girl*, written from age 13–15 while hiding with her family from the Nazis

"Diversity is a value that is shown in mutual respect and appreciation of similarities and differences."

—Public Service Enterprise Group

Diversity and Humanity

Diversity and humanity are interdependent, complementary concepts. Diversity represents the variation on the same theme that unites all humans: humanity. To understand human diversity is to understand both our differences *and* our similarities. To appreciate diversity is to appreciate the unique experiences of different groups of humans as well as the common (universal) experiences shared by all humans. Members of different ethnic and racial groups may have distinctive cultural or physical characteristics, but members of all ethnic and racial groups live in communities, develop interpersonal relationships, and undergo life experiences that shape their personal identity.

Furthermore, all human groups have the same, basic human needs—such as those identified by psychologist Abraham Maslow in his famous hierarchy of human needs (see **Figure 1.2**).

Humans of all races and all cultures also experience similar emotions and express those emotions facially in a similar way (see **Figure 1.3**).

2 *What is Diversity?*

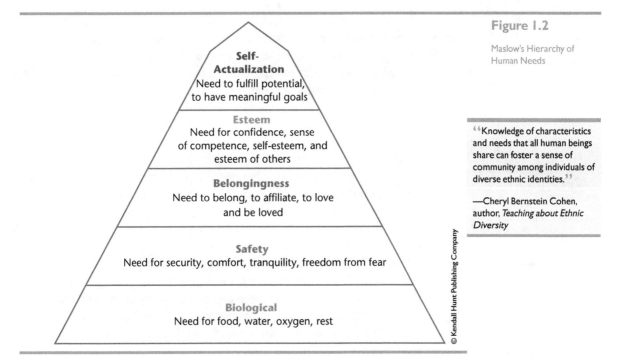

© Kendall Hunt Publishing Company

Figure 1.2

Maslow's Hierarchy of Human Needs

> "Knowledge of characteristics and needs that all human beings share can foster a sense of community among individuals of diverse ethnic identities."
>
> —Cheryl Bernstein Cohen, author, *Teaching about Ethnic Diversity*

Figure 1.3

Humans all over the world display similar facial expressions when they experience and express certain emotions. See if you can detect the universal emotions being expressed by the following faces of people from very different cultural backgrounds. (To find the answers, turn your book upside down.)

Answers: The emotions expressed by the top three faces (left to right): anger, fear, and sadness. The bottom three faces (left to right) express the following emotions: disgust, happiness, and surprise.

Anthropologists have also found that all groups of humans in every corner of the world share the following characteristics: storytelling, dance, music, decorating, adorning the body, socialization of children by elders, moral codes of conduct, supernatural beliefs, and mourning the dead (Pinker, 2000). Although different cultural groups may express these experiences in distinctive ways, these are universal experiences shared by all cultural groups.

You may have heard the question: "We're all human, aren't we?" The answer to this question is "yes and no." Yes, all humans are the same, but not in the same way. A metaphor for making sense of this apparent contradiction is picturing humanity as a quilt composed of different patches (representing multiple cultural groups) that are woven together with a common thread: their shared humanity. (See picture below.) The quilt metaphor acknowledges the identity and beauty of all cultures; at the same time, it illustrates how multicultural differences interweave to form a larger, unified tapestry. Despite the fact that these cultures are different, they come together to form a seamless, integrated whole. This is illustrated in the experiences of the earliest English immigrants to the United States, who depended heavily on Native Americans for their survival (e.g., Native farming methods and tools) and integrated components of Native American culture into the British culture they brought with them to America (Weatherford, 1991).

The quilt metaphor contrasts sharply with the old American "melting pot" metaphor, which viewed cultural differences in America as something to be melted away (eliminated) and assimilated (Cubberley, 1909). The quilt metaphor also differs from the "salad bowl" metaphor that depicted America as a hodgepodge or mishmash of cultures thrown together without any common connection (Bourne, 1916; Drachsler, 1920). In contrast, the quilt metaphor suggests that the cultures of different human groups should be preserved and recognized, yet remain unified.

According to Banks (2016), a multiculturalist "sees neither separatism (as the pluralist does) nor total integration (as the assimilationist does) to be the ideal societal goal, but envisions an open society in which individuals … can participate fully in the society while preserving their distinct ethnic and cultural traits and are able to freely initiate contacts with individuals from diverse

"We are all the same, and we are all unique."

—Georgia Dunston, African-American biologist and research specialist in human genetics

"Unity without diversity results in cultural repression and hegemony. Diversity without unity leads to ethnic and cultural separatism and the fracturing of the nation-state."

—James Banks, Founding Director for the Center of Multicultural Education, University of Washington

"We have become not a melting pot but a beautiful mosaic."

—Jimmy Carter, 39th president of the United States and winner of the Nobel Peace Prize

© steven r.hendricks/Shutterstock.com

racial, ethnic, cultural, and religious groups" (p. 127). This blending of diversity and unity is captured in the Latin expression *E pluribus unum* ("Out of many, one")—the motto of the United States. When students experience a multicultural education grounded in the context of national unity, America's noble motto is put into educational practice (National Council for the Social Sciences, 1991).

AUTHOR'S EXPERIENCE

I was a 12-year-old boy, living in New York City, when I returned home after school one Friday. My mother asked me if anything interesting happened in class that day. I told her that the teacher went around the room asking students what they had for dinner the night before. At that moment, my mother stopped what she was doing and nervously asked me: "What did you tell the teacher?" I said: "I told her and the rest of the class that I had pasta last night because my family always eats pasta on Thursdays and Sundays." My mother became very agitated and fired the following question back at me in an annoyed tone: "Why didn't you tell her we had steak or roast beef?" I was surprised and confused because I didn't understand what I had done wrong, or why I should have hidden the fact that we had eaten pasta. Then it dawned on me: My mom was embarrassed about being an Italian-American. She wanted me to conceal our family's ethnic background and make us sound more "American."

As I grew older, I understood why my mother felt the way she did. She was raised in America's "melting pot" generation—a time when different American ethnic groups were expected to melt down and melt away their ethnicity. They were not to celebrate diversity; they were to eliminate it.

Joe Cuseo

When different human groups are appreciated for both their diversity and their unity, their separate cultural streams converge and merge into a single river, harnessing the collective power of humanity.

Diversity and Individuality

All humans are unique. Just as no two snowflakes are exactly alike and no two zebras have the same pattern of stripes, each human being is a unique individual. When discussing human diversity, it's important to keep in mind that individual differences among members of the same racial or ethnic group are greater than average differences between groups. For instance, differences among individuals of the same race in terms of physical characteristics (e.g., height and weight) and psychological characteristics (e.g., temperament and personality) are greater than the average difference between their racial group and other racial groups (Caplan & Caplan, 2016).

Although it is valuable to learn about group differences, the substantial differences that exist among individuals within the same group should neither be overlooked nor underestimated. It shouldn't be assumed that individuals who are members of the same race or share the same culture also share similar personal characteristics. The tendency for people to assume that a particular person possesses the general characteristics associated with that person's cultural group is referred to by diversity scholars as "essentializing" (Smith, 2015).

"Most variation is within, not between, 'races.' That means two random Koreans may be as genetically different as a Korean and an Italian."

—California Newsreel, *Race—The Power of an Illusion*

"I realize that I'm black, but I like to be viewed as a person, and this is everybody's wish."

—Michael Jordan, Hall of Fame basketball player

Educators experiencing diversity in their personal lives and promoting diversity in their educational practices should keep the following key distinctions in mind:

▶ **Humanity.** All humans are members of the *same group*—the human species.

▶ **Diversity.** All humans are members of *different groups*—for example, different ethnic, racial, and national groups.

▶ **Individuality.** Each human is a *unique individual* who differs from all other members of any group(s) in which he or she shares membership.

Forms and Varieties of Diversity

Cultural Diversity

Culture refers to the distinctive pattern of beliefs and values learned by a group of people who share the same social heritage and traditions. In short, culture is the whole way in which a group of people has learned to live (Peoples & Bailey, 2011). It includes their style of speaking (language), fashion, food, art, and music, as well as their beliefs and values. **Box 1.1** summarizes the key components of culture typically shared by members of the same cultural group. Some of these cultural components represent internally held beliefs, values, and world views; these are as important to understand and appreciate as a culture's music, fashion, and cuisine (National Council on Social Sciences, 1991; Valenzuela, 1999).

PERSONAL INSIGHT

I was once watching a basketball game between the Los Angeles Lakers and Los Angeles Clippers. During the game, a short scuffle broke out between two members of the opposing teams: the Lakers' Pau Gasol—who is from Spain—and the Clippers' Chris Paul—who is African American. After the scuffle ended, Gasol tried to show Paul there were no hard feelings by patting him on the head. Instead of interpreting Gasol's head pat as a peacemaking gesture, Paul took it as a putdown and returned the favor by slapping (rather than patting) Gasol in the head.

This head-patting, head-slapping misunderstanding stemmed from a basic difference in nonverbal communication between two players from two different cultures. Patting someone on the head in European cultures is a friendly gesture; European soccer players often do it to an opposing player to express no ill will after a foul or collision. However, this same nonverbal message had a very different cultural meaning something to Chris Paul—an African American raised in urban America.

Joe Cuseo

Although the terms "culture" and "society" are often used interchangeably, they are not synonymous. Each of these terms refers to a different aspect of humanity. Society is a group of people organized under the same social system. For example, all members of American society are organized under the same system of government, justice, and education. In contrast, culture is what a certain group of people share with respect to its past traditions and current

Box 1.1 Key Components of Culture

▶ **Language:** How members of the culture communicate through written or spoken words, including their particular dialect and their distinctive style of nonverbal communication (body language).

▶ **Use of Physical Space:** How cultural members arrange themselves with respect to social-spatial distance (e.g., how closely they stand next to each other when having a conversation).

▶ **Use of Time:** How the culture conceives of, divides up, and uses time (e.g., the speed or pace at which cultural members conduct business).

▶ **Aesthetics:** How cultural members appreciate and express artistic beauty and creativity (e.g., their style of visual art, culinary art, music, theater, literature, and dance).

▶ **Family:** The culture's attitudes and habits with respect to family interactions (e.g., customary styles of parenting children and caring for the elderly).

▶ **Economics:** How the culture meets its members' material needs, and the customary ways in which wealth is acquired and distributed (e.g., its overall level of wealth and the wealth gap between cultural members who are very wealthy and very poor).

▶ **Gender Roles:** The culture's expectations for "appropriate" male and female behavior (e.g., how men and women are expected to dress and whether or not women are allowed to hold the same occupational positions as men).

▶ **Politics:** How decision-making power is exercised in the culture (e.g., democratically or autocratically).

▶ **Science and Technology:** The culture's attitude toward, and use of, science and technology (e.g., the degree to which the culture is technologically "advanced").

▶ **Philosophy:** The culture's ideas and views about wisdom, goodness, truth, and social values (e.g., whether its members place greater value on individual competition or collective collaboration).

▶ **Spirituality and Religion:** Cultural beliefs about the existence of a supreme being and an afterlife (e.g., its members' predominant faith and belief systems about the supernatural).

ways of living, regardless of the particular society or social system in which are living (Nicholas, 1991). Thus, cultural differences can exist within the same society, resulting a "multicultural" society.

Culture serves the positive purpose of helping to bind its members into a supportive, tight-knit community. However, culture not only can bind its members, it can also blind them from taking the perspectives of other cultures. Since culture shapes thought and perception, people from the same cultural (ethnic) group run the risk of becoming *ethnocentric*—centered so much on their own culture that they perceive the world solely through one cultural lens and fail to consider or appreciate other cultural viewpoints (Colombo, Cullen, & Lisle, 2016).

Optical illusions are a good example of how strongly our particular cultural perspective can limit our perceptions and contribute to misperceptions. Compare the lengths of the two lines depicted in **Figure 1.4**.

Figure 1.4

Optical Illusion

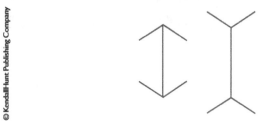

Both lines are actually equal in length. (If you don't believe it, take out a ruler and measure them.) If you misperceived the line on the right to be longer than the line on the left, it's because your perception has been shaped by your cultural background. This optical illusion is experienced only by people in Western cultures (e.g., Americans and Europeans) whose living spaces consist primarily of rectangular-shaped buildings and angled corners. The illusion isn't experienced by people living in non-Western cultures whose living spaces are predominantly circular—e.g., huts or igloos (Segall, Campbell, & Herskovits, 1966).

The optical illusion depicted in Figure 1.4 is just one of many illusions that people experience in some cultures but not others (Shiraev & Levy, 2017). Cross-cultural differences in susceptibility to optical illusions illustrate how strongly our cultural experiences can influence and sometimes misinform our perception of reality. People think they're seeing things objectively (as they actually are), but their viewpoint is actually subjective (as seen from a perspective shaped by their particular cultural background).

If our cultural experiences can shape our perception of the physical world, they can certainly shape our perception of the social world. Research in social psychology reveals that the more exposure people have to something or somebody, not only does that thing or person become more familiar to them, the more likely they are to be perceived positively and judged favorably. This phenomenon is so prevalent and powerful that social psychologists have come to

People whose cultural experiences involve living and working in circular structures are not deceived by the optical illusion in Figure 1.4.

call it the "familiarity principle"—the more familiar something is, the more favorable or likeable it is perceived to be (Zajonc, 1968, 1970, 2001). One consequence of the familiarity principle is that familiar cultural experiences can bias its cultural members to view their culture as better or more "normal" and acceptable than others. By resisting this tendency and remaining open to the viewpoints of people from other culture (who view the world from different vantage points than our own), we can uncover our cultural blind spots, expand our range of perception, and put ourselves in a position to view the world with greater objectivity and cultural sensitivity.

Multicultural education views cultural differences much differently than the old "cultural deficit" model that considered the cultures of minority and low-income students to be deficient and saw the purpose of education as remedy these deficiencies by replacing them with the mainstream (majority) American culture. In contrast to the cultural *deficit* model, multicultural education is a cultural *difference* model that acknowledges rather than ignores the variety of cultures present in the classroom, including those of minority students, and capitalizes on these cultural differences to enrich the education of all students (Banks, 2016).

Racial Diversity

A *racial group (race)* is a group of people who share distinctive physical traits—most notably, skin color. The variation in skin color we see among different human groups today is largely due to biological adaptations that have evolved over thousands of years, beginning when humans first started to migrate to different climatic regions of the world. Currently, the most widely accepted explanation for racial differences in skin color is the "Out of Africa" theory. Genetic studies and fossil evidence indicate that all *Homo sapiens* inhabited Africa 150,000–250,000 years ago; over the course of time, some migrated from Africa to other parts of the world (Mendez et al., 2013; Meredith, 2011; Reid & Hetherington, 2010). Those who lived and reproduced in hotter regions of the world nearer the equator (e.g., Africa and South America) developed darker skin color, which enabled them to better adapt and survive because it provided them with better protection from the potentially damaging effects of intense sunlight (Bridgeman, 2003). In contrast, lighter skin tones emerged over time among humans inhabiting colder climates farther from the equator (e.g., Central and Northern Europe). Their lighter skin color contributed to their survival by enabling them to absorb greater amounts of vitamin D from the less direct and intense sunlight they received in their region of the world (Jablonksi & Chaplin, 2002).

Consider this ...

The term "Caucasian" was coined by a German anthropologist who discovered a female human skull in the Caucasus Mountains, a region of Russia. The anthropologist thought that the skull he discovered was "handsome and becoming," and assumed it was associated with a white person. He then concluded (erroneously) that the Caucasus Mountains must be the birthplace of the white race.

"The story of our current usage of Caucasian is one of myth living on in defiance of science. Using the term Caucasian is no more scientific than, say, calling people of short stature Hobbits—another fictional race with European origins."

—Joe Dinerstein, Professor, Tulane University

The U.S. Census Bureau categorizes humans into five racial categories (U.S Census Bureau, 2018a):

▶ **White:** people whose lineage may be traced to the original humans inhabiting Europe, the Middle East, or North Africa.
▶ **Black or African American:** people whose lineage may be traced to the original humans inhabiting Africa.
▶ **American Indian and Alaska Native:** people whose lineage may be traced to the original humans inhabiting North and South America (including Central America), and who continue to maintain their tribal affiliation or attachment.
▶ **Asian:** people whose lineage may be traced to the original humans inhabiting the Far East, Southeast Asia, or the Indian subcontinent, including Cambodia, China, India, Japan, Korea, Malaysia, Pakistan, the Philippine Islands, Thailand, and Vietnam.
▶ **Native Hawaiian and Other Pacific Islander:** people whose lineage may be traced to the original humans inhabiting Hawaii, Guam, Samoa, and other Pacific Islands.

Attempting to categorize people into distinct racial groups has always been difficult, but it is more difficult today than at any other time in history because of the growing number of interracial families. The number of Americans who identify themselves as being of two or more races is projected to be the fastest growing racial group category over the next several decade; by 2050, it is expected to more than triple, growing to 26.7 million (U.S. Census Bureau (2013, 2018b).

PERSONAL INSIGHT

As the child of a black man and a white woman, and as someone born in the racial melting pot of Hawaii, with a sister who's half Indonesian but who's usually mistaken for Mexican or Puerto Rican, and a brother-in-law and niece of Chinese descent, with some blood relatives who resemble Margaret Thatcher and others who could pass for Bernie Mac, family get-togethers over Christmas take on the appearance of a UN General Assembly meeting. I've never had the option of restricting my loyalties on the basis of race, or measuring my worth on the basis of tribe.

Barack Obama, 44th president of the United States

It's important to keep in mind that racial categories are social classifications that humans have decided to create or construct—in other words, race is a *socially constructed* concept (Anderson & Fienberg, 2000). "Races" are merely categories that societies have elected to build based on how humans differ with respect to certain physical characteristics, particularly the color or shade of their outer layer of skin (Jacobson, 1998). Although skin color has been used as the basis for creating these social categories (and for treating people differently on the basis of these categories), humans could just as easily have been categorized on the basis of eye color (blue, brown, and green), hair color (brown, black, blonde, or red), or body size (tall, short, or mid-sized).

I was sitting in a coffee shop in Chicago O'Hare airport while proofreading my first draft of this chapter. I looked up from my work for a moment and saw what appeared to be a white girl about 18 years of age. As I lowered my head to return to work, I did a double-take and looked at her again, because something about her physical appearance seemed different or unusual. When I looked more closely at her the second time, I noticed that although she had white skin, the features of her face and hair appeared to be those of an African American. After a couple of seconds of puzzlement, I figured it out: she was an *albino* African American. That satisfied my curiosity for the moment, but then I began to wonder: Would it still be accurate to say she was "black" even though her skin was not black? Would her hair and facial features be sufficient for her to be considered or classified as black? If yes, then what would be the "race" of someone who had black skin tone, but did not have the hair and facial features characteristic of black people? Is skin color the defining feature of being African American or are other features equally important?

Joe Cuseo

My father stood approximately six feet tall and had straight, light brown hair. His skin color was that of a Western European with a very slight suntan. My mother was from Alabama; she was dark in skin color with high cheekbones and had long curly black hair. In fact, if you didn't know that my father was of African American descent, you would not think he was black.

All my life, I've thought of myself as African American, and all people who know me think of me as being African American. I've lived more than half a century with that as my racial identity. Several years ago, I carefully reviewed records of births and deaths in my family history and discovered that I had less than 50% African lineage. Biologically, I can no longer call myself black; socially and emotionally, I still am. Clearly, my "race" has been socially constructed, not biologically determined.

Aaron Thompson

No identifiable set of genes distinguishes one race from another; in fact, there continues to be disagreement among scholars about what groups of people constitute a human race or whether distinctive races actually exist (Wheelright, 2005). No blood test or any other type of biological test can be conducted on a person that will immediately and accurately indicate that person's racial category. In fact, racial categories have changed over time. When darker-skinned White immigrants first came to America in the mid-1800s from Eastern and Southern Europe in (e.g., Hungarians, Jews, Greeks and Italians), an anti-immigration movement arose called *nativism* (Bennett, 1988) that led to categorizing these new immigrants as "non-White" by Western Europeans (e.g., English and Scottish) who were already in the U.S. and were socially dominant (Martin, 2011). Eventually, Eastern and Southern European immigrants began to refer to themselves as "White" as they moved up to higher levels of socioeconomic and political status (Roediger, in Feagin & Feagin, 2011). Such racist views of immigrants and resistance to their assimilation have persisted throughout American history (Giroux, 1998; Moghaddam, 2008).

Although the color of humans' external layer of skin may be dissimilar, all members of the human species are remarkably similar at an internal,

> "Biologically, race is an illusion Sociologically, it is a pervasive phenomenon."
>
> —Jane Fried, Professor of Counseling and Student Development

biological level. More than 98 percent of the genes found in humans are exactly the same, regardless of what their particular racial category may be (Bronfenbrenner, 2005). This large amount of genetic overlap among us accounts for the fact that humans are clearly distinguishable from all other animal species. The tremendous amount of genetic overlap among humans also explains why our internal body parts look the same and whatever the color of our outer layer of skin may be, when it's cut, we all bleed in the same color. Differences between human races in their external appearance are superficial and easily detectable; commonalities across races in their internal biological makeup are less obvious and often more meaningful.

> **Consider this . . .**
>
> After initially banning African American blood donations, the American Red Cross eventually admitted in 1942 that blood donated by Blacks was acceptable for transfusion into White bodies. This change in policy enabled the Red Cross to overcome its blood shortage during World War II and save the lives of wounded White soldiers.

Ethnic Diversity

An *ethnic group* refers to a group of people who share the same culture. Thus, "culture" is *what* members of an ethnic group have in common (e.g., common language and traditions) and "ethnic group" refers to a group of *people* who share the same cultural characteristics—which are acquired (learned) through shared social experiences. Members of different ethnic groups can be members of the same racial group, whose shared physical characteristics have been *inherited*. For example, White Americans constitute the same racial group, but are members of different ethnic groups (e.g., French, German, Irish). Similarly, Asian Americans constitute the same racial group, but are members of different ethnic groups (e.g., Japanese, Chinese, Korean). European Americans are still the majority ethnic group in the United States; they account for more than 50 percent of the American population (U.S. Census Bureau, 2015).

Members of White ethnic groups have the option of choosing whether they want to identify with and reveal their ethnic identity to the dominant culture because their ethnicity cannot be easily inferred from the color of their skin. As a result, ethnic minority groups of European ancestry (e.g., Armenians and Croatians) can more easily "blend into" and assimilate into the majority (dominant) culture because their skin color (white) is like that of the majority group. In fact, many White immigrants of Eastern and Southern European ancestry attempted to further ease their assimilation into American culture by changing their last names to appear to be Americans of Western European descent—as illustrated by the personal experience shared below. In contrast, the minority status of African Americans, or darker-skinned Hispanics and Native Americans, doesn't allow them the option of presenting themselves as members of an already-assimilated majority group (National Council for the Social Sciences, 1991).

My grandparents changed their name from the very Italian-sounding "DeVigilio" to the more American-sounding "Vigilis," and my mother had her first name changed from the Italian-sounding Carmella to Mildred. Similarly, my father's first name was changed from Biaggio to Blase; my father also chose to list his first name (Blase), not his last name (Cuseo), on the sign outside his watch-repair office in New York City because he thought that would conceal his Italian ethnicity and increase the likelihood that people would not discriminate against him and bring their business elsewhere.

Thus, my parents were able to minimize their risk of appearing "different" and encountering prejudice, while maximizing their chances of being accepted and assimilated into the dominant American culture. If my parents were members of a non-White ethnic group, they would not have been able to "hide" their ethnicity and reduce their risk of encountering prejudice or discrimination. I learned later that some Jewish Americans used the same name-changing strategies as did my parents and grandparents. For example, the parents of my favorite guitarist, Peter Green, changed their last name from Greenbaum to Green to avoid being victims of anti-Semitism.

Joe Cuseo

As with categorizing people into racial groups, classifying humans into ethnic groups is often subject to different, socially constructed interpretations (or misinterpretations). Currently, the U.S. Census Bureau classifies Americans into three racial categories: White, Black, and Asian. Hispanics are considered to be an ethnic group and member of the White race. However, when Hispanics complete national census surveys and see these three racial categories listed, the overwhelming majority of them check the box "some other race." For example, 97 percent of Americans who checked this box in the 2000 national census survey were Hispanic. This finding suggests that Hispanic Americans do not view themselves as an ethnic group, but as a racial group, likely because they feel their ethnicity is often clearly visible to others and influences how others perceive and treat them (Cianciotto, 2005). Supporting their viewpoint was the use of the term "racial profiling" by American media to describe Arizona's controversial 2010 law that allowed police to target people who "look" like illegal aliens from Mexico, Central America, or South America. This example illustrates again how race and ethnicity are subjective, socially constructed concepts that depend on how society decides to perceive and treat certain social groups, which, in turn, affects how members of these groups perceive themselves.

"I'm the only person from my 'race' in class."

—Hispanic student commenting on why he felt uncomfortable being the only Latino in his class on Race, Ethnicity, & Gender

America's Growing Racial and Ethnic Diversity

In 2011, for the first time in history, more than half (50.4%) of all children born in the United States were members of racial and ethnic minority groups. Racial and ethnic minorities now account for more than 45 percent of the total American population—an all-time high (Brookings Institution, 2019). By the middle of the 21st century, minority groups are projected to comprise 57% of the American population and more than 60% of American children (U.S. Census Bureau, 2015). This diversity within America's native-born population is accompanied by its rich diversity of immigrants. The U.S. is home to more immigrants than any other nation in the world; about 1 in 4 people living in America today is foreign born or the child of immigrants

("Immigrants from 1776 Onward," 2019). At the turn of the 21st century, over 80% of U.S. immigrants were non-European and non-White (Camorata, 2012).

There is also more student diversity in America's schools today than at any other time in U.S. history, and our schools will continue to grow more diverse. By 2021, it's projected that students of color will comprise 52% of America's K–12 system (U.S. Department of Education, 2013). This projection is particularly noteworthy when viewed in light of the educational history of racial and ethnic minority groups in the United States. In the early 19th century, education was not a right, but a privilege granted only to Americans who could afford to attend private schools. That privilege was reserved largely for Protestants of European descent. Later, White immigrants from other national and religious backgrounds began migrating to America. Private education then became mandatory public education—one goal of which was to acculturate or "Americanize" these new immigrants and obliterate their former cultural identities (Luhman, 2007).

In many U.S. states, Americans of color were left out of the educational process altogether or were educated in separate, racially segregated schools with inferior educational facilities. The groundbreaking Supreme Court case in 1954 (*Brown v. Board of Education*) changed the face of public education in America when the Court ruled that "separate educational facilities are inherently unequal." That judicial decision made it illegal for Kansas and 20 other states to deliver education to African Americans in segregated classrooms. As important as the *Brown v. Board of Education* ruling was, an often overlooked earlier development in the historical quest for equal educational opportunity in America took place in 1947, when a California judge ruled in the case of *Mendez v. Westminster* that the segregation of Mexican American school children was unconstitutional. The *Mendez* case was critical to the legal arguments used in the *Brown* case and illustrates how equity struggles of different minority groups have intersected to dismantle segregation and promote equal educational opportunity for students of all colors (Blanco, 2010).

America's historic attempts to ensure equal educational opportunity for its citizens, coupled with the changing demographics of its population, make it paramount that its school system educates students from all cultural backgrounds equally and effectively. This is an ongoing challenge because there has been, and continues to be, a longstanding gap between the academic achievement of White students and students of color. Research conducted by the National Assessment of Educational Progress (NAEP) (2019) has revealed significant gaps between White students and students of color in reading and math achievement scores at the fourth-grade, eighth-grade and twelfth-grade levels. These gaps have remained stubbornly in place since 1992 (NAEP, 2015a; 2015b).

"Of all the civil rights for which the world has struggled and fought for 5,000 years, the right to learn is undoubtedly the most fundamental."

—W. E. B. DuBois, African American sociologist, historian, and civil rights activist

Socioeconomic Diversity

In addition to racial and ethnic diversity, diversity exists among different human groups in terms of socioeconomic status (SES)—a measure of their level of education, level of income, and the occupational prestige of the jobs they hold (American Psychological Association, 2019).

Human societies are typically stratified into three different levels of socio-economic status: upper, middle, and lower (working) classes. Groups occupying lower social strata have fewer economic resources and less access to social privileges (Feagin & Feagin, 2011). One of America's deepest-held ideals is that all people are created equal and that the pursuit and achievement of socio-economic prosperity should be attained through individual initiative and personal merit, rather than by birthright or heritage. To believe in the *American Dream* is to believe that all Americans, regardless of where they were born or what class they were born into, have the same opportunity to attain success in a country where upward mobility is possible for everyone. According to Ginsberg and Wlodkowski (2009), this dream is "rooted in cultural mythology that overlooks the social, political, and economic forces that favor certain groups over others [and] has at least as much to do with privilege as to personal desire and effort" (p. 14). The reality is that not all Americans start the race to success at the same starting line; some start much closer to the finish line than others. Said in another way, some are born with the privilege of having a silver spoon in their mouth, others a plastic spoon, and others no spoon at all.

Sharp socioeconomic differences exist across different racial and ethnic groups in America, and the gap between rich and poor Americans is widening (Stiglitz, 2012). For example, in 2018, the median household income for non-Hispanic White households was $70,642, compared to $51,450 for Hispanics and $41,361 for African Americans (Peter G. Peterson Foundation, 2019). The great housing and mortgage collapse after the turn of the 21st century had its most damaging impact on lower-income, ethnic minorities. Household wealth fell by 66% for Hispanics and 53% for Blacks, compared to 16% for Whites (Kochlar, Fry, & Taylor, 2011).

Since 1980, rates of intergenerational socioeconomic mobility in America have steadily declined. America is now one of the hardest industrialized nations in the world for children born into poverty to escape poverty by the time they reach adulthood (Corak, 2010). Research conducted by Mitnik and Gruskey (2015) revealed that a child born to parents in the lowest income quintile in America is more than ten times likely to end up in the lowest quintile than the highest quintile. Although people of all groups experience poverty, members of racial and ethnic minority groups experience it at significantly higher rates than the White majority. In 2018, poverty rates for different ethnic and racial groups were as follows: Whites (10.1%), Asians (10.1%), Hispanics (17.6%), Blacks (20.8%), and Native Americans (25.4%). It's estimated that by 2020, almost one-half of the nation's school-age population will be students of color, and about 27% of these students will be living below the poverty line. More than 60% of Black and Hispanic students attend high-poverty schools (defined as schools in which more than 50% of the student body lives below the poverty line), compared to 30% of Asian students and 18% of White students (U.S. Department of Education, 2013). For students attending extreme-poverty schools (defined as having more than 90% of their student body living in poverty), only 1% are White—compared to 12% of Black and Hispanic students (Orfield & Lee, 2005).

"In my younger and more vulnerable years, my father gave me some advice that I've been turning over in my mind ever since:'Whenever you feel like criticizing anyone,' he told me, 'just remember that all the people in this world haven't had the advantages you've had.'"

—F. Scott Fitzgerald, in *The Great Gatsby*, an American literary classic

"We cannot be content, no matter how high the general standard of living may be, if some fraction of our people … is ill-fed, ill-housed, ill-clothed, and insecure."

—Franklin Delano Roosevelt, 32nd president of the United States

The fact that students of color are also more likely to be students from low-income or impoverished families highlights the concept of *intersectionality*—membership in two or more disadvantaged social categories (e.g., race and social class) often intersect to exert a combined effect that further disadvantages people who hold joint membership in these intersecting categories (Cho, Crenshaw, & McCall, 2013; Crenshaw, 1991).

PERSONAL INSIGHT

When I was a four-year-old boy living in the mountains of Kentucky, it was safe for a young lad to walk the roads and railroad tracks alone. Knowing this, my mother was comfortable sending me on long walks to the general store to buy a variety of small items we needed for our household. Since we had very little money, she made sure that whatever money we had should be spent on the most basic necessities. I could only buy items from the general store that my mother strictly ordered me to buy. In the early 1960s, most of these items cost less than a dollar and many times you could buy multiple items for a dollar. At the store's checkout counter, there were jars with different kinds of candy or gum. Since you could buy two pieces for one cent, I didn't think there would be any harm in rewarding myself for the long walk to the grocery store with just two pieces of candy. I could even devour the evidence of my disobedience on my slow walk home.

When I returned from the store, my mother— the protector of the vault and the sergeant-of-arms in our household— would carefully check each item I bought to make sure I had been charged correctly. She never failed to notice if the total was off by a single cent. After discovering that I had spent an extra cent on something unessential, she scolded me and said in no uncertain terms: "Boy, you better learn how to count your money if you're ever going to be successful in life!"

Growing up in poverty wasn't fun, but we managed. What we ate had to be reasonable in price and bought in bulk. Every morning my mother fixed rice or oatmeal for breakfast, along with wonderful buttermilk biscuits. At night, she fixed pinto beans and cornbread for dinner. We also had fresh vegetables from the garden and apples, hickory nuts, and walnuts from surrounding trees. Meat was not readily available and was only eaten when we killed a chicken or hog that we had raised.

Aaron Thompson

"Being born in the elite in the U.S. gives you a constellation of privileges that very few people in the world have ever experienced. Being born poor in the U.S. gives you disadvantages unlike anything in Western Europe, Japan, and Canada."

—David I. Levine, economist and social mobility researcher

With higher social-class status also comes greater privileges. A *privilege* may be defined as an advantage acquired without being earned, such as inheriting money or being admitted to a college because a family member previously attended the college or donated money to the college (Minnich, 2005). Higher SES (socioeconomic status) families are privileged with two major forms of capital: (a) *economic* capital—*what* they have (e.g., homes, health benefits, and discretionary income for travel and other enriching experiences for their children), and (b) *social* capital—*who* they know (e.g., contacts with employers and access to people in powerful legal, political, and educational positions) (Conley, 2005). Children born into higher-income families acquire these privileges without earning them and they will benefit from these privileges throughout life. For instance, children with parents of higher socioeconomic status have greater social capital for getting into college (e.g., personal connections with private counselors and admissions officers) and greater economical capital to help them complete college (e.g., financial resources to pay for college tuition and to participate in special college programs, such as study-abroad experiences).

In addition to, and often correlated with, achievement gaps between students from different ethnic and racial groups are achievement gaps among students from families of different socioeconomic status. The achievement gaps between children from high and low SES families are large and have remained almost constant for a almost half a century (Hanushek et al., 2019). Children from high SES groups enter kindergarten with average cognitive test scores that are 60 percent higher than children from the lowest socioeconomic groups. By the third grade, children from middle class families with well-educated parents possess a vocabulary of about 12,000 words; in contrast, children from low-income families with poorly educated parents have a vocabulary of about 4,000 words (Snow, 2005). By the fourth grade, the math achievement gap for students living below and above the poverty line is 22 points; by the eighth grade, it grows to 27 points (Kopkowski, 2006).

Educational achievement is likely to be the only available route through which economically disadvantaged children can escape lower socioeconomic status and gain upward social mobility for themselves and their future families. America's school system has the potential to narrow the achievement gap for students from low-income families by providing them with the social capital and educational resources that are not available to them at home. **Box 1.2** supplies some school-based strategies that have the potential to close the achievement gap for low-income students and open up their opportunities for educational advancement and upward social mobility.

> "Deep in America's soul lies the promise of opportunity, of liberty and freedom for every person [and] education is the path to the table of opportunity in 21st century America."
>
> —Peter Smith, *The Quiet Crisis*

Box 1.2 How Can Schools Close the Achievement Gap for Low-Income Students?

1. Utilize an intentional curriculum that:
   - ▶ is research-based
   - ▶ is content-driven
   - ▶ is developmentally appropriate
   - ▶ responds to cultural diversity and ESL students
   - ▶ emphasizes active learning
   - ▶ is attentive to social and self-regulatory (self-management) skills
   - ▶ promotes positive interaction among students, teachers, and parents.

2. Outreach to Students' Families
   - ▶ Establish family centers at schools and other community locations
   - ▶ Hire staff from the community who speak the language spoken by students' families at home
   - ▶ Supply families with transportation to and from school events
   - ▶ Offer adult education and parenting courses

3. Provide ongoing professional development for school-based leaders that focus on:
   - ▶ Research on how children develop and learn

- ▶ Strategies for closing the achievement gap
- ▶ Diversifying instructional methods to accommodate the learning styles of students from different cultural backgrounds
- ▶ Strategies for working effectively with students' families and communities

4. Cultivate Cultural Competence

- ▶ Foster a school climate in which student diversity is perceived as an asset and opportunity, rather than a liability
- ▶ Demonstrate sensitivity to students' home cultures
- ▶ Capitalize on students' cultures to enhance learning
- ▶ Engage teachers in professional development relating to diversity, cultural competence, cultural traditions, and the teaching of immigrant and limited English-proficient students

5. Create a Comprehensive Student Support System

- ▶ Screen children early for medical/social services and collaborate with medical, social services, and community agencies
- ▶ Identify and reach out to students who need additional instructional support
- ▶ Support students with mentors, tutoring, peer support networks, and role models
- ▶ Provide full-day kindergarten and pre-kindergarten programs
- ▶ Offer extended learning experiences in the form of before-school, after-school, and summer school programs

(Adapted from: Klein & Knitzer, 2007; National Education Association, 2002-2019.)

Consider This ...

More detailed discussion of the practices cited in Box 1.2 is provided throughout the remaining chapters of this book. When students attain higher rates of academic achievement, their children are more likely to demonstrate higher levels of academic achievement, graduate from high school, and complete a postsecondary college degree or credential—which is becoming increasingly important passport for gainful employment in the twenty-first century. Thus, closing the achievement gap not only increases the employment prospects of today's low-income children, it has a positive cross-generational "ripple effect" on the educational and occupational attainment of their own children.

Internet Resources

Dimensions of diversity:
http://sgba-resource.ca/en/concepts/diversity/describe-the-various-dimensions-of-diversity/

Dimensions of culture:
https://www.cleverism.com/understanding-cultures-people-hofstede-dimensions/

http://changingminds.org/explanations/culture/hall_culture.htm

Race and ethnicity:
https://www.diffen.com/difference/Ethnicity_vs_Race

Socioeconomic status and education:
https://iris.peabody.vanderbilt.edu/module/div/cresource/q2/p06/

Understanding privilege:
https://msw.usc.edu/mswusc-blog/
diversity-workshop-guide-to-discussing-identity-power-and-privilege/

Closing the achievement gap:
https://www.theedadvocate.org/creative-ways-close-achievement-gap/
https://www.edutopia.org/closing-achievement-gap
http://www.nea.org/home/13550.htm

References

American Psychological Association. (2019). *Socioeconomic status*. Retrieved from https://www.apa.org/topics/socioeconomic-status/

Anderson, M., & Fienberg, S. (2000). Race and ethnicity and the controversy over the U.S. Census. *Current Sociology, 48*(3), 87–110.

Banks, J. A. (2016). *Cultural diversity and education: Foundations, curriculum, and teaching* (6th ed.) New York: Routledge.

Bennett, D. H. (1988). *The party of fear: From nativist movements to the new right in American history.* Chapel Hill, NC: University of North Carolina Press.

Bourne, R. S. (1916). Trans-national America. *Atlantic Monthly, 118,* p. 95

Blanco, M. (2010). *Before Brown there was Mendez: The lasting impact of Mendez v. Westminster in the struggle for desegregation.* Immigration Policy Center, American Immigration Council. Retrieved from https://www.americanimmigrationcouncil.org/sites/default/files/research/Mendez_vWestminster_032410.pdf

Bridgeman, B. (2003). *Psychology and evolution: The origins of mind.* Thousand Oaks, CA: Sage.

Bronfenbrenner, U. (Ed.) (2005). *Making human beings human: Bioecological perspectives on human development.* Thousand Oaks, CA: Sage.

Brookings Institution (2019). *The US will become 'minority white' in 2045, census projects.* Retrieved from Camorata, S. A. (2012). *Immigrants in the United States, 2010: A profile of America's foreign-born population.* Washington, DC: Center for Immigration Studies. Retrieved from http://www.cis.org/2012-profile-of-America-foreign-born-population

Caplan, P. J., & Caplan, J. B. (2009). *Thinking critically about research on sex and gender* (3rd ed.). New York: HarperCollins College Publishers.

Cho, S., Crenshaw, K. W., McCall, L. (2013). Toward a field of intersectionality studies: theory, applications, and praxis. *Journal of Women in Culture and Society, 38*(4), 785–810.

Cianciotto, J. (2005) *Hispanic and latino same-sex couple households in the United States: A report from the 2000 census.* New York: The National Gay and Lesbian Task Force Policy Institute and the National Latino/a Coalition for Justice.

Colombo, G., Cullen, R., & Lisle, B. (2013). *Rereading America: Cultural contexts for critical thinking and writing* (9th ed.). Boston: Bedford Books of St. Martin's Press.

Conley, D. (2005). *The pecking order: A bold new look and how family and society determine who we become.* New York: Random House.

Corak, M. (2010). *Chasing the same dream, climbing different ladders: Economic mobility in the United States and Canada.* Washington, DC: Economic mobility project of the Pew Charitable Trusts. Retrieved from http://www.pewtrusts.org/en/research-and-analysis/reports/0001/01/01/chasing-the-same-dream-climbing-different-ladders

Crenshaw, K. (1991). Mapping the margins: intersectionality, identity politics, and violence against women of color. *Stanford Law Review. 43*(6): 1241–1299.

Cubberly, E. P. (1909). *Changing conceptions of education.* Boston, MA: Houghton Mifflin.

Drachsler, J. (1920). *Democracy and assimilation.* New York, NY: Macmillan.

Feagin, J., & Feagin, J. B. R. (2011). *Race and ethnic relations* (9th ed.). Upper Saddle River, NJ: Pearson.

Giroux, H. A. (1998). The politics of national identity and the pedagogy of multicultralism in the USA. In D. Bennett (Ed.), *Multicultural states: Rethinking difference and identity* (pp. 178–194). New York: Routledge.

"Immigrants from 1776 Onward" (2019). *Los Angeles Times,* July 4, pp. A10.

Hanushek, E. A., Peterson, P. F., Tapepy, L. M., Woessmann, L. (2019). *The unwavering SES achievement Gap: Trends in U.S. student performance.* NBER Working Paper No. 25648. National Bureau of Economic Research. Retrieved from https://www.nber.org/papers/w25648

Jablonski, N. G., & Chaplin, G. (2002). Skin deep. *Scientific American* (October), 75–81.

Jacobson, M. F. (1998). *Whiteness of a different color: European immigrants and the alchemy of race.* Cambridge, MA: Harvard University Press.

Klein, L. G., & Knitzer, J. (2007). *Promoting effective learning: What every policymaker and educator should know.* National Center for Children in Poverty. Retrieved from http://nccp.org/publications/pub_695.html

Kochlar, R., Fry, R., & Taylor, P. (2011). Wealth gaps rise to record highs between Whites, Blacks, Hispanics, twenty-to-one. *Pew Research Social and Demographics Trends* (July). Retrieved from http://www.pewsocialtrends.org/2011/07/26/wealth-gaps-rise-to-record-highs-between-whites-blacks-hispanics/

Koplowski, C. (2006, November). Talk about it. *NEA Today Magazine.* Retrieved from http://www.nea.org/home/14449.htm

Luhman, R. (2007). *The sociological outlook.* Lanham, MD: Rowman & Littlefield.

Martin, S. F. (2011). *A nation of immigrants.* New York, NY: Cambridge University Press.

May, S. (2012). Critical multiculturalism and education. In J. A. Banks (Ed.), *Encyclopedia of diversity in education* (volume 1, pp. 472–478). Thousand Oaks, CA: Sage.

Mendez, F., Krahn, T., Schrack, B., Krahn, A. M., Veeramah, K., Woerner, A., Fomine,

F. L. M., Bradman, N., Thomas, M., Karafet, T., & Hammer, M. (2013). An African American paternal lineage adds an extremely ancient root to the human Y chromo-some phylogenetic tree. *The American Journal of Human Genetics, 92,* 454–459.

Meredith, M. (2011). *Born in Africa: The quest for the origins of human life.* New York: Public Affairs.

Minnich, E. K. (2005). *Transforming knowledge* (2nd ed.) Philadelphia: Temple University Press.

Mitnik, P. A., & Gruskey, D. B. (2015). *Economic mobility in the United States.* The Pew Charitable Trusts and the Russell Sage Foundation. Retrieved from http://www.pewtrusts.org/~/media/assets/2015/07/fsm-irs-report_artfinal.pdf

Moghaddam, F. (2008). *Multiculturalism and intergroup relations: Psychological implications for democracy in global context.* Washington, DC: American Psychological Association.

National Assessment of Educational Progress (NAEP) (2015a). *2015 Reading Grade 12 Assessment Report Card: Summary Data Tables for National and Pilot State Sample Sizes, Participation Rates, Proportions of SD and ELL Students Identified, Demographics, and Performance Results.* Retrieved from https://www.nationsreportcard.gov/reading_math_g12_2015/files/Appendix_20

National Assessment of Educational Progress (NAEP) (2015b). *2015 Mathematics Grade 12 Assessment Report Card: Summary Data Average scores and achievement-level results in*

NAEP mathematics for twelfth-grade students, by selected characteristics: Various years, 2005–2015. Retrieved from https://www.nationsreportcard.gov/reading_math_g12_2015/files/Appendix_20

National Assessment of Educational Progress (NAEP) (2019). *Results from the 2019 mathematics and reading assessments. The National Report Card.* National Center for Education Statistics. Retrieved from https://www.nationsreportcard.gov/mathematics/supportive_files/2019_infogra

National Center for Education Statistics (2008). Table 41: Percentage distribution of enrollment in public elementary and secondary schools by race/ethnicity and state or jurisdiction: Fall 1996 and fall 2006. Washington, DC: U.S. Department of Education. National Council for the Social Sciences (NCSS) (1991). *Curriculum guidelines for multicultural education.* Prepared by the NCSS Task Force on Ethnic Studies Curriculum Guidelines. Retrieved from www.socialstudies.org/positions/multicultural

National Education Association (2002–2019). *Strategies for closing the achievement gaps.* Retrieved from http://www.nea.org/home/13550.htm

Nicholas, R. W. (1991). Cultures in the curriculum. *Liberal Education, 77*(3), 16–21.

Orfield, G., & Lee, C. (2005). *Why segregation matters: Poverty and educational inequality.* Cambridge, MA: The Civil Rights Project at Harvard University.

Peoples, J. & Bailey, G. (2011). *Humanity: An introduction to cultural anthropology.* Belmont, CA: Wadsworth, Cengage Learning from http://www.aacu.org/leap/documents/2009-employersurvey.pdf

Peter G. Peterson Foundation (2019, October 4). *Income and wealth in America: An overview of recent data.* https://www.pgpf.org/blog/2019/10/income-and-wealth-in-the-united-states-an-overview-of-data

Pinker, S. (2000). *The language instinct: The new science of language and mind.* New York: Perennial.

Reid, G. B. R., & Hetherington, R. (2010). *The climate connection: Climate change and modern evolution.* Cambridge, UK: Cambridge University Press.

Segall, M. H., Campbell, D. T., & Herskovits, M. J. (1996). *The influence of culture on visual perception.* Indianapolis: Bobbs-Merrill.

Shiraev, E. D., & Levy, D. (2013). *Cross-cultural psychology: Critical thinking and contemporary applications* (5th ed.).Upper Saddle River, NJ: Pearson Education.

Smith, D. (2015). *Diversity's promise for higher education: Making it work* (2nd ed.). Baltimore, MD: Johns Hopkins University Press.

Snow, C. (2005). From literacy to learning. *Harvard Education Letter*, July/August.

Stiglitz, J. E. (2012). The price of inequality: How today's divided society endangers our future. New York, NY: Horton.

U.S. Census Bureau (2008). "An older and more diverse nation by midcentury." Retrieved from http://www.census.gov/Press-release/www/releases/archives/population/012496.html

U.S. Census Bureau. (2013). "About race." Retrieved from https://www.census.gov/topics/population/race/about.html

U.S. Census Bureau. (2018). "Race." Retrieved from https://www.census.gov/topics/population/race/about.html

U.S. Census Bureau (2018b). Newsroom. Retrieved from https://www.census.gov/newsroom/press-releases/2018/cb18-41-population-projections.html

U.S. Census Bureau (2015, March). *Projections of the Size and Composition of the U.S. Population: 2014 to 2060.* Retrieved from http://www.census.gov/content/dam/Census/library/publications/2015/demo/p25-1143.pdf

U.S. Department of Education, National Center for Education Statistics. (2013). *The condition of education 2013.* Retrieved from https://nces.ed.gov/pubs2013/2013037.pdf

Valenzuela, A. (1999). *Subtractive schooling: U.S.-Mexican youth and the politics of caring.* Albany, NY: State University of New York Press.

Weatherford, J. (1991). *Native roots: How the Indians enriched America.* New York, NY: Crown Publishers.

Wheelright, J. (2005). Human, study thyself. *Discover,* (March), pp. 39–45.

Zajonc, R. B. (1968). Attitudinal effects of mere exposure. *Journal of Personality and Social Psychology, 9,* Monograph Supplement, No. 2, Part 2.

Zajonc, R. B. (1970). Brainwash: Familiarity breeds comfort. *Psychology Today* (February), pp. 32–35, 60–62.

Zajonc, R. B. (2001). Mere exposure: A gateway to the subliminal. *Current Directions in Psychological Science,* 10, 224–228.

Reflections and Applications

1.1 When people hear the word "diversity," what do you think is the first thought that comes to their mind? Why?

1.2 Review the diversity spectrum depicted in Figure 1. (p. 2). Do you notice any groups missing from the list that should be included because they have distinctive educational needs, or because they have been victims of prejudice and discrimination?

1.3 Review the sidebar quotes contained in this chapter and select two that you think are particularly meaningful or inspirational. For each quote you selected, provide an explanation why you chose it.

1.4 In addition to the universally shared human characteristics cited on p. 02, can you think of any other human characteristic(s) shared by all people, no matter what their race or culture may be?

1.5 Review the components of culture cited in Box 1.1 (p. 7):
   (a) Identify a component that you think is most important for educators to be mindful of, and explain why you chose it.
   (b) Make note of another cultural component that you think should be added to the list, and explain why you added it.

1.6 What race(s) do you consider yourself to be? Would you say you identify strongly with your racial identity, or do you rarely think about it? How do you think your students would respond to these two questions?

1.7 Review the strategies for how schools can *close the achievement gap for low-income students* cited in Box 1.2 (p. 17). Select two strategies that you think would have the most direct and dramatic impact on closing the gap, and explain why you selected each of these strategies.

2 The Benefits of Diversity Education

Chapter Purpose and Preview

This chapter defines multicultural education and articulates how it not only promotes acceptance and appreciation of minority groups, but also deepens learning and elevates the critical and creative thinking skills of all students. In addition to documenting the social and cognitive benefits of diversity, the chapter demonstrates how multicultural education preserves democracy, enhances emotional intelligence and self-awareness, and cultivates intercultural competencies essential for career success in the twenty-first century.

What is Diversity Education?

The term "multicultural education" is often associated with cultural appreciation activities, such as schools celebrating Black History Month or students bringing artifacts to school representing their culture. While these are useful experiences and should be continued, bona fide diversity education involves more than periodic celebrations of cultural differences. Diversity education empowers students to evaluate ideas in terms of their cultural validity and cultural bias, and engages students in learning experiences that foster interaction among diverse student groups (Banks et al., 2001). Education for and with diversity is an ongoing learning process that takes place consistently throughout the school year and is integrated across the curriculum. When students are exposed to multiple perspectives and engage with diverse viewpoints during the learning process the learning of any academic subject is broadened and deepened.

> "One of the most compelling arguments for the importance of diversity has framed it as an educational opportunity for groups from different backgrounds to learn from and with one another."
>
> —Daryl G. Smith, *Diversity's Promise for Higher Education*

Benefits of Diversity Education

In addition to pursuing the important objective of ensuring equitable treatment of cultural groups that have been and continue to be oppressed, diversity education has the broader purpose of enriching the learning experience and future success of *all* students, preparing them for further education and future success in their careers. These and other benefits of diversity education are discussed in the following sections of this chapter. By intentionally articulating these benefits to students, educators can increase their motivation to learn about and from diversity. When students are more consciously aware of the benefits of diversity, they are more likely to attend to, seek out, and profit from experiencing diversity.

Diversity Education Increases Self-Awareness and Self-Knowledge

Know Thyself

© Kendall Hunt Publishing Company

Gaining greater self-awareness (self-knowledge) is one of the major benefits of diversity education.

One of the most frequently cited outcomes of higher education is to "know thyself" (Cross, 1982), and this ability to engage in introspection to gain greater self-awareness and self-knowledge has been identified as a distinctive form of human intelligence, i.e., "intrapersonal intelligence" (Gardner, 1999).

Multicultural experiences supply students with multiple opportunities to deepen self-knowledge. When students encounter people and ideas from different cultures, those encounters shed brighter light on their own identities, prompting self-searching questions such as: *Who am I? How am I different from others? What has made me the person I am?* As a result, "students develop more sophisticated understandings of why they are the way they are, why their ethnic and cultural groups are the way they are, and what ethnicity and culture mean in their daily lives" (National Council for the Social Studies, 1991, p. 18).

The nature of the people with whom we interact can deepen our self-knowledge and self-insight (Tatum, 2007). As Ginsberg and Wlodkowski (2009) point out: "When we meet others whose family or community norms vary from our own, it is akin to holding up a mirror, provoking questions we might not otherwise think to ask. Contrast and dissonance present [opportunities] to examine assumptions, making it possible to more deeply understand who we are in relation to one another" (p. 7). Postsecondary research shows that when students interact with students of different races and ethnic backgrounds, they often experience "unexpected" or "jarring" self-insights which enable them to learn more about themselves (Light, 2001).

Consider This . . .

The more opportunities educators create for students to learn about and from cultures different from their own, the more opportunities they create for students to learn about themselves.

Students' self-knowledge is deepened by experiences with others from diverse backgrounds because it enables them to compare and contrast their life experiences with others whose experiences differ sharply from their own. Viewing themselves in relation to others from different backgrounds helps liberate students from ethnocentrism, enabling them to gain a *comparative cultural perspective*—a reference point that positions them to see more clearly how their particular cultural background has shaped who they are.

PERSONAL INSIGHT

By 1969 my third-grade class was integrated. That year, Black students were bused to my school in the predominantly White neighborhood I lived in. The next three years I was bused to a school in a predominantly Black neighborhood. There has been much said about Black people benefitting from integration. What has not been expressed is the huge advantage integration gave to White students. Attending integrated public schools had a profound, positive effect on who I am ... this integration was liberating for all involved.

John Chichester, letter to the editor, *Los Angeles Times*, July 4, 2019

When students gain greater insight into what is distinctive about their personal experiences, they're also more likely to see how they may be uniquely advantaged or disadvantaged relative to others. For example, by learning about the limited educational opportunities that people in other countries have today, and the limited opportunities that certain groups of people once had in our own country, students today are more likely to appreciate the opportunity they now have to be educated, to continue their education, and influence their future quality of life.

Educators can also gain greater insight into their personal and professional identity by contrasting their life experiences with students from different cultural backgrounds. (Chisholm, 1994). Gaining greater self-awareness though diversity experiences serves as the critical first step toward overcoming personal biases that may interfere with culturally-inclusive and culturally-responsive teaching.

Diversity Education Deepens and Accelerates Learning

Simply stated, humans learn more from diversity than they do from similarity or familiarity. In contrast, when we restrict the diversity of people with whom we interact because of stereotypes or prejudices, we restrict the variety of our social diet, and in so doing, restrict the breadth and depth of our learning. Similar to how physical performance is strengthened by supplying the body with a diversified diet of foods from different nutritional groups, mental performance is strengthened by supplying the mind with a diversified diet of ideas from different cultural groups. For example, our knowledge about stress and how to manage it has been strengthened by learning from Indian Buddhist culture that meditation is an effective, drug-free, stress-management strategy (Bodian, 2006). Indian Buddhist culture has also fueled the current use of mindfulness in America as a self-awareness and self-growth strategy (Gunaratana, 2011). We have also learned from Eskimos that their extraordinarily low rate of cardiovascular disease is related to the natural oil contained in their fish-rich diet—which contains a type of unsaturated fat that flushes out and washes away cholesterol-forming fats from the bloodstream (Feskens & Kromhout, 1993; Khoshaba & Maddi, 1999–2004). We have also learned from studying the culture of Intuits or Yupiks (a.k.a. Eskimos) that a diet high in unsaturated fats (and low in saturated fats) reduces our risk for non-genetic forms of cardiovascular disease, such as high blood pressure, heart attacks, and strokes (American Heart Association, 2006). These examples illustrate how learning about and from different cultures serves to make our knowledge base more diversified, nuanced, and comprehensive.

Deep learning takes place when strong neurological connections are made between what students are learning and the knowledge or experiences they have already stored in the their brain (see **Figure 2.1**). It's easier for students to assimilate new information and integrate it with prior knowledge when a wider range of interconnections have already been formed in their brain (Rosenshine, 1997). When students experience diversity, it broadens and

"A comparison of American cultural products, practices, and perspectives to those of another culture will lead to a more profound understanding of what it means to be an American."

—David Conley, *College Knowledge: What It Really Takes for Students to Succeed and What We Can Do to Get Them Ready*

"The more eyes, different eyes, we can use to observe one thing, the more complete will our concept of this thing, our objectivity, be."

—Friedrich Nietzsche, German philosopher

Figure 2.1

Knowledge is stored in the brain in the form of neurological connections. Diversity education adds to the multiplicity and variety of the brain's neural network, providing more pathways through which students can connect new ideas.

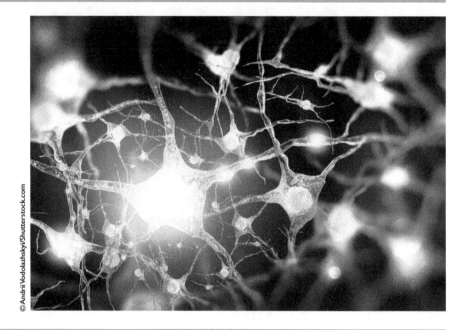

©Andrii Vodolazhskyi/Shutterstock.com

differentiates their base of knowledge, which facilitates the brain's capacity for making new connections. In other words, diversity education adds to the multiplicity and variety of the brain's neural pathways, providing it with more routes through which to assimilate new ideas, and in so doing, accelerates and deepens learning.

Experiencing diversity "stretches" the brain beyond its normal comfort zone, pushing it to work harder. When encountering something unfamiliar, the brain has to take an extra step to make sense of it—by comparing, contrasting, and trying to relate it to something it already knows (Acredolo & O'Connor, 1991; Nagda, Gurin, & Johnson, 2005). This added expenditure of mental energy results in the creation of deeper and more durable neurological connections (Willis, 2006). Research indicates that one instructional practice shared by K–12 teachers who promote the greatest gains in student achievement is they encourage students to compare and contrast ideas (Dean et al., 2012; Marzano, Pickering, & Pollock, 2001).

Diversity Education Strengthens Students' Ability to Think Critically from Multiple Perspectives

"Mono-perspective analyses of complex ethnic and cultural issues can produce skewed, distorted interpretations and evaluations."

—National Council for the Social Sciences, *Curriculum Guidelines for Multicultural Education*

When the world is viewed through the lens of a single (monocultural) perspective, it's seen from the narrow, ethnocentric perspective of the viewer (Paul & Elder, 2002). Diversity emancipates the viewer from the tunnel vision of an ethnocentric perspective, replacing it with a kaleidoscopic lens that includes a mixture of multicultural and cross-cultural perspectives.

When such diverse perspectives are brought into the thinking process, it enhances the quality and accuracy of decision-making (Banks, 2016; Smith, 2015). If group discussion takes place among diverse people with multiple perspectives, group decisions become less polarized (one-sided) (Baron, 2005). Multicultural perspectives combat "groupthink"—the tendency for people with similar viewpoints not to challenge their shared perspective, which can lead to faulty decisions that overlook the flaws or biases in the group members' thought processes (Janis, 1982). Groupthink is what led American doctors to erroneously conclude that acupuncture was quackery (International Wellness Directory, 2009), which delayed recognition and approval of this Chinese method of pain relief as an effective alternative to pain-killing drugs.

> "When all men think alike, no one thinks very much."
>
> —Walter Lippmann, distinguished journalist and originator of the term "stereotype"

Consider This . . .

Because our views are shaped, limited, and often biased by our own cultural vantage point, exposing students to multicultural perspectives creates multiple opportunities for students to think beyond the boundaries of their ethnocentric perspective, empowering them to become more open-minded, multi-dimensional thinkers.

Research on educational programs designed to promote students' critical thinking skills indicates that the most successful programs are those in which "divergent views are aggressively sought" (Kurfiss, 1988, p. 2). Studies also show that students who have more experiences with diversity—such as taking multicultural courses, participating in diversity programs on campus, and interacting with peers from different racial and ethnic backgrounds—are more likely to experience greater gains in:

- ▶ thinking *complexity*—ability to think about all parts of a problem and approach issues from multiple vantage points (Association of American Colleges & Universities, 2004; Gurin, 1999),
- ▶ *reflective* thinking—ability to think deeply about both personal and global issues (Kitchener, Wood, & Jensen, 2000), and
- ▶ *critical* thinking—ability to evaluate the validity of one's own reasoning and the reasoning of others (Gorski,1995-2019; Pascarella et al., 2001).

These cognitive benefits of diversity experiences stem from the fact that encountering perspectives different from our own creates "cognitive dissonance"—a state of mental disequilibrium or imbalance that disrupts our habitual ways of thinking (Langer, 1997). This internal disequilibrium requires the mind to deal with contrasting perspectives simultaneously, which displaces single-dimensional thinking with thinking that is more multidimensional and complex (Brookfield, 1987; Gorski, 1995–2019).

> "The nation's future depends upon leaders trained through wide exposure to that robust exchange of ideas which discovers truth 'out of a multitude of tongues."
>
> —William J. Brennan, former Supreme Court Justice

When subject matter is approached from diverse cultural perspectives, students become more critically aware of how knowledge is "constructed" from the knowledge reporter's particular cultural perspective, and how it may be challenged (Banks, 1995). As Gorski (1995–2019) points out, a multicultural curriculum helps students critically evaluate what they read and view by asking such questions as: "Whose voice is speaking, and whose voice am I not hearing?" and "What cultural perspective (or bias) is the author or producer bringing to their book, website, or movie?" When such multicultural perspective-taking is seen as a potent tool for promoting the critical thinking skills of all students, the multicultural curriculum can be woven seamlessly into the traditional (mainstream) curriculum, ensuring that both curricula are covered simultaneously and synergistically (McKay School of Education, 2010).

Diversity Cultivates Creative Thinking

Besides promoting critical thinking, diversity has been found to foster creative thinking (Leung et al; 2008; Maddux & Galinsky, 2009). When students acquire knowledge about multiple cultures and become cognizant of diverse cultural perspectives, it positions them to think "outside the box" of their own cultural framework, equipping them with more varied vantage points to view problems and more tools to solve them (Kelly, 1994).

Furthermore, when people from different cultural backgrounds exchange ideas, it can have a "cross-stimulation" effect—the sharing of these diverse ideas combine in such a way that they stimulate creation of new ideas which transcend the boundaries of any one culture (Brown, Dane, & Durham, 1998). Said in another way cross-cultural ideas "cross-fertilize" and germinate new ideas for attacking old problems (Harris, 2010). Research also suggests that when people seek out diverse perspectives and alternative viewpoints, they become more open to considering different goal options and more willing to experiment with different goal-achievement strategies (Stoltz, 2014).

In contrast, when cultural perspectives other than our own are dismissed or devalued, the number and variety of lenses through which we can view issues or problems is reduced. This reduced range of viewpoints restricts opportunities for divergent thinking—thinking that moves in different directions—which is a signature feature of creative thinking. When interactions and conversations take place exclusively among groups of people with similar cultural experiences, their ideas are less likely to diverge; instead, they're more likely to converge and merge into the same lane or line of thought—the one occupied by the homogeneous cultural group doing the thinking. Thus, segregation of racial and ethnic groups not only separates people socially, it also separates them mentally, and suppresses their collective creativity. This is well illustrated in the book (and movie) *Hidden Figures,* which documents how a group of talented black female mathematicians were initially and intentionally segregated from their white male coworkers at NASA, but when eventually integrated into the work team, they made crucial, creative contributions to the successful launching of America's first astronaut (Shetterly, 2017).

"When the only tool you have is a hammer, you tend to see every problem as a nail."

—Abraham Maslow, psychologist, best known for his theory of human self-actualization

"What I look for in musicians is generosity. There is so much to learn from each other and about each other's culture. Great creativity begins with tolerance."

—Yo-Yo Ma, French-born, Chinese-American virtuoso cellist, composer, and winner of multiple Grammy Awards

> Consider this ...
> When people from diverse backgrounds are given the opportunity to bounce ideas off one another, it stimulates divergent (out-of-the-box) thinking, generates synergy (multiplication of ideas), and leads to serendipity (unexpected discoveries of innovative ideas).

Diversity Expands Social Networks and Builds Emotional Intelligence

When students acquire more knowledge about cultures other than their own people and have more interaction with member of other cultural groups, they widen their social circle and expand the pool of people to whom they can relate and form friendships. Research in postsecondary settings indicates that the more frequently students engage with diversity and experience positive intergroup contact, the more likely they are to report higher levels of satisfaction with campus life and their college experience (Astin, 1993; Cheng & Zhao, 2006; Dovidio, Kawakami, & Gaertner, 2000; Enberg, 2004). Reinforcing these findings is research in social psychology, which indicates that less-prejudiced people report higher life satisfaction (Feagin & McKinney, 2003), likely because they are less distrustful or fearful of others and more open to new social experiences (Baron, Byrne, & Branscombe, 2006).

Furthermore, studies show that when students widen the cultural circle of peers with whom they interact, they gain greater self-confidence and ability to adapt to new people and situations (Miville, Molla & Sedlacek, 1992). In contrast, students who limit their social experiences to members of their own culture are left with "few opportunities to acquire more than stereotypes about ethnic and cultural groups other than their own" (National Council for Social Sciences, 1991, p. 22).

Lastly, interaction with people whose life experiences, circumstances and challenges differ from one's own serves to promote empathy—awareness of, and sensitivity to, the feelings of others (Levine, 2005). Empathy is an essential ingredient of *emotional intelligence,* an attribute that has been found to be a better predictor of personal and professional success than intellectual ability (Goleman, 1995, 2006).

> "Variety is the spice of life."
>
> —An old American proverb

> "Viva la difference!" (Long live difference!)
>
> —A famous French saying

> "When diverse and conflicting perspectives are juxtaposed, students are able to develop empathy and an understanding of each group's perspective and point of view."
>
> —James Banks, Founding Director of the Center for Multicultural Education at the University of Washington

Diversity Education Enhances Career Preparation

Learning about, with, and from diverse people also has a very practical long-term benefit: It prepares students for future work in the current century. Whatever line of work today's students eventually pursue, they are likely to find themselves working with employers, co-workers, customers, and clients from diverse cultural backgrounds. America's workforce is now more racially and ethnically diverse than at any other time in history and will grow ever more diverse throughout the twenty-first century. By 2050, the proportion of American workers from minority ethnic and racial groups will jump to 55% (U.S. Census Bureau, 2008).

National surveys show that today's policymakers, business leaders, and employers are seeking to hire people who are more than just "aware" or "tolerant" of diversity. They want employees who have actual *experience* with diversity and are able to collaborate with diverse co-workers, clients, and customers

Students' future coworkers are likely to come from diverse cultural backgrounds.

© adriaticfoto/Shutterstock.com

(Association of American Colleges & Universities, 2002; Education Commission of the States, 1995; Hart Research Associates, 2013).

In addition to the growing domestic diversity within the United States, the current "global economy" calls for cross-cultural skills relating to international diversity. Due to unprecedented and ongoing advances in electronic technology, today's work world is characterized by more economic interdependence among nations, more international trading, more multinational corporations, more international travel, and almost instantaneous worldwide communication (Dryden & Vos, 1999; Friedman, 2005). Even smaller companies and corporations are becoming more international in nature (Brooks, 2009). As a result, employers in all sectors of the economy are seeking job candidates with the following skills and attributes: sensitivity to human differences, ability to understand and relate to people from different cultural backgrounds, international and intercultural knowledge, and ability to communicate in a second language (NACE, 2019; Hart Research Associates, 2013; Job Outlook, 2018; Office of Research, 1994).

The growth in both domestic and international diversity has made intercultural competence an essential twenty-first century skill (Bennett, 2004; Thompson & Cuseo, 2014). *Intercultural competence* may be defined as the ability to appreciate and learn from human differences and to interact effectively with people from diverse cultural backgrounds. It includes "knowledge of cultures and cultural practices (one's own and others), complex cognitive skills for decision making in intercultural contexts, social skills to function effectively in diverse groups and personal attributes that include flexibility and openness to new ideas" (Wabash National Study of Liberal Arts Education, 2007). The ability to step across cultural boundaries and view the world from multiracial and multiethnic perspectives has also been identified as a key political leadership skill in the twenty-first century (Blackwell, Kwoh, & Pastor, 2002).

Consider This ...

Intercultural competence has two powerful qualities:

1. *Transferability*: it's a portable skill that "travels well"—it can be carried and applied across a wide range of learning experiences, work situations, and life roles.
2. *Durability*: it's a sustainable skill with long-lasting value—it can be used continuously throughout life.

Diversity Education Reduces Societal Prejudice and Discrimination

Schools serve as the starting place for promoting social justice and equity in the larger society (Gorski, 1995–2019). When students have positive interpersonal interactions with peers from different cultures and engage in open conversations with them about diversity-related topics that challenge their previously held beliefs, it reduces prejudice and increases openness to diversity (Pascarella et al., 1996; Whitt et al., 2001). These positive outcomes do not take place simply by mixing minority and majority students together in the same school environment. School-integration research strongly indicates that mere exposure to, or incidental contact between, majority and minority students does not automatically reduce prejudice and improve interracial relations (Stephan, 1978).

Research shows that simply integrating students of different racial groups in the same school environment doesn't automatically reduce prejudice. It requires a school climate that fosters positive interracial interaction.

Integrating students into the same school district is necessary but sufficient condition for promoting interracial student interaction because minority and majority students can (and will) self-segregate within the same school setting (Gerard & Miller, 1975; Rogers et al., 1984). In a comprehensive review of all school-desegregation research conducted over a 30-year period, it was discovered that forced desegregation in schools whose cultures were not receptive to diversity actually increased racial prejudice (Stephan, 1986). Studies also show that on integrated college campuses where the culture is hostile toward students from minority groups, students have lower rates of college satisfaction and lower rates of college completion—for both minority and majority students (Cabrera et al, 1999; Eimers & Pike, 1997; Nora & Cabrera, 1996).

Thus, the benefits of diversity cannot be achieved solely through policy decisions mandating that minority students be admitted to the same schools as majority students. School integration and a multicultural curricula need to be accompanied by a school climate that fosters positive, prosocial *interaction* between minority and majority students. For the goals of multicultural education to be fully realized, schools need to move beyond incidental intergroup contact to intentional intergroup interaction. As Patrick Hill (1991) puts it,

> Meaningful multi-culturalism transforms the curriculum. While the presence of persons of other cultures and subcultures is a virtual prerequisite to that transformation, their "mere presence" is primarily a political achievement, not an intellectual or educational achievement. Real educational progress will be made when multi-culturalism becomes *interculturalism* [emphasis added] (p. 41).

Research strongly suggests that when members of diverse groups engage in cooperative learning activities in which they pursue a unified goal, have equal status (equally important and positively interdependent roles) that are supported by school authorities (e.g., teachers or principals), student prejudices decrease and interracial friendships increase. These results have been found for elementary and high school students (Aronson, 1978; Banks, 1997; Slavin, 1980), college students (Nagda, Gurin, Soresen, & Zúñiga, 2009; Worchel, 1979), and workers in business settings (Blake & Mouton, 1979). More specific information on how to implement the cooperative learning is provided in Chapter 7, pp. 156.

By remaining mindful of the power of intercultural interaction and by using teaching methods that promote collaborative interaction among students from different cultural groups, educators not only help students learn more deeply and think more critically, they also help reduce stereotypes and prejudices held by students by engaging them in the collaborative learning process.

Diversity Education Preserves Democracy

Prejudice and discrimination should be vigorously resisted as both contradictions and threats to the foundational principles of any nation that calls itself a democracy (Myrdal, 1944; Smith, 2004). As a democratic nation, American is built on the principles of social justice, equal rights, and equal opportunity for *all* citizens. America's ability to continue to thrive as a democracy in the twenty-first century will depend on an educational system that develops and deploys the talents and civic participation of all its citizens, including those from historically underrepresented and disadvantaged backgrounds (American Council on Education, 2008). Educators who commit themselves to cultural pluralism "make a strong, unequivocal commitment to democracy, to basic American values of justice and equality" (Banks in Brandt, 1994, p. 31). Lest we forget, it was the vigorous efforts of minority groups to combat prejudice and discrimination, such as the civil rights movement in the 1960s and 70s, which effectively compelled America to live up to its democratic ideals—as stated in its Declaration of Independence, Constitution, and Bill of Rights (Okihiro, 1994).

Members of minority groups are more likely to develop allegiance to their country and pride in their country, and more likely to participate in their country's governance when their group identity and culture are valued (Kymlicka, 2004). Multicultural education serves to validate the culture of minority groups, and in so doing, deepens their awareness of social justice issues and increases the likelihood that they become citizens who cast votes for political leaders that are committed to ensuring equal rights, promoting social justice, and fulfilling the full promise of democracy.

"The Constitution of the United States knows no distinction between citizens on account of color."

—Frederick Douglass, former slave and subsequent abolitionist, author, and advocate for equal rights for all American citizens

> **Consider This ...**
> Diversity education elevates student awareness that diversity and democracy go hand-in-hand; when the former is valued, the latter is preserved.

Internet Resources

Educational benefits of ethnic diversity:
https://sudikoff.gseis.ucla.edu/ethnic-diversity-in-schools-benefits-everyone/

Benefits of integrated schools:
https://tcf.org/content/facts/the-benefits-of-socioeconomically-and-racially-integrated-schools-and-classrooms/?agreed=1

Benefits of diversity for democratic citizenship:
http://www-personal.umich.edu/~pgurin/benefits.html

Importance and value of diversity in STEM fields:
https://blogs.scientificamerican.com/voices/diversity-in-stem-what-it-is-and-why-it-matters/

Benefits and challenges of diversity in the workplace;
https://inside.6q.io/benefits-of-cultural-diversity-in-the-workplace/
https://www.hult.edu/blog/benefits-challenges-cultural-diversity-workplace/

References

Acredolo, C., & O'Connor, J. (1991). On the difficulty of detecting cognitive uncertainty. *Human Development, 34,* 204–223.

American Council on Education (2008). *Making the case for affirmative action* Retrieved from http://www.acenet.edu/bookstore/descriptions/making_the_case/works/research.cfm.

American Heart Association (2006). *Fish, levels of mercury and omega-3 fatty acids* Retrieved from http://americanheart.org/presenter.jthml?identifier =3013797.

Aronson, E. (1978). *The jigsaw classroom.* Beverly Hills, CA: Sage.

Association of American Colleges & Universities (AAC&U) (2002). *Greater expectations: A new vision for learning as a nation goes to college.* Washington, DC: Author.

Association of American Colleges & Universities (AAC&U) (2004). *Our students' best work.* Washington, DC: Author.

Astin, A. W. (1993). *What matters in college?* San Francisco: Jossey-Bass.

Banks, J. A. (2016). *Cultural diversity and education: Foundations, curriculum, and teaching* (6th ed.). New York: Routledge.

Banks, J. A. (1995). Multicultural education and curriculum transformation. *The Journal of Negro Education, 64*(4), 390–400.

Banks, C. A. M. (1997). Parents and teachers: Partners in school reform. In J. A. Banks & C. A. M. Banks (Eds.), *Multicultural education: Issues and perspectives* (3rd ed.) (pp. 408–426). Boston: Allyn and Bacon.

Banks, J. A., Cookson, P., Gay, G., Hawley, W., Irvine, J. J., Nieto, S., Schofield, J. W., & Stephan, W. (2001). Diversity within unity: Essential principles for teaching and learning in a multicultural society. *Phi Delta Kappan, 83*(3), 196–203,

Baron, R. S. (2005). So right it's wrong: groupthink and the ubiquitous nature of polarized group decision making. *Advances in Experimental Social Psychology, 37,* 219–253.

Baron, R. A., Byrne, D., & Brauscombe, N. R. (2006). *Social psychology* (11th ed.). Boston: Pearson.

Bennett, M. J. (2004). From ethnocentrism to ethnorelativism. In J. S. Wurzel (Ed.), *Toward multiculturalism: A reader in multicultural education* (2nd ed.) (pp. 62–78). Newton, MA: Intercultural Resource Corporation.

Blackwell, A. G., Kwoh, S., & Pastor, M. (2002). *Searching for the uncommon common ground: New dimensions on race in America.* New York: Norton.

Blake, R., & Mouton, J. (1979). Intergroup problem solving in organizations: From theory to practice. In W. Austin & S. Worchel (Eds.), *The social psychology of intergroup relations.* Monterey, CA: Brooks/Cole.

Bodian, S. (2006). *Meditation for dummies* (2nd ed.) Indianapolis, IN: Wiley Publishing.

Brandt, R. (1994). On educating for diversity: A conversation with James Banks. *Educational Leadership, 52*(9), 31–35.

Brookfield, S. D. (1987). Developing critical thinkers. San Francisco: Jossey-Bass.

Brooks, I. (2009). *Organizational behavior* (4th ed.). Englewood Cliffs, NJ: Prentice Hall.

Brown, T. D., Dane, F. C., & Durham, M. D. (1998). Perception of race and ethnicity. *Journal of Social Behavior & Personality, 13*(2), 295–306.

Cabrera, A., Nora, A., Terenzini, P., Pascarella, E., & Hagedorn, L. S. (1999). Campus racial climate and the adjustment of students to college: A comparison between White students and African American students. *The Journal of Higher Education, 70*(2), 134–160.

Cheng, D. X., & Zhao, C. (2006). Cultivating multicultural competence through active participation, multicultural activities, and multicultural learning. *NASPA Journal, 43*(4) 13–38.

Chisholm, I. M. (1994). Preparing teachers for multicultural classrooms. *Journal of Educational Issues of Language Minority Students, 14*, 43–68.

Cross, K. P. (1982). Thirty years passed: Trends in general education. In B. L. Johnson (Ed.), *General education in two-year colleges* (pp. 11–20). San Francisco: Jossey-Bass.

Cuseo, J. (1992, Spring). Cooperative learning vs. small-group discussions and group projects: The critical differences. *Cooperative Learning & College Teaching Newsletter, 2*(3), pp. 4–10. (Reprinted in Jones & Price [1995], *Introduction to accounting: A user's perspective.* Englewood Cliffs, NJ: Prentice-Hall.)

Dean, C. B., Hubbell, E. R., Pitler, H., & Stone, B. (2012). *Classroom instruction that works: Research-based strategies for increasing student achievement* (2nd ed.) Alexandria, VA: Association for Supervision and Curriculum Development.

Dovidio, J. F., Kawakami, K., & Gaertner, S. L. (2000). Reducing contemporary prejudice: Combating explicit and implicit bias at the individual and intergroup level. In S. Oskamp (Ed.), *Reducing prejudice and discrimination* (pp. 137–164). Mahwah, NJ: Erlbaum.

Dryden, G. & Vos, J. (1999). *The learning revolution: To change the way the world learns.* Torrance, CA & Auckland, New Zealand: The Learning Web.

Education Commission of the States (1995). *Making quality count in undergraduate education.* Denver, CO: ECS Distribution Center.

Eimers, M. T., & Pike, G. R. (1997). Minority and nonminority adjustment to college: Differences or similarities. *Research in Higher Education, 38*(1), 77–97.

Enberg, M. E. (2004). Improving intergroup relations in higher education: A critical examination of the influence of educational interventions on racial bias. *Review of Educational Research, 74*(4), 473–524.

Feagin, J. R., & McKinney, M. D. (2003). *The many costs of racism.* Lanham, MD: Rowman & Littlefield.

Feskens, E. J. & Kromhout, D. (1993). Epidemiologic studies on Eskimos and fish intake. *Annals of the New York Academy of Science, 683,* 9–15.

Friedman, T. L. (2005). *The world is flat: A brief history of the twenty-first century.* New York: Farrar, Straus & Giroux.

Gardner, H. (1999). *Intelligence reframed: Multiple intelligences for the 21st century.* New York: Basic Books.

Gerard, H., & Miller, N. (1975). *School desegregation.* New York: Plenum Press.

Ginsberg, M. B., & Wlodkowski, R. J. (2009). *Diversity & motivation* (2nd ed.). San Francisco: Jossey-Bass.

Goleman, D. (1995). *Emotional intelligence: Why it can matter more than IQ.* New York: Random House.

Goleman, D. (2006). *Emotional intelligence: Why it can matter more than IQ* (2nd ed.). New York: Bantam Books.

Gorski, P. C. (1995–2019). *Key characteristics of a multicultural curriculum.* Critical Multicultural Pavilion: Multicultural Curriculum Reform (An EdChange Project). Retrieved from *www.edchange.org/multicultural/curriculum/characteristics.html*

Gunaratana, B. (2011). *Mindfulness in plain English.* Boston: Wisdom Publications.

Gurin, P. (1999). New research on the benefits of diversity in college and beyond: An empirical analysis. *Diversity Digest* (spring). Retrieved November 21, 2008, from http://www.diversityweb.org/Digest/Sp99/benefits.html.

Harris, R. (2010). *On the purpose of a liberal arts education.* Retrieved from wisdomandfolly-blog.com/.../seven-reasons-for-the-liberal-arts-part-2/

Hart Research Associates (2013). *It takes more than a major: Employer priorities for college learning and student success.* Washington, DC: Author.

Hill, P. J. (1991). Multiculturalism: The crucial philosophical and organizational issues. *Change, 23*(4), 38–47.

International Wellness Directory (2009). *The history of quackery.* Retrieved from http://www.mnwelldir.org/docs/history/quackery.htm

Janis, I. L. (1982). *Groupthink: Psychological studies of policy decisions and fiascoes.* (2nd ed.). Boston: Houghton Mifflin.

Job Outlook (2018). *Are college graduates "career ready?"* National Association of Colleges & Employers. Retrieved from https://www.naceweb.org/career-readiness/competencies/are-college-graduates-career-ready/

Johnson, D. W., & Johnson, R. T. (1989). *Cooperation and competition: Theory and research.* Edina, MN: Interaction Book Company.

Kelly, K. (1994). *Out of control: The new biology of machines, social systems, and the economic world.* Reading, MA: Addison-Wesley.

Khoshaba, D. M. & Maddi, S. R. (1999–2004). *HardiTraining: Managing stressful change.* Newport Beach, CA: The Hardiness Institute.

Kitchener, K., Wood, P., & Jensen, L. (2000, August). *Curricular, co-curricular, and institutional influence on real-world problem-solving.* Paper presented at the annual meeting of the American Psychological Association, Boston.

Kurfiss, J. G. (1988). *Critical thinking: theory, research, practice, and possibilities.* ASHE-ERIC, Report No. 2. Washington, D.C.: Association for the Study of Higher Education.

Kymlicka, W. (2004). *Multicultural citizenship: A liberal theory of minority rights.* New York, NY: Oxford University Press.

Langer, E. (1997). *The power of mindful learning. Cambridge,* MA: De Capo Press.

Leung, A. K., Maddux, W. W., Galinsky, A. D., & Chie-yue, C. (2008). Multicultural experience enhances creativity: The when and how. *American Psychologist, 63*(3), 169–181.

Levine, D. (2005). *Teaching empathy.* Bloomington, IN: Solution Tree Press.

Light, R. J. (2001). *Making the most of college: Students speak their minds.* Cambridge, MA: Harvard University Press.

Maddux, W. W., & Galinsky, A. D. (2009). Cultural borders and mental barriers: The relationship between living abroad and creativity. *Journal of Personality and Social Psychology, 96*(5), 1047–1061.

Marzano, R., Pickering, D. J., & Pollock, J. (2001). *Classroom instruction that works: Research-based strategies for increasing student achievement.* Alexandria, VA: Association for Supervision and Curriculum Development.

McKay School of Education (2010). *How to transform curriculum to be more multicultural.* Retrieved April 22, 2010, from http://www.education.byu.edu

Miville, M. L., Molla, B., & Sedlacek, W. E. (1992). Attitudes of tolerance for diversity among college students. *Journal of the Freshman Year Experience, 4*(1), 95–110.

Myrdal, F. (1944). *An American dilemma: The Negro problem and modern democracy.* New York, NY: Harper and Row.

NACE (National Association of Colleges & Employers). (2019). *Career readiness defined.* Retrieved from http://www.naceweb.org/career-readiness/competencies/career-readiness-defined/

Nagda, B. R., Gurin, P., & Johnson, S. M. (2005). Living, doing and thinking diversity: How does pre-college diversity experience affect first-year students' engagement with college diversity? In R. S. Feldman (Ed.), *Improving the first year of college: Research and practice* (pp. 73–110). Mahwah, NJ: Lawrence Erlbaum Associates.

Nagda, B., Gurin, P., Soresen, N., & Zúñiga, X. (2009). Evaluating intergroup dialogue: Engaging diversity for personal and social responsibility. *Diversity & Democracy, 12*(1), 4–6.

National Council for the Social Sciences (NCSS) (1991). *Curriculum guidelines for multicultural education.* Prepared by the NCSS Task Force on Ethnic Studies Curriculum Guidelines. Retrieved from www.socialstudies.org/positions/multicultural

Nora, A., & Cabrera, A. (1996). The role of perceptions of prejudice and discrimination on the adjustment of minority college students. *The Journal of Higher Education, 67* (2), 119–148.

Office of Research (1994). *What employers expect of college graduates: International knowledge and second language skills.* Washington, D.C.: Office of Educational Research and Improvement (OERI), U.S. Department of Education.

Okihiro, G. (1994). *Margins and mainstreams: Asians in American history and culture.* Seattle, WA: University of Washington Press.

Pascarella, E. Edison, M., Nora, A., Hagedorn, L, & Terenzini, P. (1996). Influences on students' openness to diversity and challenge in the first year of college. *Journal of Higher Education, 67,* 174–195.

Pascarella, E., Palmer, B., Moye, M., & Pierson, C. (2001). Do diversity experiences influence the development of critical thinking? *Journal of College Student Development, 42,* 257–291.

Paul. R. & Elder, L. (2002). *Critical thinking: Tools for taking charge of your professional and personal life.* Upper Saddle River, NJ: Pearson Education..

Putnam, R. (2007). 'E pluribus unum: Diversity and community in the twenty-first century. The 2006 Johan Skytte Prize Lecture', *Scandinavian Political Studies 30,* 137–74.

Rogers, M., Hennigan, K., Bowman, C., & Miller, N. (1984). Intergroup acceptance in classroom and playground settings. In N. Miller & M. B. Brewer (Eds.), *Groups in contact: The psychology of desegregation* (pp. 187–212). Orlando, FL: Academic Press.

Rosenshine, B. (1997). Advances in research on instruction. In J. W. Lloyd, E. J., Kameanui, & D. Chard (Eds.), *Issues in educating students with disabilities* (pp. 197–221). Mahwah, NJ: Lawrence Erlbaum.

Shetterly, M. L. (2017). *Hidden figures: The American dream and the untold story of the black women mathematicians who helped win the space race.* New York: HarperCollins.

Slavin, R. E. (1980). *Cooperative learning: What research says to the teacher.* Baltimore, MD: Center for Social Organization of Schools.

Slavin, R. E. (1990). *Cooperative learning: Theory, research, and practice.* Englewood Cliffs, NJ: Prentice-Hall

Smith, P. (2004). *The quiet crisis: How higher education is failing America.* Boston: Anker.

Smith, D. (2015). *Diversity's promise for higher education: Making it work* (2nd ed.). Baltimore, MD: Johns Hopkins University Press.

Stephan, W. (1978). School desegregation: An evaluation of predictions made in Brown vs. Board of Education. *Psychological Bulletin, 85,* 217–238.

Stephan, W. (1986). The effects of school desegregation: An evaluation 30 years after Brown. In M. J. Saks & L. Saxe (Eds.), *Advances in applied social psychology* (pp. 181-206). Hillsdale, NJ: Erlbaum.

Stoltz, P. G. (2014). *Grit: The new science of what it takes to persevere, flourish, succeed.* San Luis Obispo: Climb Strong Press.

Tatum, B. D. (2017, September 11). "Diverse but segregated." *Los Angeles Times,* p. A11.

Thompson, A., & Cuseo, J. (2014). *Diversity and the college experience.* Dubuque, IA: Kendall Hunt.

U.S. Census Bureau (2008). *An older and more diverse nation by midcentury.* Retrieved from http://www.census.gov/Press-Release/www/releases/archives/population/012496.html.

Wabash National Study of Liberal Arts Education (2007). *Liberal arts outcomes.* Retrieved from http:www.liberalarts.wabash.edu/ study-overview/

Whitt, E., Edison, M., Pascarella, E., Terenzini, P., & Nora, A. (2001). Influences on students' openness to diversity and challenge in the second and third years of college. *Journal of Higher Education, 72,* 172–204.

Willis, J. (2006). *Research-based strategies to ignite student learning: Insights from a neurologist and classroom teacher.* Alexandria, VA: ASCD.

Worchel, S. (1979). Cooperation and the reduction of intergroup conflict: Some determining factors. In W. Austin & S. Worchel (Eds.), The *social psychology of intergroup relations* (pp. 262–273). Monterey, CA: Brooks/Cole.

Reflections and Applications

2.1 Review the sidebar quotes contained in this chapter and select two that you think are particularly meaningful or inspirational. For each quote you selected, provide an explanation of why you chose it.

2.2 Prepare a brief (30-second) elevator pitch that supports the following statement: Diversity is not just a "PC" issue that involves certain groups of students; it's an educational issue that enhances the learning experience and future success of *all* students.

2.3 Reflect on the following benefits of diversity education cited in this chapter and rate them on a scale of 1–5 in terms of their importance to your educational role (1 = low importance; 5 = high importance).
a) Increases students' self-awareness and self-knowledge
b) Deepens and accelerates student learning
c) Strengthens students' ability to think critically
d) Fosters creative thinking
e) Expands students' social networks and builds emotional intelligence
f) Enhances career preparation
g) Reduces societal prejudice and discrimination
h) Preserves democracy

For any item you gave a rating of "5," briefly explain why you gave that item the highest possible rating.

2.4 How would you defend, support, or explain the following statement? "Humans learn more from diversity than they do from similarity or familiarity."

2.5 Intercultural competence has been defined as the ability to appreciate and learn from human differences and to interact effectively with people from diverse cultural backgrounds. How would you make the case to students that developing intercultural competence with respect to both *domestic* and *international* diversity is critical for career success in the twenty-first century?

2.6 What would you say is the key point being made by the author of the following quote? "Meaningful multi-culturalism transforms the curriculum. While the presence of persons of other cultures and subcultures is a virtual prerequisite to that transformation, their 'mere presence' is primarily a political achievement, not an intellectual or educational achievement. Real educational progress will be made when multi-culturalism becomes *interculturalism*."

2.7 Defend or support the following statement: "Diversity and democracy go hand-in-hand; when the former is valued, the latter is preserved."

3 Barriers to Diversity Appreciation: Stereotypes, Prejudice, and Discrimination

Chapter Purpose and Preview

This chapter identifies and synthesizes the most common forms of bias, stereotyping, prejudice, and discrimination that take place at both the individual and institutional (systemic) level. Also examined are the roots of prejudice: what causes it to form in the first place and what holds it in place once it has been formed. The chapter concludes by underscoring how gaining insight into the root causes of bias is a key element of multicultural education and how it can intercept prejudice formation, combat prejudice-driven discrimination, and promote diversity appreciation.

Introduction

Prejudice and discrimination displayed by humans toward other members of their own species has a long and continuing trail. (See p. 41, Box 3.1) Although some of the more flagrant forms of prejudice and discrimination have been eliminated (e.g., slavery and lynchings), the United States still remains a country fraught with more subtle forms prejudice and continues to be deeply divided along the lines of race, culture, and social class. Studies show that these divisions are increasing as the proportion of ethnic and racial minorities in the American population is increasing (Brookings Institute, 2008). America's public schools, for instance, are more segregated today than they were in the late 1960s (Kisida & Piontek, 2019; Vox Media, 2019).

Stereotyping

The word *stereotype* derives from two roots: *stereo*—to look at in a fixed way, and *type*—to categorize or group together (as in the word "typical"). Thus, stereotyping a group is to view individuals of the same type (group) in the same (fixed) way. To stereotype is to overlook or dismiss individuality; instead, all individuals of the same group (e.g., race or gender) are viewed as having similar personal characteristics—as reflected in comments like: "You know how they are; they're all alike."

At the root of stereotypes is *bias*, meaning "slant." This bias (slant) can tilt toward the positive or the negative, and it can be conscious or unconscious—known as *implicit bias*. Positive bias results in favorable stereotypes (e.g., "Asians are great in science and math"); negative bias leads to unfavorable stereotypes (e.g., "Asians are nerds who do nothing but study"). While most people would reject such blatant stereotypes, people can (and do) hold overgeneralized beliefs about social groups. When these overgeneralizations are negative, they can be internalized by the members of the stereotyped group and have adverse effects on their self-confidence and performance (Steele, 2004)—as illustrated by the following personal experience.

PERSONAL INSIGHT

I was six years old when a six-year-old girl (a member of a different racial group than me) told me that people of my race (Black) could not swim. Since I couldn't swim at that time and she could, I assumed she was correct. I asked a boy (a member of the same racial group as the girl) whether her statement was true. He responded emphatically: "Yes, it's definitely true!" Since I grew up in an area where few other African Americans were around to counteract this belief about my racial group, I continued to buy into this stereotype until I finally took swimming lessons as an adult. After many lessons, I am now a lousy swimmer because I didn't even attempt to swim until reaching an advanced age. Moral of the story: Negative group stereotypes can limit the personal confidence and performance potential of individuals in the group that has been stereotyped.

Aaron Thompson

The above story illustrates a particular form of stereotyping known as "stereotype threat"—a negative stereotype about members of a group can threaten the performance of individuals in that group and increase the likelihood they will confirm or conform to the negative stereotype. Stereotype threat was first demonstrated in a series of experiments conducted by Steele and Aronson (1995), in which it was discovered that if Black students were told prior to a test that there were racial differences on tests like the one they were about to take, it resulted in their performing more poorly than White students. However, if no mention was made prior to the test about racial differences in performance, African American students performed better and at a level that was more similar to the performance of White students. Similarly, when female students were told prior to taking a math test that there were gender differences in performance on such tests, they performed more poorly than females who were not given this information before the test (Steele, 2004). These research findings strongly suggest that educators should be mindful about holding equally high expectations for students from all social groups. (Further information on the power of holding high educational expectations is provided in chapter 5.)

New teachers typically begin their careers in schools where (a) a high percentage of students are members of minority groups, (b) at least 75% of students receive free or reduced-price lunches, and (c) many students are English-language learners with limited English proficiency (Planty et al., 2009). Yet, the majority of K–12 teachers in the American school system are white and come from middle-class socioeconomic backgrounds. For example, during a recent school year, 82 percent of all public school teachers were white, while 51 percent of all public school students were white. In contrast,

16 percent of public school students were black, while 7 percent of teachers were Black, and 24 percent of the students were Hispanic, while 8 percent of teachers were Hispanic (U.S. Department of Education, 2016).

Although teachers from non-minority groups can effectively promote the academic achievement of minority students, all teachers bring the perspective of their own cultural and socioeconomic background—either consciously or unconsciously—to their school's culture (National Collaborative on Diversity in the Teaching Force, 2004; Villegas & Lucas, 2002). It is difficult for teachers not to be influenced by their own cultural background, and this influence can lead to lead to bias, sometimes to such a degree that they disregard or devalue minority students' home culture. If students detect such a bias, they are often forced to make an uncomfortable choice: choose to value their family, friends, and community; or choose to adopt the school culture and face alienation from their own family, friends, and community (Bowman, 1995).

Numerous studies confirm that students' cultural background can influence how they respond to the teacher and the teacher's instructional methods (Gonzalez & Maez, 1995; Moss & Puma, 1995; Speidel, 1992; Wong-Fillmore, 1991). For example, Rivera and Rodgers-Adkinson (1997) report that the home culture of children from Asian and Native American backgrounds commonly stress obedience and submissiveness to authority figures (e.g., teachers). Students from these backgrounds may express this cultural norm in the classroom by not speaking up during class discussions, not feeling comfortable about asking questions, or not approaching the teacher for help. In contrast, the cultural experiences of African American children often encourage them to be strong, outspoken, and not automatically follow authority figures' rules without first questioning the rule's equity. Such behavior can sometimes be incongruent with, or in conflict with, the dominant school culture; thus, teachers may need to anticipate the possibility of cultural mismatch and be ready to respond to it with sensitivity (Cartledge, Singh, & Gibson, 2008). As Scharf (2018) notes, "Culture also plays a role in disciplinary judgments; in some cases, 'inappropriate behaviors' may reflect a cultural mismatch between the norms of the school and the norms of a student's home culture" (p. 12).

There may also be differences in linguistic norms between the student's home culture and the school culture. While it is important for students to learn standard English, teachers should acknowledge, not disparage, the language spoken in the student's home and local community. For example, in standard English, double negatives are grammatically unacceptable; however, in standard Spanish, they are perfectly acceptable and are used to convey greater emphasis. For example, "Yo no sabe" ("I don't know nothing") is used to express lack of knowledge or innocence in a more emphatic way than "I don't know anything" (Banks, 2016).

Teachers should also keep in mind that students from different socioeconomic backgrounds may respond to the same curricular content in very different ways. Research indicates that students from minority cultures learn concepts more effectively when they are taught via culturally-based modules, particularly with respect to their learning of mathematical concepts and their ability to transfer newly acquired knowledge to real-life situations (Lipka et al., 2005).

Culturally sensitive and responsive teachers are also careful not to interpret the achievement gap between students of different cultural groups as an indication of group differences in their innate ability to learn or as an unalterable byproduct of their family and community circumstances, but as a gap that that is reducible through high-quality instruction (Kober, 2001; Smith, 2005). A substantial body of research has shown that the school environment can shrink the achievement gap, or it can magnify it—particularly if the environment consists of teachers who: (a) lack multicultural respect or acceptance, (b) display a privileged attitude, (c) have low expectations for student success, (d) misperceive or misjudge minority students' behavior, and/or (e) have poor relationships with their students (Gordon, Piana & Keleher, 2000; Revilla & Sweeney, 1997, Thompson & Luhman, 1997; Weissglass, 2001).

Prejudice

If members of a stereotyped group are *judged* or *evaluated* in a certain way, the result is *prejudice*. The word *prejudice* literally means to "pre-judge." Thus, prejudice may be defined as a stereotype held about a group of people that's formed before the facts are known. Typically, prejudice is negative and involves

PERSONAL INSIGHT

I was 15 years old when I first became aware of the racial prejudice that existed among members of my extended family. I grew up in New York during the 1950s and became an avid fan of the New York Giants baseball team. When I was 8, the team left New York and become the San Francisco Giants. Even though the Giants left my hometown, I still considered them to be my team. As a result, I was teased frequently by members of my extended family about rooting for an out-of-town team and not being loyal to New York.

During one teasing episode that took place in the presence of my cousins and uncles, I defended my team by saying that they were in first place and that I expected them to win the double-header they were going to play later that day. My 19-year-old cousin, Jimmy, interrupted me and sarcastically proclaimed that the Giants double-header was going to be cancelled because Malcolm X (black civil rights leader) was holding a meeting that day! Several of my older cousins and my uncles began laughing, but I couldn't figure out what was so funny. Then I suddenly got the "joke." At that time, the Giants were a team that had more black and Latino players than any other team in baseball. They were the first major league team to have multiple players from the Dominican Republic, and they had players from Puerto Rico and Cuba. I began to realize that all the teasing I received about being a Giants fan had less to do with the fact that I was rooting for an out-of-town team and more to do with the fact that I was rooting for a "colored" team.

Before hearing that joke about Malcolm X at my family get-together, I never thought of the Giants, players as colored; I just thought they were colorful. They had unique playing styles as well as distinctive surnames and nicknames, such as: Willie Mays ("The Say Hey Kid"), Willie "Stretch" McCovey, Orlando Cepeda (the "Baby Bull"), and Juan Marichal (the "Dominican Dandy"). As a young boy, I saw these players as being refreshingly different and exciting.

My cousin's wisecrack that day, and the encouraging reaction it received from many of my family members, instantly and permanently changed me from being color-blind to color-conscious. It also transformed me from a Giants fan to Giants fanatic. I was not only rooting for a team; I was rooting for a cause. Later that year, the Giants added a pitcher by the name of Masanori Murakami—the first Asian player ever to play major league baseball in America. I was proud to be rooting for the most diverse team in history. I didn't know it at the time, but I was appreciating (and advocating for) diversity.

Joe Cuseo

stigmatizing—ascribing inferior or unfavorable traits to people belonging to the same group (Goffman, 1963). Studies show that stigmatizing can affect students' behavior in general and their academic performance in particular (Inzlicht & Good, 2006; Mendoza-Denton, Page-Gould, & Pietrak, 2006). Studies also show that young children often enter school with prejudicial attitudes that reflect those held by the adults in their family and community (Aboud, 1998; 2009; Stephan & Stephan, 2004).

Discrimination

The term *discrimination* means to "divide" or "separate." In contrast to prejudice, which is a biased belief, attitude, or opinion, discrimination is a biased *action*. Technically, discrimination can be either negative or positive—for example, a discriminating eater may be careful about eating only healthy foods and avoiding unhealthy foods. However, the term is most often associated with negative forms of discriminatory behavior in which prejudiced people engage in unfair or unjust acts toward another group of people. For example, not hiring someone because of the person's race, gender, or sexual orientation is an act of discrimination. Thus, it could be said that discrimination transforms latent prejudice into blatant action.

Other forms of discrimination are more subtle and may take place without people being fully aware that they're discriminating. For example, in a series of classic studies, it was discovered that a number of white, male college professors were treating white male students differently than female students and students of color. These studies showed that females and minority students taught by white male instructors:

▶ received less eye contact in class,
▶ were called on less frequently in class,
▶ were given less time to respond to questions that the instructors asked in class, and
▶ had less contact with the instructors outside of class (Hall & Sandler, 1982, 1984; Sedlacek, 1987; Wright, 1987).

In the vast majority of these cases, the discriminatory treatment that female and minority students received was subtle and was not done intentionally or consciously by the instructors (Green, 1989). Nonetheless, these unintended actions were still discriminatory because they sent a tacit message to students from certain groups that less was expected of them or they were less capable than other students (Sadker & Sadker, 1994).

> "A lot of us never asked questions in class before—it just wasn't done, especially by a woman or a girl, so we need to realize that and get into the habit of asking questions and challenging—regardless of the reactions of the professors and other students."
>
> —Adult female college student

Discrimination can take place on a personal or institutional (structural) level. African Americans now have the same personal rights as whites in the United States; however, for almost 200 years, they did not. Nearly two centuries worth of racial prejudice, discrimination, and exploitation has left long-standing structures, policies, and practices embedded in our nation's economic and social system that still leave black vulnerable to prejudice and discrimination in a less direct but still damaging form known as *institutional racism*—racial discrimination rooted in organizational policies and practices. For example, studies show that institutional racism exists in the

© Monkey Business Images/Shutterstock.com

healthcare industry. Compared to white patients, black patients with similar income and socioeconomic status are less likely to receive: (a) quality medical care during childbirth, (b) breast cancer screening, (c) follow-up visits after hospitalization for mental illness, and (d) maximum-strength pain medication when reporting high levels of pain (Chabria, 2019; Friedman, Kim, & Schneberk, 2019; Schneider, Zaslavsky, & Epstein, 2002).

Institutional racism also manifests itself in real estate practices that demonstrate race-based discrimination in mortgage lending, housing, and bank loans. After World War II, the federal government passed the GI Bill to provide returning veterans with financial assistance that would enable them to attend college and obtain low-interest home loans. The bill was "color blind" in that it was to be applied to veterans of all races. However, politicians from southern states insisted that the implementation of the Bill not be administered by the federal government, but by local political officials who implemented the bill in a way that denied black GIs (veterans) access to state universities, and allowed local bank executives to deny black and Latino GIs access to low-interest home loans. As Daryl Smith (2015) points out, "implementation of the housing policies of the GI Bill is a perfect example of institutional racism under cover of state's rights" (p. 38). This discriminatory real estate practice was compounded by "redlining"—the practice of marking red lines on a map to indicate neighborhoods where banks in the South (and other parts of the country as well) would not invest or lend money, many of which were neighborhoods occupied predominantly by African Americans (Shapiro, 1993).

Most economists agree that the GI Bill stimulated the growth of home ownership, built up the American middle class, and allowed whites to accumulate wealth over time. Thirty years after the passage of the GI Bill, almost 7 of 10 whites owned homes and had a net household worth of over $39,000; in contrast, black households had a net worth of less than $4,000. Most of this racial disparity in wealth was accounted for by home ownership (Katznelson, 2005). As Smith (2015) notes: "There is far less resilience in a family that does not own property than in a family that can leverage assets to get through hard times. It is difficult not to speculate whether, if the GI Bill had provided as many African Americans with opportunities for home ownership and higher education as it did whites, there would be more resiliency, stability, and equity within American society today" (p. 15).

Institutional racism and sexism can also take place with respect to employment opportunities. An interesting illustration of race-based and gender-based employment discrimination once took place in the musical industry. Auditions for orchestras were originally conducted with the identity of the applicants visible to the judges (employers). However, in one audition, the son of a man who worked for the orchestra was applying for a position as a musician and there was concern that if his identity were visible, nepotism (favoring a relative) would bias the hiring process. To guard against this unfair practice, screens were placed in front of the auditioning musicians to conceal their identities. Other orchestras heard about this practice and soon began implementing the same procedure for all their auditions. After the practice of concealing the identity of auditioning musicians became common, something unexpected happened: more women and racial minorities were hired by classical orchestras. Since the applicants' identity was concealed, employment decisions that were previously biased by institutional racism or sexism began to be replaced by applicants' actual qualifications—the merit of their performance (Gladwell, 2005).

Even if job applicants are not intentionally discriminated against in the hiring process on the basis of race, research reveals that people of color still have less access to jobs, particularly higher-paying ones, because many of these positions are obtained through word of mouth. This networking advantage (sometimes referred to as "social capital") favors people who live and socialize with people holding similar positions and who make hiring decisions for such positions—people who are predominantly white. Research shows that employers in most organizations tend to hire people like themselves, either consciously or unconsciously, because they perceive them to be better qualified (Harper, 2012). Sociologists refer to this phenomenon as *homosocial reproduction*—the tendency to replace departing members of an organization with candidates whose characteristics are similar to the departing employee or the employer doing the hiring (Elliott & Smith, 2004; Kanter, 1977). This works to the advantage of white job candidates, providing them with a *privilege* (an unearned advantage) that people of color are denied. Similarly, privileged legacies—people who benefit their relationship to a family member, such as inheriting money from a wealthy parent or being admitted to a college because a family member previously attended the college, are benefits not available to students of color whose family members grew up during times of segregation, discrimination, and civil rights violations (Minnich, 2005).

Such historically-rooted and still lingering forms of institutional racism suggest that even if individuals do their best to be "race blind" and treat people in a non-discriminatory way on a person-by-person basis, it will not eliminate discrimination because much of it takes place at a systemic and institutional level. These persistent, structural forms of racism contradict the argument that minority-group members who have been discriminated against historically do not need affirmative action today because they now have equality. This argument confuses equality with equity. *Equality* refers to treating everyone the *same*; *equity* refers to treating everyone *fairly* so that they have equal opportunities to compete (e.g., start the race at the same starting line). Treating everyone equally after the race has begun doesn't ensure they're being treated equitably if some have already begun the race with an unearned advantage (e.g., starting the race on steroids or starting closer to the finish line). (See figure 3.1) As Banks (2016) puts it: "A significant problem . . . is the assumption that treating groups the same will result in equity, even though some groups have been historic victims of racism and discrimination. Some groups must be treated differently in order for them to attain equity" (p. 26).

> "The route to achieving *equity* will not be accomplished through treating everyone *equally*. It will be achieved by treating everyone justly according to their circumstances."
>
> —Paula Dressel, Ph.D., Race Matters Institute

Thus, it's important to keep in mind that racial discrimination extends beyond individual biases to biases that are ensconced in larger organizational structures and societal systems. An anti-*bias* curriculum helps students understand and appreciate race, class, gender, and other differences on a *personal* level; an anti-*racist* curriculum engages both educators and students in the process of detecting and dismantling *structural* oppression the classroom, school and community ("Ask Teaching Tolerance," 2019). Survey research suggests that American citizens have difficulty understanding or accepting structural causes of discrimination because individualism is a long-held and ingrained value of American culture (Sumida & Gurin, 2001). One goal of multicultural education is to help students understand longstanding structural inequities and empower students with knowledge and skills to eventually change societal systems that continue to perpetuate injustice and inequality (Gorski 1995–2019).

Segregation

Segregation may be defined as the decision of one group to separate itself, either socially or physically, from another group. Well after slavery was abolished, whites created formal and informal laws to allow them to separate themselves from blacks; for example, blacks could not attend the same schools, eat at the same restaurants, or use the same bathroom as whites). These "Jim Crow" laws (named after "Jump Jim Crow"—a song-and-dance character played by a white man in blackface) were enacted after the Civil War to preserve the prejudicial ideology that blacks should be kept separate from and subordinate to whites (Thompson, 2009).

© Everett Historical/Shutterstock.com

Racial segregation still exists in American society today (Massey, 2003; Nagda, Gurin, & Johnson, 2005). Even with the increasing diversity in our society and our schools, students of color are much more likely than white students to attend schools where students of color comprise the majority of the school's population. For example, it has been found that 80% of Hispanic students and 74% of black students attend schools in which they are the majority group at their school; in contrast, white students attend schools where 75% of their schoolmates are white (Orfield, Kucsera, & Siegel-Hawley, 2012). Today, more than half of the nation's schoolchildren are enrolled in schools where over 75 percent of students are either white or non-white (Mervosh, 2019). In a long-term study of more than 2,500 African American, Asian American, Latino, and white students who attended the University of Michigan, it was found that the white students came from highly segregated high schools and neighborhoods and had the most segregated friendship patterns (Matlock, 1997).

While segregation itself may not represent a blatant, malicious form of discrimination, it can lead to and perpetuate prejudice by minimizing (or eliminating) contact between members of the segregated groups. When there is little or no contact between members of a segregated or isolated minority group, it increases the likelihood that the minority group will be perceived them as "unfamiliar" (or "strange"), which can trigger negative feelings toward them (e.g., uncertainty or anxiety) (Zajonc, 2001). Because uncertainty and anxiety are unpleasant feelings, they can then lead to avoidance and dislike of the avoided (segregated) group (Pettigrew, 1998). In contrast, research shows that when children grow up in interracial communities with less prejudicial racial attitudes, they are more likely to live in interracial neighborhoods as adults and are more likely to send their children to interracial schools (Braddock & Mikulyuk, 2012).

 Box 3.1 Summary of Biases, Prejudices, and Discriminatory Behaviors

This box contains a summary of biases, prejudicial beliefs, and discriminatory behaviors that have plagued humankind and serve as barriers to acceptance and appreciation of diversity. As you read through the list, place a checkmark next to any form of prejudice that you have experienced, have seen others experience, or have seen others demonstrate.

▶ **Ethnocentrism:** viewing one's own culture or ethnic group as "normal" or "superior" and another culture as "deficient" or "inferior."

Example: Our viewing another culture as "abnormal" or "uncivilized" because its members eat animals that our culture views unacceptable to eat, even though we eat animals that their culture views unacceptable to eat.

▶ **Stereotyping:** viewing all (or virtually all) members of the same group in the same way—as having the same personal qualities or characteristics.

Example: "If you're Italian, you must be in the Mafia or have a family member who is."

▶ **Prejudice:** negative pre-judgment about members of a social group.

Example: Black football players cannot play quarterback because they lack the intelligence.

▶ **Discrimination:** unequal and unfair treatment of a group of people.

Example: Paying women less than men for performing the same job, even though they have the same level of education and job qualifications.

▶ **Racism:** belief that one's racial group is superior to another group, which is expressed as an attitude (prejudice) or an action (discrimination).

Example: Confiscating land from American Indians based on the belief that they're "savages" or enslaving African Americans based on the belief that they're "subhuman."

> "Let us all hope that the dark clouds of racial prejudice will soon pass away and ...in some not too distant tomorrow the radiant stars of love and brotherhood will shine over our great nation."
>
> —Martin Luther King, Jr., civil rights leader, humanitarian, and recipient of the Nobel Peace Prize

▶ **Institutional Racism:** racial discrimination rooted in organizational policies and practices that disadvantage certain racial groups.

Example: Race-based discrimination in mortgage lending, bank loans, and housing opportunities.

▶ **Racial Profiling:** investigating or arresting someone based solely on the person's race, ethnicity, or national origin—without observing them engaging in actual criminal behavior or without incriminating evidence.

Example: Police making a traffic stop or conducting a personal search based solely on an individual's racial features.

▶ **Slavery:** forced labor in which people are viewed as property, held against their will, and deprived of the right to receive wages.

Example: The legal enslavement of African Americans in the United States until 1865.

▶ **"Jim Crow" Laws:** formal and informal laws created by whites to segregate blacks after the abolition of slavery.

Example: laws in certain parts of the U.S. that required blacks to use separate bathrooms and be educated in separate schools.

▶ **Colorism:** a form of racism that involves bias toward people of color who have darker-colored skin.

Example: Darker-skinned Mexican Americans being more likely to be targeted with "go back to Mexico" chants than lighter-skinned Mexican Americans.

▶ **Segregation:** intentional decision made by a group to separate itself (socially or physically) from another group.

Example: "White flight"—white people moving out of neighborhoods when people of color move in.

▶ **Apartheid:** an institutionalized system of "legal racism" supported by a nation's government. (Apartheid derives from a word in the Afrikaans language, meaning "apartness.")

Example: South Africa's national system of racial segregation and discrimination that was in place from 1948 to 1994.

"Never, never, and never again shall it be that this beautiful land will again experience the oppression of one by another."

—Nelson Mandela, anti-apartheid revolutionary, first black president of South Africa after apartheid, and recipient of the Nobel Peace Prize

▶ **Hate Crimes:** criminal action motivated solely by prejudice toward the victim.

Example: Acts of vandalism or assault aimed at members of a particular ethnic group or persons of a particular sexual orientation.

▶ **Hate Groups:** organizations whose primary purpose is to stimulate prejudice, discrimination, or aggression toward certain groups of people based on their ethnicity, race, religion, etc.

Example: The Ku Klux Klan—an American terrorist group that perpetrates hatred toward all non-white races.

▶ **White Supremacy:** the view that whites are a genetically superior group and should dominate other racial groups or live in a whites-only society.

Example: The view held by hate groups, such as the Ku Klux Klan and neo-Nazi groups.

▶ **Genocide:** mass murdering of a particular ethnic or racial group.

Example: The Holocaust, in which millions of Jews were systematically murdered in Nazi Germany. Other examples include the murdering of Cambodians under the Khmer Rouge regime, the murdering of Bosnian Muslims in the former country of Yugoslavia, and the slaughter of the Tutsi minority by the Hutu majority in Rwanda.

"A war of extermination will continue to be waged ... until the Indian race becomes extinct."

—Peter Burnett, first elected governor of California, 1851

▶ **White Genocide:** (a.k.a. "Replacement Theory") a racist conspiracy theory contending that white people all over the world are being displaced by immigrants and people of color, with the secret assistance of prominent Jews.

Example: Erroneous claims that the South African government is attacking and seizing the land of white farmers.

▶ **Classism:** prejudice or discrimination based on social class, particularly toward people of lower socioeconomic status.

Example: Acknowledging the contributions made by politicians and wealthy industrialists to America, while ignoring the contributions of poor immigrants, farmers, slaves, and pioneer women.

▶ **Religious Intolerance:** denying the fundamental human right of people to hold religious beliefs, or to hold religious beliefs that differ from one's own.

Example: Atheists who force non-religious (secular) beliefs on others, or members of religious groups who believe that people holding different religious beliefs are infidels or "sinners."

"Rivers, ponds, lakes and streams—they all have different names, but they all contain water. Just as religions do—they all contain truths."

—Muhammad Ali, three-time world heavyweight boxing champion, member of the International Boxing Hall of Fame, and recipient of the Spirit of America Award as the most recognized American in the world

▶ **Anti-Semitism:** prejudice or discrimination toward Jews and other people who practice the religion of Judaism.

Example: Disliking or disdaining Jews because are the people who "killed Christ."

▶ **Xenophobia:** fear or hatred of foreigners, outsiders, or strangers.

Example: Believing that immigrants must be banned from entering the country or deported from the country because they undermine the economy and escalate crime.

▶ **Regional Bias:** prejudice or discrimination based on the geographical region in which an individual is born and raised.

Example: A northerner who thinks that all southerners are racists.

▶ **Nationalism a.k.a. Jingoism:** excessive interest and belief in the superiority of one's own nation (without acknowledging its mistakes or weaknesses), often accompanied by favoring aggressive foreign policy that neglects the needs of other nations or the common needs of all nations.

Example: "Blind patriotism"—not seeing the shortcomings of one's own nation and viewing any questioning or criticism of it as being disloyal or "unpatriotic." (As reflected in such slogans as: "America: right or wrong!" "America: love it or leave it!")

> "The teaching of nationalism often results in students learning misconceptions, stereotypes, and myths about other nations and acquiring negative and confused attitudes toward them."
>
> —James Banks, Founding Director of the Center or Multicultural Education at the University of Washington

▶ **Nativism:** a political policy of preserving or advancing the interests of native inhabitants at the expense of immigrants, including opposing immigration based on fears that immigrants—particularly those from certain nations—will distort or displace the home nation's existing cultural norms and values. (Note: People holding this political position do not view it as prejudice, but as patriotism.)

Example: The Chinese Exclusion Act—a federal law passed in 1882 that banned all Chinese immigrants from entering the United States. It was the first law implemented in America that prohibited all members of a specific ethnic or national group from entering the country.

▶ **Terrorism:** intentional acts of violence committed against civilians that are motivated by political or religious prejudice.

Example: The September 11th, 2001 attacks on the United States.

▶ **Sexism:** prejudice or discrimination based on sex or gender.

Example: Believing that women should not pursue careers in fields traditionally occupied by men (e.g., engineering or politics) because they lack the innate qualities or natural skills to be successful.

▶ **Heterosexism:** belief that heterosexuality is the only acceptable sexual orientation.

Example: Believing gays should not have the same legal rights as heterosexuals.

▶ **Homophobia:** extreme fear or hatred of homosexuals.

Example: Creating or contributing to anti-gay websites, or "gay bashing"—engaging in acts of violence aimed at gays.

▶ **Ageism:** prejudice or discrimination toward certain age groups, particularly toward the elderly.

Example: believing that "old" people have dementia and should not be allowed to drive a car or make important decisions.

▶ **Ableism:** prejudice or discrimination toward people who are disabled or handicapped (physically, mentally, or emotionally).

Example: Intentionally avoiding social contact with people in wheelchairs.

Causes of Prejudice and Discrimination

What all forms of prejudice and discrimination have in common is they involve biases that are unsupported by factual evidence and critical thinking. Less clear, however, is why or how these biases develop in the first place. There is no single, definitive answer to this question, but research does suggest that the following factors play a contributing role to the formation and preservation of negative biases:

1. Experiencing feelings of discomfort with the unknown or unfamiliar
2. Use of selective perception and selective memory to preserve prejudicial beliefs
3. Mentally categorizing people into "in" groups and "out" groups
4. Perceiving members of unfamiliar groups as being more alike than members of one's own group
5. Tendency for majority group members to overestimate negative behaviors exhibited by members of minority groups
6. Rationalizing prejudice and discrimination as justifiable
7. Strengthening self-esteem by assuming membership in a "superior" group.

Experiencing Feelings of Discomfort with the Unknown or Unfamiliar

Studies show that when humans encounter something unfamiliar or uncommon, they're likely to experience feelings of discomfort or anxiety; in contrast, when people experience repeated exposure to something and become more familiar with it, it is perceived more positively and judged more favorably (Zajonc, 2001). This phenomenon is so prevalent and powerful that social psychologists have come to call it the "familiarity principle" (Zajonc, 1968, 1970). It is the principle that underlies the slogan "advertising pays"—the more exposure a product receives, the more familiar the product becomes, and the more likely people are to favor it—and buy it (Grimes & Kitchen, 2007). The familiarity principle also accounts for why research on voting patterns reveal that there is strong relationship between the amount of public exposure a candidate receives and the number of votes the candidate receives (Bornstein & Carver-Lemley, 2004).

Comfort with familiarity is likely "wired into" the human brain because it played an important role in the survival and evolution of the human species (Kahneman, 2011). When our early ancestors encountered something or somebody unfamiliar, it was advantageous for them to react with anxiety because it released a rush of adrenaline that prepared them to deal with what might be a potential predator. This adrenaline rush put them in a better position to deal with the threat by them to fight it or flee from it (known the "fight- or -flight" response), thus helping to ensure their survival and the future survival of the human species (Cannon, 1932; Jansen et al., 1995). The fight-or-flight response to the unfamiliar is so deeply rooted in our evolutionary history that it continues to manifest itself in newborn babies. Between 6–12 months, most infants experience "stranger anxiety"—when they encounter someone unfamiliar, it triggers anxiety—they cry, their heart rate accelerates, and their breathing rate increases rapidly (Brooker et al., 2013). The fight-or-flight response to the unfamiliar may also explain why people of all ages tend to form rapid judgments (within 40 milliseconds) about anyone they encounter who they think may be personally threatening (Bar, Neta, & Linz. 2006; Gladwell, 2005).

It may also help explain why negative pre-judgments (prejudice) can form so quickly toward members of less familiar racial or cultural groups (Aronson, Wilson, & Akert, 2013). We may not be able to prevent this automatic emotional reaction from initially kicking in because it's initiated in lower (subconscious) centers of the brain and takes place before higher sections of the brain (responsible for conscious awareness and rational thinking) can get involved (see Figure 3.1). However, if we remain mindful of this fear-of-the-unfamiliar reaction, we can make a conscious effort to react to it rationally and prevent it from morphing into biased judgments, attitudes, and actions toward members of groups who are unfamiliar to us, or with whom we've have had limited contact.

"See that man over there?
Yes, I hate him.
But you don't know him.
That's why I hate him."

—Gordon Allport, social psychologist, *The Nature of Prejudice*

How Selective Perception and Selective Memory can Preserve Prejudicial Beliefs

People who are prejudiced toward a social group typically avoid contact with members of that group, leaving them with little or no opportunity to have positive experiences with members of the group that could contradict or disprove their prejudice. This results in a self-perpetuating cycle in which the prejudiced person continually avoids contact with members of the stigmatized group, which, in turn, continues to maintain and reinforce the person's prejudice.

In addition, personal prejudice is likely to be held intact through a psychological process known as *selective perception*—the tendency for biased people to see what they *expect* to see and fail to see what contradicts their bias (Hugenberg & Bodenhausen, 2003). Have you ever noticed how fans rooting

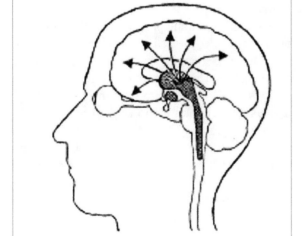

© Kendall Hunt Publishing Company

Figure 13.1

How Information is Processed in the Brain Information entering the human brain is first processed emotionally at a subconscious level (lower shaded area) before reaching higher areas of the brain responsible for conscious, rational thinking. By being consciously aware of, and reacting rationally to, fear or anxiety triggered by encounters with unfamiliar social groups, irrational prejudices can be short-circuited before becoming enduring attitudes.

for their favorite sports team tend to focus on, "see" and react strongly to calls by referees that go against their own team, but don't seem to react (or even notice) calls that go against the opposing team? This is an innocuous everyday example of selective perception. In the more pernicious case of prejudice, selective perception takes the old adage, "seeing is believing" and turns it into "believing is seeing." It leads prejudiced people to continue "seeing" things that are consistent with their prejudicial belief while remaining "blind" to experiences and pieces of evidence that contradict it.

Making matters worse, selective perception is often accompanied by *selective memory*—the tendency for prejudiced people to recall information that reinforces their prejudicial belief and forget information that refutes it (Judd, Ryan, & Parke, 1991). The two prejudice-preserving processes of selective perception and selective memory reinforce one another and often operate *unconsciously* (Baron, Branscombe, & Byrne, 2009). As a result, people holding a prejudice may not even be aware that they are using these processes and that their use of them is perpetuating their prejudice, ensuring it will go unchallenged and unchanged. The power of this prejudice-preserving process can be so strong that even if the prejudiced people happen to have a positive experience with a person from the stigmatized group, that person is perceived to be an "exception" to the general rule (Crisp & Hewstone, 2007; Hewstone, 1994) or as an individual exception that actually "proves" the general rule (Aronson, Wilson, & Akert, 2013).

Mentally Categorizing People into "In" Groups and "Out" Groups

Human societies have a long history of grouping fellow humans into social categories, probably because the human brain has a natural tendency to (a) seeks patterns and associations to make the complex social world simpler to understand—a phenomenon referred to as "implicit social cognition" (Greenwald & Banaji, 1995; Bless, Fiedler, Strack, 2004), and (b) take mental shortcuts so it can more efficiently manage all the outside information has to deal with and process—a phenomenon called "cognitive bias" (Haselton, Nettle, & Andrews, 2005).

The good news is that grouping people into categories can help organize and simplify our social world; the bad news is that it can also lead to group stereotypes that blind us to the uniqueness of individuals who compose the social categories we create. The tendency to create group classifications can also create *in*-groups ("us") and *out*-groups ("them"), resulting in *ethnocentrism*—viewing one's own cultural group as the central in-group and other cultures as marginal out-groups. The norms of our own cultural group then tends to be viewed as "normal" while the norms of other cultures come to be seen as "abnormal"—deviant or deficient (National Council for the Social Sciences, 2001). Thus, ethnocentrism can lead to prejudice and discrimination toward members of other cultural groups (Bigler & Hughes, 2009; Stephan & Stephan, 2004).

Perceiving Members of Unfamiliar Groups as More Alike than Members of One's Own Group

Research in the field of social psychology demonstrates that humans tend to perceive members of different (less familiar) groups as more alike in attitudes and behavior than members of their own (familiar) group (Baron, Byrne, & Branscombe, 2006). For example, members of younger age groups perceive members of older age groups to be more alike in their attitudes and beliefs than members of their own age group (Linville, Fischer, & Salovey, 1989).

This tendency may stem from the fact that we have more experience with members of our own group, which gives us more opportunities to observe and interact with a wide variety of individuals within our group. In contrast, we have less frequent contact with individuals from an unfamiliar group, so we don't have as many opportunities to witness the variety of individual differences within that group. As a result, we may arrive at the conclusion that members of an unfamiliar group are more alike in attitudes and behavior than members of our own group.

When people have very limited contact with individuals from other racial groups, it can also lead them to the erroneous conclusion that "they all look alike." Studies show that humans are better able to recognize individual differences among members of their own race than members of other races—a phenomenon known as "own-race bias" (Aronson, Wilson, & Akert, 2013). However, these identification errors are much less likely to take place among members of different races who interact and become familiar with one another, particularly at an early age (Sangrigoli et al., 2005).

People of all races are susceptible to making more facial identification errors when identifying individuals of races with whom they have limited interaction and familiarity (Malpass, 1992). The greater likelihood of cross-race facial recognition errors may be due to the fact that when viewing a member of an unfamiliar race, the viewer's perception is influenced less by the member's individual facial features and more by the general facial features associated with the member's racial group (e.g., Asian eyes or African lips) (Levin, 2000).

Cross-race identification errors have led to false criminal convictions of individuals from racial minority groups that were based on eyewitness testimony provided by a member of the majority racial group. DNA evidence discovered later proved that the crime was committed by another member of the same racial group as the falsely accused person (Ramsey & Frank, 2007). A famous example of such a cross-race identification error is the case of Lenell Geter, an African American engineer who received a life sentence for a crime he never committed. The arresting officer (a white man) mistakenly swore under oath that Geter was a career criminal suspected of dozens of holdups. Four other white witnesses also misidentified him for a different black man who actually committed the crime and was later apprehended.

Such miscarriages of justice resulting from the misperception that minority-group members "all *look* alike" are stunning and have received national attention. Yet, the belief that they "all *act* alike" is a much more pervasive, prejudice-forming misconception. This misconception is the underlying foundation on which negative group stereotyping (e.g., Indians are savages; blacks are violent) and it has led to the most extreme forms of racial discrimination and domination (Baron, Byrne, & Brancombe, 2006).

Tendency for Majority Group Members to Overestimate Negative Behaviors Exhibited by Members of Minority Groups

Studies show that if negative or socially threatening behavior occurs at the same rate among members of both a majority and minority group (e.g., the rate of criminal behavior in both groups is 10 percent), members of the majority group are more likely to perceive the rate as being higher in the minority group and are more likely to develop negative attitudes (prejudice) toward the minority group (Baron, Byrne, & Brauncombe, 2006). For example, it has been found that whites in the United States underestimate the crime rate of white men and overestimate the crime rates of black men (Hamilton & Sherman, 1989).

One possible explanation for this overestimation error is that minorities represent a smaller proportion of the population and, therefore, are more likely to stand out. Thus, behavior exhibited by members of a minority group is more likely to be noticed (and remembered). If the behavior they exhibit happens to be negative or potentially threatening, it is more likely to attract the attention of the majority group and trigger prejudice toward the minority group (McArthur & Friedman, 1980).

Rationalizing Prejudice and Discrimination as Justifiable

Rationalization is a psychological strategy used to try to explain or justify personal behavior that is clearly illogical or unethical. Rationalization was used to justify slavery in the United States despite the fact that our nation was built on the foundational principle that "all men are created equal and from that equal creation they derive rights inherent and inalienable, among which are the preservation of life, & liberty, & the pursuit of happiness." At the time that this principle was enunciated in our nation's Declaration of Independence, slavery was legal and an established feature of America's colonial economy. In fact, our country's first president, George Washington, "owned" more than 300 slaves at the time of his death (Hirschfeld, 1997).

Slavery clearly contradicted the democratic ideals on which America was founded. To reconcile this contradiction and allow the United States to use unpaid labor in pursuit of economic prosperity, the concept of different human "races" was introduced. Americans of a darker color (race) were deemed to be inferior to the "white race," therefore, it was justifiable (and legal) to enslave them. The United States continued with its slave-based economy and became the first nation in the world to use a system of slavery based exclusively on skin color. The same rationalization was used to justify the extermination of Native Americans, the forced takeover of Mexican land, and the exclusion of Asian immigrants (California Newsreel, 2003).

These historical examples illustrate the extent to which humans can rationalize unconscionable beliefs and actions and how can lead to the formation and perpetuation of prejudice. What is offered as a rationale (rational explanation) for flagrant acts of discrimination is often nothing more than a rationalization (self-serving justification) that is neither rational nor ethical.

Strengthening Self-Esteem by Assuming Membership in a "Superior" Group

Personal identity (Who am I?) and self-esteem (How do I feel about myself?) are strongly influenced by the group(s) to which a person belongs. By believing one's own group is better than or superior to other groups, one's self-image is strengthened (Tafjel, 1982; Tafjel & Turner, 1986). It allows members of the self-proclaimed "superior" group to develop a more positive self-image by comparing themselves members of other groups—who are seen as being "less than" or inferior to their own group (Brislin, 1993). The reasoning goes like this: My group is better, and since I belong to a better group, I am better (I feel better about myself).

Building up one's self-image by identifying with a "superior" group is particularly attractive to people who may have low self-esteem, are experiencing frustration, or are struggling. Their self-esteem can be boosted by finding flaws or weaknesses in members of another group (Rudman & Fairchild, 2004). Members of the flawed (stigmatized) group can also serve as an excuse or scapegoat for one's frustrations and failures (Gemmil, 1989). The word *scapegoat* has its roots in Biblical times, when a goat was released into the wilderness as part of the Jewish ceremony of Yom Kippur (Day of Atonement). Before the goat was released, a high priest symbolically laid the sins of the people on its head; when the goat was set free, the people were then symbolically freed (forgiven) for their sins. This ritual led to the term "scapegoat," which now refers to an innocent person or group of people on whom the flaws and misfortunes of others are transferred, thereby absolving the flawed or guilty party of blame and responsibility.

Research in social psychology has shown that when people experience self-esteem-deflating events (e.g., when their employment rate or income level income goes down), their prejudice toward other groups goes up (Aronson, Wilson, & Akert, 2013). This is illustrated by a study in which individuals were given either positive or negative feedback on a task they just performed. After receiving such feedback, they evaluated a female job applicant who was introduced as being Jewish. The experiment's results revealed that individuals who received negative feedback on their task performance (lowering their self-esteem) were more likely to evaluate the Jewish job applicant negatively, but if they were later allowed to point out the weaknesses and shortcomings of the Jewish job applicant (the scapegoat), their reported sense of self-esteem increased (Fein & Spencer, 1997). The results of this study demonstrate that lower levels of self-esteem lead to higher likelihood of scapegoating, which, in turn, serves to heighten self-esteem. By finding flaws and shortcomings in someone else (a scapegoat), people felt better about themselves. These experimental results are consistent with arguably the most extreme and horrific example of scapegoating in human history. During his Nazi regime, Adolf Hitler's prejudicial ideology about Jews (and other "defective" groups) stirred up ethnic pride among Germans, instilling in them the idea that they were members of a "master race." At the same time, Jews and other "inferior" groups were blamed for the country's economic problems, making them the scapegoats and subsequent targets of the Holocaust.

PERSONAL INSIGHT

One of the best-attended extracurricular events at my school was a presentation delivered by a guest speaker named Floyd Cochran. Originally a member of and recruiter for "Aryan Nation" (a white-supremacist hate group), he eventually quit the group, then became a nationally known civil rights activist and educator, touring the country, speaking out against racist organizations and hate crimes at high schools and colleges. After giving his talk on my campus, he asked the jam-packed room of students if they had any questions. No student raised a hand, probably because the audience was so large and the topic so sensitive. I thought that if I broke the ice and asked a question, then students would feel comfortable doing the same. So, I asked Cochran: "Based on your experience with the hate-group members you associated with and new members you recruited, what would you say is the number-one reason *why* people join a hate group?" Without the slightest pause, he immediately and firmly stated that most members of his hate group had a poor self-image and many came from dysfunctional families where their need for social acceptance was never met. Cochran's answer strongly suggests that one root cause of prejudice is the need for people with low self-esteem to strengthen their weak self-image by identifying with a "stronger" or more "superior" group.

Joe Cuseo

> Consider This ...
> Understanding the root causes of bias, prejudice, and discrimination should be a key component of multicultural education. It can help prevent the formation of prejudice, combat its continuation, and serve as a stepping stone to multicultural appreciation.

Internet Resources

Combating stereotype threat: www.reducingstereotypethreat.org/

Critical practices for anti-bias education: www.tolerance.org/sites/default/files/general/PDA Critical Practices.pdf

LGBTQ Acceptance and Support: "It Gets Better Project," at *www.itgetsbetter.org*

Preservation of human rights in America:
www.tolerance.org
www.splcenter.org/

Preservation of human rights worldwide: www.amnesty.org/en/discrimination

References

Aboud, F. E. (1998). *Children and prejudice*. New York: Basil Blackwell.

Aboud, F. E. (2009). Modifying children's racial attitudes. In J. A. Banks (Ed.), *The Routledge international companion to multicultural education* (pp. 199–209). New York & London: Routledge.

Aronson, E., Wilson, T. D., & Akert, R. M. (2013). *Social psychology* (8th ed.). Upper Saddle River, NJ: Pearson/Prentice Hall.

"Ask Teaching Tolerance" (2019, Fall). *Teaching Tolerance*, Issue 63, p. 9.

Banks, J. A. (2016). *Cultural diversity and education: Foundations, curriculum, and teaching* (6th ed.). New York: Routledge.

Bar, M., Neta, M., & Linz, H. (2006). Very first impressions. *Emotion*, 6(2), 269–278.

Baron, R. A., Brauncombe, N. R., & Byrne, D. R. (2009). *Social psychology* (12th ed.). Hoboken, NJ: Pearson.

Baron, B. A., Byrne, D., & Branscombe, N. R. (2006). *Mastering social psychology*. Boston: Pearson/Allyn and Bacon.

Bigler, R. A., & Hughes, J. M. (2009). The nature and origins of children's racial attitudes. In J. A. Banks (Ed.), *The Routledge international companion to multicultural education* (pp. 186–198). New York: & London: Routledge.

Bless, H., Fiedler, K., & Strack, F. (2004). *Social cognition: How individuals construct social reality*. Hove and New York: Psychology Press

Bornstein, R. F., & Craver-Lemley, C. (2004). Mere exposure effect. In R. F. Pohl, (Ed.), *Cognitive illusions: A handbook on fallacies and biases in thinking, judgement and memory* (pp. 215–234). Hove, UK: Psychology Press.

Bowman, B. T. (1995). Cultural diversity and academic achievement. Retrieved from http://www.ncrel.org/sdrs/areas/issues/educatrs/leadrshp/le0bow.htm#author

Braddock, J, M. II., & Mikulyuk, A. B. (2012). Segregation, desegregation, and resegregation. In J. A. Banks (Ed.), *Encyclopedia of diversity in education* (volume 4) (pp. 1930–1934). Thousand Oaks, CA: Sage.

Brislin, R. W. (1993). *Understanding culture's influence on behavior*. Fort Worth, TX: Harcourt Brace Jovanovich College Publishers.

Brooker, R. J., Buss, K. A., Lemery-Chalfant, K., Aksan, N., Davidson, R. J., & Goldsmith, H. H. (2013). The development of stranger fear in infancy and toddlerhood: Normative development, individual differences, antecedents, and outcomes. *Developmental Science, 16* (6): 864–78

Brookings Institute (2008). *Demographic keys to the 2008 election*. Washington, DC: Brookings Institute. Retrieved from www.brookings.edu/~/media/Files/events/2008/1020_demographics/20081020_demographics.pdf

California Newsreel (2003). *Race-the power of an illusion*. Retrieved April 11, 2009, from http://www.PBS.org/Race

Cannon, W. (1932). *The wisdom of the body*. United States: W.W. Norton & Company.

Cartledge, G., Singh, A., & Gibson, L. (2008). Practical behavior management techniques to close the accessibility gap for students who are culturally and linguistically diverse. *Preventing School Failure, 52*(3), 29–38.

Chabria, A. (2019, September 14). 3 bills on bias are sent to Gov. *Los Angeles Times*, pp. B1, B4.

Crisp, R. J., & Hewstone, N. (2007). Multiple social categorizations. In M. P. Sanna (Ed.), *Advances in experimental and social psychology* (Vol. 39, pp. 163-254). Orlando, FL: Academic Press.

Elliot, J. R., & Smith, R. A. (2004). Race, gender, and workplace power. *American Sociological Review, 69*(3), 365–386.

Fein, S., & Spencer, S. J. (1997). Prejudice as self-image maintenance: Affirming the self through derogating others. *Journal of Personality and Social Behavior, 73*(1), 31–44.

Friedman, J., Kim, D. & Schneberk, T. (2019). Assessment of racial/ethnic and income disparities in the prescription of opioids and other controlled medications in California. *JAMA Internal Medicine, 179*(4), 469–476. Retrieved from https://jamanetwork.com/journals/jamainternalmedicine/fullarticle/2723625

Gemmil, G. (1989). The dynamics of scapegoating in small groups. *Small Group Behavior, 20,* 406–418.

Gladwell, M. (2005). *Blink: The power of thinking without thinking.* New York: Little, Brown and Company.

Goffman, E. (1963). *Stigma: Notes on the management of spoiled identity.* Englewood Cliffs, NJ: Prentice-Hall.

Gonzalez, G., & Maez, L. (1995, Fall). Advances in research in bilingual education. *Directions in Language and Education, 1*(5), 694–701.

Gordon, R., Piana, L. D., & Keleher, T. (2000). *Facing the consequences: An examination of racial discrimination in U.S. public schools.* Oakland, CA: Applied Research Center.

Gorski, P. C. (1995-2018). *Key characteristics of a multicultural curriculum.* Critical Multicultural Pavilion: Multicultural Curriculum Reform (An EdChange Project). Retrieved from www.edchange.org/multicultural/curriculum/characteristics.html

Green, M. G. (Ed.) (1989). *Minorities on campus: A handbook for enhancing diversity.* Washington, DC: American Council on Education.

Greenwald, A. G., & Banaji, M. R. (1995). Implicit social cognition: Attitudes, self-esteem and stereotypes. *Psychological Review, 102*(1), 4–27.

Grimes, A., &. Kitchen, P. J. (2007). Researching mere exposure effects to advertising. *International Journal of Market Research, 4*(2): 191–221.

Hall, R. M. & Sandler, B. R. (1982). *The classroom climate: A chilly one for women.* Association of American Colleges' Project on the Status of Women. Washington, D.C.: Association of American Colleges.

Hall, R. M. & Sandler, B. R. (1984). *Out of the classroom: A chilly campus climate for women.* Association of American Colleges' Project on the Status of Women. Washington, D.C.: Association of American Colleges.

Hamilton, D. L. & Sherman, S. J. (1989). Illusory correlations: Implications for stereotype theory and research. In D. Bar-Tal, C. F. Graumann, A. W. Kruglanski, & W. Stroebe (Eds.), *Stereotyping and prejudice: Changing conceptions* (pp. 59–82). New York: Springer-Verlag.

Harper, S. R. (2012). Race without racism: How higher education researchers minimize racist institutional norms. *Review of Higher Education, 36*(1), 9–30.

Haselton, M. G., Nettle, D., & Andrews, P. W. (2005). The evolution of cognitive bias. In D. M. Buss (Ed.), *The handbook of evolutionary psychology* (pp. 724–746.). Hoboken, NJ: John Wiley & Sons Inc.

Hewstone, M. (1994). Revision and change of strereotypic beliefs. In search of the elusive subtyping model. In W. Stroebe & M. Hewstone (Eds.), *European Review of Social Psychology, 5*(1), 69–109.

Hirschfeld, F. (1997). *George Washington and slavery.* University of Missouri Press.

Hugenberg, K., & Bodenhausen, G. V. (2003). Facing prejudice: Implicit prejudice and the perception of facial threat. *Psychological Science, 14,* 640–643.

Inzlicht, M., & Good, C. (2006). How environments can threaten academic performance, self-knowledge, and sense of belonging. In S. Levin & C. van Laar (Eds.), *Stigma and group inequality* (pp. 129-150). Mahwah, NJ: Erlbaum.

Jansen, A. S. P., Nguyen, X. V., Karpitsky, V., Mettenleiter, T. C., & Loewy, A. D. (1995). Central command neurons of the sympathetic nervous system: Basis of the fight-or-flight response. *Science, 27*(5236), 644-646.

Judd, C. M., Ryan, C. S., & Parke, B. (1991). Accuracy in the judgment of in-group and out-group variability. *Journal of Personality and Social Psychology, 61,* 366–379.

Kahneman, D. (2011). *Thinking, fast and slow.* New York: Farrar, Straus & Giroux.

Kanter, R. (1977). *Men and women of the corporation.* New York: Basic Books.

Katznelson, I. (2005). *When affirmative action was white: An untold history of racial inequality in twentieth-century America.* New York; Norton.

Kisida, B., & Piontek, O. (2019, May 22). Is segregation really getting worse? Education Next. Retrieved from https://www.educationnext.org/is-school-segregation-really-getting-worse/

Kober, N. (2001, April). *It takes more than testing: Closing the achievement gap. A report of the Center on Education Policy.* Washington, DC: Center on Education Policy.

Levin, D. T. (2000). Race as a visual feature: Using visual search and perceptual discrimination tasks to understand face categories and the cross-race recognition deficit. Journal of Experimental Psychology: General, 129(4), 559–574.

Linville, P. W., Fischer, G. W., & Salovey, P. (1989). Perceived distributions of the characteristics of in-group and out-group members: Empirical evidence and a computer simulation. *Journal of Personality and Social Psychology, 57,* 165–188.

Lipka, J., Hoganm M. P., Webster, J. P., Yanez, E., Adams, B., Clark, S, et al. (2005). Math in a cultural context: Two case studies of a successful culturally based math project. *Anthropology and Education Quarterly, 36*(4), 367-385.

Malpass, R. S. (1992). "They all look alike to me". In M. Merrens & G. Brannigan (Eds.) *The undaunted psychologist.* (pp. 74–88). New York: McGraw-Hill.

Massey, D. (2003). *The source of the river: The social origins of freshmen at America's selective colleges and universities.* Princeton, NJ: Princeton University Press.

Matlock, J. (1997). Student expectations and experiences: The Michigan study. *Diversity Digest* (summer). Retrieved from http://www.diversityweb.org/Digest/Sm97/research.html.

McArthur, L. Z., & Friedman, S. A. (1980). Illusory correlation in impression formation: Variations in the shared distinctiveness effect as a function of the distinctive person's age, race, and sex. *Journal of Personality and Social Psychology, 39,* 615–624.

Mendoza-Denton, R., Page-Gould, E., & Pietrak, J. (2006). Mechanisms for coping with status-based rejection expectations. In S. Levin & C. van Laar (Eds.), *Stigma and group inequality* (pp. 151-170). Mahwah, NJ: Erlbaum.

Mervosh, S. (2019, February 27). How much wealthier are white school districts than nonwhite ones? $23 billion, report says. *The New York Times.* Retrieved from https://www.nytimes.com/2019/02/27/education/school-districts-funding-white-minorities.html?module=inline

Minnich, E. K. (2005). *Transforming knowledge* (2nd ed.) Philadelphia: Temple University Press.

Moss, M., & Puma, M. (1995). *Prospects: The congressionally mandated study of educational growth and opportunity: First year report on language minority and limited English proficient students.* Washington, DC: U.S. Department of Education.

Nagda, B. R., Gurin, P., & Johnson, S. M. (2005). Living, doing and thinking diversity: How does pre-college diversity experience affect first-year students' engagement with college diversity? In R. S. Feldman (Ed.), *Improving the first year of college: Research and practice* (pp. 73–110). Mahwah, NJ: Lawrence Erlbaum.

National Collaborative on Diversity in the Teaching Force. (2004). *Assessment of diversity in America's teaching force.* Washington, DC: Author

National Council for the Social Sciences (NCSS) (1991). *Curriculum guidelines for multicultural education.* Prepared by the NCSS Task Force on Ethnic Studies Curriculum Guidelines. Retrieved from www.socialstudies.org/positions/multicultural

Orfield, G., Kucsera, J., & Siegel-Hawley, G. (2012). *E pluribus . . . separation: Deepening double segregation for more students.* The Civil Rights Project/Proyecto Derechos Civiles, University of California, Los Angeles. Retrieved from http://civil- rightsproject.ucla.edu/research/k-12-eduction/integration-and-diversity/mlk-national/e-pluribus . . . separation-deepening-double-segregation-for-more-students

Ormseth, M., Parvini, S., Do, A., & Tchekmedyian, A. (2019, March 5). "Shock in O.C. over photos." *Los Angeles Times,* pp. A1 & A12.

Pettigrew, T. F. (1998). Intergroup contact theory. *Annual Review of Psychology, 49,* 65–85.

Planty, M., Hussar, W., Snyder, T., Kena, G., KewalRamani, A., Kemp, J., Bianco, K., & Dinkes, R. (2009). *The condition of education 2009.* Washington DC: National Center for Education Statistics. Retrieved from https://nces.ed.gov/pubs2009/2009081.pdf

Ramsey, R. J., & Frank, J. (2007). Wrongful conviction: Perceptions of criminal justice professionals regarding the frequency of wrongful conviction and the extent of system errors. *Crime & Delinquency, 53,* 436–470.

Revilla, A. T., & Sweeney, Y. D. L. G. (1997). Low income does not cause low school achievement: Creating a sense of family and respect in the school environment. Retrieved from http://www.idra.org/IDRA_Newsletter/June_-_July_1997_High_-_Performing_High_Poverty_Schools/Low_Income_Does_Not_Cause_Low_School_Achievement/

Rivera, B .D., & Rogers-Adkinson, D. (1997). Culturally sensitive interventions: Social skills training with children and parents from culturally and linguistically diverse backgrounds. *Intervention in School and Clinic, 33,* 75–80.

Rudman, L. A. & Fairchild, K. (2004). Reactions to counter-stereotypic behavior: The role of backlash in cultural stereotype maintenance. *Journal of Personality and Social Psychology, 87,* 157–176.

Sadker, M. & Sadker, D. (1994). *Failing at fairness: How America's schools cheat girls.* New York: Charles Scribner's Sons.

Sangrigoli, S., Pallier, C., Argenti, A. M, Ventureya, V.A.G., & de Schonen, S. (2005). Reversibility of the other-race effect in face recognition during childhood. *Psychological Science, 16,* 440–444.

Scharf, A. (2018). *Critical practices for anti-bias education.* Teaching Tolerance: A Project of the Southern Poverty Law Center. Retrieved from https://www.tolerance.org/.../2019-04/TT-Critical-Practices-for-Anti-bias-Education.pdf

Schneider, E. C., Zaslavsky, A. M., & Epstein, A. M. (2002). Racial disparities in the quality of care for enrollees in Medicare managed care. *Journal of the American Medical Association, 287,* 1288–1294.

Sedlacek, W. (1987). Black students on white campuses: 20 years of research. *Journal of College Student Personnel, 28,* 484–495.

Shapiro, S. R. (1993). *Human rights violations in the United States: A report on U.S. compliance.* Human Rights Watch, American Civil Liberties Union. New York, NY.

Smith, R. (2005). Saving black boys: Unimaginable outcomes for the most vulnerable students require imaginable leadership. *School Administrator, 62*(1), 1–7.

Smith, D. (2015). *Diversity's promise for higher education: Making it work* (2nd ed.). Baltimore, MD: Johns Hopkins University Press.

Steele, C. M. (2004). A threat in the air: How stereotypes shape intellectual identity and performance. In J. A. Banks & C. A. M. Banks (Eds.), Handbook of research on multicultural education (2nd ed., pp. 692-698). San Francisco: Jossey-Bass.

Steele, C. M., & Aronson, J. (1995). Stereotype threat and the intellectual test performance of African–Americans. *Journal of Personality and Social Psychology, 69,* 797–811.

Stephan, W. G., & Stephan, C. W. (2004). Intergroup relations in multicultural education programs. In J. A. Banks & C. A. M. Banks (Eds.), *Handbook of research on multicultural education* (2nd ed., pp. 782–798). San Francisco: Jossey-Bass.

Sumida, S., & Gurin, P. A. (2001). Celebration of power. In D. L. Schoem & S. Hurtado (Eds.), *Intergroup dialogue: Deliberative democracy in school, college, community, and workplace* (pp. 280-293). Ann Arbor: University of Michigan.

Tafjel, H. (1982). *Social identity and intergroup behavior.* Cambridge, England: Cambridge University Press.

Tafjel, H., & Turner, J. C. (1986). The social identity theory of intergroup behavior. In S. Worchel & W. G. Austin (Eds.), *Psychology of intergroup relations* (2nd ed.). Chicago, IL: Nelson-Hall,

Thompson, A. (2009). *White privilege.* In H. Greene & S. Gabbidon (Eds.), *Encyclopedia of race and crime.* Thousand Oaks, CA: Sage.

Thompson, A., & Luhman, R. (1997). Familial predictors of educational attainment: Regional and racial variations. In P. Hall (Ed.), *Race, ethnicity, and multiculturalism* (pp. 63–88). New York: Garland Publishing.

U.S. Department of Education. (2016). *The state of racial diversity in the educator workforce.* Retrieved from https://www2.ed.gov/rschstat/eval/highered/racial-diversity/state-ra-cial-diversity-workforce.pdf

Villegas, A. M., & Lucas, T. (2002). *Educating culturally responsive teachers.* Albany, NY: State University of New York Press.

Vox Media (2019). *The data proves that segregation is getting worse.* Retrieved from https://www.vox.com/2018/3/5/17080218/school-segregation-getting-worse-data

Weissglass, J. (2001). Racism and the achievement gap. *Education Week, 20*(43), 49–72.

Wong-Fillmore, L. (1991). When learning a second language means losing the first. *Early Childhood Research Quarterly, 6,* 323–346.

Wright, D. J. (Ed.) (1987). *Responding to the needs of today's minority students.* New Directions for Student Services, No. 38. San Francisco: Jossey-Bass.

Zajonc, R. B. (1968). Attitudinal effects of mere exposure. *Journal of Personality and Social Psychology, 9,* Monograph Supplement, No. 2, part 2.

Zajonc, R. B. (1970). Brainwash: Familiarity breeds comfort. *Psychology Today* (February), pp. 32-35 & 60-62.

Zajonc, R. B. (2001). Mere exposure: A gateway to the subliminal. *Current Directions in Psychological Science,10,* 224–228.

Reflections and Applications

3.1 Review the sidebar quotes contained in this chapter and select two that you think are particularly meaningful or inspirational. For each quote you selected, provide an explanation of why you chose it.

3.2 Reflect on the following factors discussed in this chapter that play a role in the development of prejudice. Suggest an educational strategy that might be used with students to prevent or combat these potential causes of prejudice.

    a) Experiencing feelings of discomfort with the unknown or unfamiliar

    b) Mentally categorizing people into "in" groups and "out" groups

    c) Strengthening self-esteem by identifying or associating with a "superior" group

    d) Using selective perception and selective memory to support prejudicial beliefs

3.3 Rate the amount or variety of diversity you have experienced in the following settings:

The high school you attended	High	Moderate	Low
The college or university attended	High	Moderate	Low
The neighborhood in which you grew up	High	Moderate	Low
Places where you have been employed	High	Moderate	Low

Which of these settings had the *most* and *least* diversity? What do you think accounted for this difference?

3.4 Have you ever been stereotyped based on your appearance or group membership?
  a) If yes, what was the stereotype? How did being stereotyped make you feel?
  b) If no, why do you think you have not been stereotyped?

3.5 Have you ever perceived or treated someone in terms of a stereotype associated with that person's group rather than as an individual?
  a) If yes, what assumptions did you make about the person? Was that person aware of or affected by your stereotyping?
  b) If no, why do you think you have always been able to treat others individually rather than stereotypically?

3.6 Have you ever witnessed someone using selective perception or selective memory—seeing or recalling what they believe to be true (due to bias) rather than what is actually true?
  a) If yes, what bias was involved and how was selective perception or selective memory used to support the bias?
  b) If no, what do you think is a common bias held by people that is maintained through use of selective perception or selective memory?

3.7 **Case Study: Anti-Semitic Incident at High School Party**

At a house party in southern California, a group of high school juniors played a drinking game with red cups and ping-pong balls. As the students were adding and moving around cups on the floor, one student noted that it was starting to look like a swastika, so he rearranged a few more cups to create the shape of a swastika. About a dozen students then gathered around it, raised their arms in a Nazi salute, and had their photo taken. One student put a caption on the photo (titled "German rage") and posted it on Snapchat. The picture quickly spread throughout social media and triggered outrage among other students, parents, and politicians. Some of the partying students then took to social media to criticize students who condemned the Nazi display, saying that it was just a joke and questioning why people who weren't even Jewish were so upset.

Because the incident happened off campus on a weekend, school officials were uncertain about what disciplinary action could or should be taken. The director of a regional Anti-Defamation League reported that he hadn't seen any evidence that these students were Nazis or Nazi sympathizers, but felt their actions were still reprehensible because they served to "normalize" hate. He said: "What starts as jokes then becomes social exclusion then becomes discrimination."

The incident called attention to a nationwide trend of increasing anti-Semitic incidents at American schools. In 2017 alone, there were 457 anti-Semitic incidents in non-Jewish schools across the country, making K–12 schools the number-one public place where such incidents occurred.

Source: Ormseth et al. (2019).

Reflection Questions

1. Why do you think this incident took place in the first place?
2. What action (if any) do you think the school district should have taken in response to this incident?
3. Could this incident have been prevented? If yes, how? If no, why not?
4. How likely do you think an incident like this could take place in your school district?
5. If this event were to take place in your school district, how do you think members of your community would react?
6. Why do you think anti-Semitic incidents (and hate crimes toward minority groups in general) are on the rise?

Overcoming Bias, Combating Prejudice, and Developing Cultural Competence

Chapter Purpose and Preview

This chapter lays out a systematic, four-step process for helping educators and their students detect bias, decrease prejudice, and appreciate diversity. Research-based interpersonal communication skills are presented for strengthening human relations in general and relationships with members of diverse groups in particular. Lastly, strategies are provided for developing cultural competence—the ability to effectively relate to, learn from, and collaborate with people of diverse cultural backgrounds.

Introduction

As discussed in the previous chapter, *bias* means slant—a leaning toward viewing something or someone without accurate or complete information, and often without conscious awareness (Fiarman, 2016). All human beings, including educators, can hold biases rooted in their cultural backgrounds. Bowman (1995) warns that teachers who are not willing to reflect on and become aware of their culturally-bound preconceptions become vulnerable to interacting with students in ways that can limit their potential to learn. Taking action to minimize or eliminate bias is integral to holding high expectations for all students, particularly students from minority cultural backgrounds.

A Four-Stage Model for Overcoming Biases and Appreciating Diversity

Only a deep sense of self-awareness can uproot and correct bias: We need to continually and consciously ask ourselves *what* we believe about a subject, person, or group, as well as *why* we hold that belief and what evidence there is to support it. Taking time to introspect and inspect our biases represents the critical first step in the process of accepting and appreciating diversity. This reflective process may be conceptualized as unfolding in a systematic sequence of steps that begins first with gaining *awareness* of group differences, followed by: *acknowledging* biases (explicit or implicit) toward certain groups, *accepting* group differences, and putting acceptance into *action* by engaging in authentic interaction with members of diverse groups. Thus, the process of diversity appreciation may be conceived of as a process composed of the following four steps or stages:

1. **Awareness** of our personal beliefs and attitudes toward diverse groups;
2. **Acknowledgement** of how our beliefs and attitudes may affect our interactions with members of diverse groups;
3. **Acceptance** of (including empathy for) members of diverse groups; and
4. **Action** taken to engage with members of diverse groups.
   (See **Figure 4.1**)

This four-step process is not only sequential, it's also hierarchical—each step builds on the step preceding it in such a way that advancing to a higher step isn't possible until the previous step has been taken. By completing all steps, the person moves beyond mere acceptance or tolerance of diversity to valuing diversity and reaping its benefits.

Stage 1. Awareness

Biases can be held without people being aware that they hold them (Fiarman, 2016) and these unconscious biases can lead to acts of discrimination, unintentional though they may be (Baron, Byrne, & Branscombe, 2006; Butler, 1993). Teachers, for example, can bring unconscious biases to the classroom (Cochran-Smith, 2012), which in turn can lead to inadvertent discriminatory behavior toward particular groups of students (Green, 2012). When educators gain deeper awareness of the subtle, subconscious biases they may hold, and help their students do the same, they achieve a key objective of multicultural education: deepening self-insight (Gorski, 1995-2019).

Starting at a very young age, a variety of social agents (family members, peers, media, etc.) shape our attitudes, beliefs, and behaviors, and shape them to such a degree that we no longer evaluate them. In fact, to question or challenge culturally acquired beliefs may make us feel as if we're dismissing or disrespecting our upbringing and heritage. However, by taking time to

"We must learn to be vulnerable enough to allow our world to turn upside down in order to allow the realities of others to edge themselves into our consciousness."

—Lisa Delpit, "The Silenced Dialogue: Power and Pedagogy in Educating Other People's Children." *Harvard Educational Review*

Figure 4.1

The cycle of diversity appreciation.

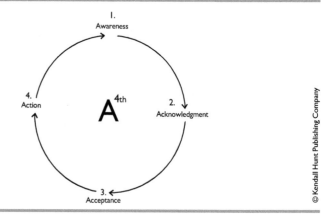

© Kendall Hunt Publishing Company

carefully examine our beliefs and consciously challenge that are biased, we become less blind to and bound by those biased beliefs, and less likely to engage in discriminatory behavior that may arise from them.

Thus, the first step toward culturally inclusive education is for educators to gain deeper awareness of their culturally influenced beliefs and how those beliefs may affect their expectations of, and interactions with, students from different cultural groups. Before effective multicultural education can take place, educators need to gain awareness of any subconscious biases they hold that may sabotage their treatment of students from different social groups in an impartial and equitable manner.

PERSONAL INSIGHT

I've become more aware of a deep-seated bias that was rooted in my childhood experiences. I recall that when I was 11 years old, I was comparing baseball cards with a friend of mine who was of Irish descent. As he was showing me his cards, he pulled out certain ones and said "he's good." After he pulled out the fourth or fifth card, I finally figured out what his criterion for determining who was "good." All the cards he pulled out had Irish surnames (e.g., O'Toole, McMahon, Maloney). He certainly didn't pull out any cards that had Italian-sounding names like mine. Later that year, I noticed that some of my Italian classmates were being derisively called "wops" and "guineas." On one particular occasion, someone in our crowded schoolyard shouted out the following question at me: "Hey, Cuseo, you know why you don't have any freckles? It's because they'd slide right off your greasy Italian face!" Laughter then broke out among a bunch of kids who overheard the comment.

These childhood incidents have left me with a lingering bias against Irish-Americans. To this day, I cannot bring myself to root for Notre Dame's sports teams because their nickname is the "fighting Irish," or root for Boston's professional basketball team because they're called the Celtics.

The good news is that I'm aware of this bias and haven't let it lead to full-blown prejudice or discrimination toward people of Irish descent. In fact, the young Irish American boy who showed me only the baseball cards of "good" (Irish-named) players has remained a close, lifelong friend.

Joe Cuseo

Figure 4.2

Self-awareness is the first step in the process of overcoming personal biases.

Exploring and unearthing our unconscious biases doesn't mean we're engaging in a self-induced "guilt trip." It also doesn't mean we're holding ourselves personally responsible for the extreme forms of prejudice and discrimination that have long plagued, and continue to plague, us at a societal level. Instead, it's simply an introspective process designed to promote deeper self-insight and potential discovery of subtle beliefs or attitudes can disadvantage members of diverse groups, even if it's without malicious intent (Butler, 1993). As Ginsberg and Wlodowksi (2009) point out:

> The first requisite for culturally responsive teaching [is] a sincere sense of self-scrutiny, not to induce guilt but to deepen sensitivity to the range of ways educators are complicit with inequitable treatment of others and to open ourselves to knowing the limitations of our own perspectives .... Mindfulness of who we are and what we believe culturally can help us examine the ways in which we may be unknowingly placing our good intentions within a dominant and unyielding framework—in spite of the appearance of openness and receptivity (pp. 13 & 330).

One effective way to increase self-awareness of feelings, beliefs, and biases about diverse groups is to do the following:

▶ Take a moment to list all things that come to mind about a social group of which you are not a member and with whom you've had very little contact. (You can use the diversity spectrum on **p. 56** to identify one such group.)

▶ Write down all thoughts and feelings you have about the group. Be sure it's what you truly believe and not what seems like the right thing or socially acceptable to say. Try to be totally honest; don't worry about how your thoughts and feelings might be judged because you will not be sharing them with anyone else.

▶ Reflect back on the ideas you wrote down in the previous step, go deeper into the thought process, and dig up any subtle beliefs you may have about that group.

▶ Once you've carefully examined your deepest thoughts and feelings, and have recorded them in writing, answer the following questions as honestly as possible:

Would you say that any of the thoughts or feelings you wrote down represents a negative bias, stereotype, or prejudice? If yes, (a) Why do you think you hold it? (b) How do you think it developed in the first place?

Once you've honestly answered the above questions, you're ready to advance to the next stage in the process of diversity appreciation: *Acknowledgement*.

Stage 2. Acknowledgement

Diversity cannot be appreciated without first acknowledging the diverse groups that make up our social environment and how their life experiences differ from our own. This involves moving beyond the diversity-dismissive question: "We're all human, aren't we?" This statement denies the reality of group identity and that an individual's group identity can strongly influence that individual's life experiences and personal identity. Minimizing or ignoring group differences also ignores the fact that members of different groups experience different personal privileges, such as access to different amounts of social and economic resources. For instance, to ignore differences between socioeconomic groups is to fail to acknowledge the reality that individuals born into families with greater wealth and socioeconomic status have the privilege of tapping into networks of influential people who can help them gain access to employment, loans, educational services, and legal assistance.

This "acknowledgment" stage of the diversity appreciation process also involves acknowledging how our attitudes and behavior toward different groups can, in turn, affect how members of these groups view themselves. George Cooley, famous sociologist, coined the term "looking glass self" to capture the idea that when people see how others act toward them and react to them, it's like looking at a mirror—the actions and reactions (positive or negative) reflect back on them and affect how they view themselves (positively or negatively) (Cooley, 1922). Applying Cooley's concept to educational settings, if children come to the school environment with a positive view of their academic ability and aspirations for success and see that educators have low expectations of them and treat them accordingly, they internalize these observations—which, in turn, adversely affects their academic self-image and performance (Bowman, 1995). For example, teachers who believe that females cannot perform as well as males in math and science have been found to hold lower expectations of female students in these subject areas—which, in turn, lowers their levels of academic aspiration and achievement in math and science (Clewell, Anderson, & Thorpe, 1992; Tobias, 1978). Teachers can help guard against such unconscious biases that lead to their holding lower expectations for students from different groups by observing videotapes of their teaching behavior, or by having a colleague visit class and provide objective "third party" feedback about whether they are treating certain groups of students differently, albeit unknowingly.

Culturally competent educators *acknowledge* that:

- ► attitudes and actions toward different students from different social groups can affect their academic self-concept and level of achievement
- ► learning is maximized in classroom environments that are inclusive and personally validating
- ► one of their key roles is to serve as a bridge builder between the cultures of the student, the school, and the surrounding community
- ► the families of students from all social groups have a vested interest in the educational success of their children
- ► students' language and culture are interrelated
- ► cultural and linguistic diversity are essential elements of the learning experience
- ► cultural dialect is a valid expression of language that should neither be dismissed nor devalued, but acknowledged and utilized to enhance a student's ability to learn, read, and communicate.

After acknowledging how our thoughts, feelings, and actions impact members of different groups (particularly if that impact may disadvantage them), we are positioned to move to the next stage in the cycle of diversity appreciation: *Acceptance*.

Stage 3. Acceptance

This stage of diversity appreciation involves sensitivity to, and empathy for, others who have been adversely affected by biases or prejudices. In this stage, we accept the fact that although we cannot actually feel what victims of prejudice have felt, we can still understand how they feel and why they feel the way they do. In other words, we exhibit empathy—which is a critical component of emotional intelligence (Goleman, 2006) and a powerful predictor of personal and professional success (Goleman, 1995).

To increase your empathy for the experiences of members of a disadvantaged group, imagine that you are a member of that group and attempt to visualize yourself having the same experiences. Better yet, place yourself in a role, position or situation of a member of the disadvantaged group. For example, spend a day in a wheelchair to experience what it's like for someone who has a physical disability, or wear an eye mask for a day to experience what it's like to be blind.

A third-grade school teacher from Iowa by the name of Jane Elliot once devised a famous and daring classroom exercise to develop her students' empathy for victims of racial discrimination. In 1968, after Martin Luther King, Jr. had been assassinated, Elliot was struck by white reporters' lack of empathy for what black Americans were experiencing after the assassination. So, she decided to conduct an experiment in her class of all-white students that came to be called the "blue eyes—brown eyes" exercise. Elliott constructed brown fabric collars and asked the blue-eyed students to wrap them around the necks of their brown-eyed peers so they can be easily identified as members of an "inferior" minority group. The "superior" blue-eyed children were given such privileges as front-row seats in class, opportunity to participate in class discussions, access to a new jungle gym, extra recess time, and extra helpings of food at lunch. The brown-eyed children had none of these privileges; they were forced to sit in the back of class and were more severely reprimanded for the same type of behavior that blue-eyed children were allowed to get away with. The blue-eyed children were also encouraged to ignore the brown-eyed students, play only with other blue-eyed children, and drink from different water fountains than the brown-eyed students.

At first, the disadvantaged group (brown-eyed students) resisted the idea that blue-eyed children were superior to them. However, their resistance faded when the class was told that there was scientific evidence "proving" that a body chemical causes a person's eyes to be blue and that it's also associated with higher levels of intelligence.

The results of the classroom exercise were stunning. The "inferior" group became more timid, submissive, and their academic performance declined. In contrast, the school performance of the "superior" blue-eyed students improved, but they also became more arrogant, dominating, and unpleasant when interacting with their "inferior" brown-eyed classmates (Peters, 1987).

Later, Elliot reversed the roles she assigned to the blue-eyed and brown-eyed students, giving the brown-eyed students the accolades and privileges previously given to the blue-eyed students. Similar results took place, but in the opposite direction; the only difference being that the brown-eyed students didn't taunt their blue-eyed classmates quite as viciously as they had been taunted, likely because their prior experience of being victims of prejudice and discrimination equipped them with greater empathy.

As soon as the classroom exercise ended, Elliot gave her students a detailed explanation about the purpose of the exercise and what the results suggested. The blue-eyed and brown-eyed children then hugged and apologized to one another. Their teacher had effectively helped a class of all-white students develop empathy for what minority racial groups that experience when they encounter prejudice and discrimination.

The children wrote stories about their experiences as a class assignment, and a news reported heard about the stories and they were later published in a local newspaper. The children's stories then received attention from the national media, which launched Elliot into a career as a public speaker against discrimination. In 1970, ABC produced a documentary about her classroom experiment, titled *The Eye of the Storm* (https://vimeo.com/153858146). Fifteen years later, the film inspired a reunion of the 1970 class members with their teacher. Two books were also written about the classroom experiment: *A Class Divided* and *A Class Divided: Then and Now* (https://www.pbs.org/wgbh/frontline/film/class-divided/), and the experiment reenacted by adults on the Oprah Winfrey show in 1992 (https://www.huffingtonpost.com/2015/01/02/jane-elliott-race-experiment-oprah-show_n_6396980.html) (Huffpost, 2018).

More formal research studies were later conducted on Elliot's classroom exercise that supported its effectiveness as a strategy promoting students' empathy toward members of disadvantaged groups (Byrnes & Kiger, 1990).

> "God created one race: The human race. Human beings created racism."
>
> —Jane Elliot, third-grade schoolteacher, anti-racism activist, and nationally-known diversity educator

PERSONAL INSIGHT

As I mentioned previously, one of the best attended events that ever took place at my school was a presentation made by Floyd Cochran, a former member and recruiter for "Aryan Nation" (a White-supremacist hate group), who eventually left the group and went on to become a nationally known civil rights activist and educator. While he was speaking at my school, Cochran pointed to a key experience that caused him to change his bigoted views. It occurred when his pregnant wife had an ultrasound that revealed his unborn son had a cleft palate. In the minds of the white supremacist group of which he was a member, the baby was "defective" and if he were to become the father of that defective child, he could no longer be a member of the supremacist group. This left Cochran with two choices: (a) abort his son and remain a member of the group, or (b) keep his son and be ostracized by a group whose supremacist beliefs he endorsed. Cochran chose to quit the group, renounced his racist beliefs, and then began speaking out publically against the hateful prejudices he once firmly believed and taught.

After hearing Cochran's story, it struck me that the experience which triggered his incredible transformation was an exercise in role reversal. When his son was deemed "inferior," he was thrust into a reversed role—he became the recipient rather than the perpetrator of hateful discrimination. Cochran's radical reversal from hateful racist to civil rights activist is a dramatic illustration of how being placed in the role or position of a person experiencing prejudice is a powerful way to promote empathy for victims of prejudice.

Joe Cuseo

Stage 4. Action

Once we: (a) become aware of our biases, (b) acknowledge how our biases have affected members of other social groups, and (c) accept the feelings of others who may have been adversely affected by our biases, we can (d) take action to capitalize on the benefits of diversity. This fourth and most advanced stage of diversity appreciation involves stepping beyond just tolerating and accepting diversity. A person who merely tolerates diversity, or simply co-exists with diverse groups, might say something like: "Let's just get along." In contrast, this Action Stage of diversity appreciation involves *cultural competence*—deeper, authentic diversity-related action and interaction with respect to diverse groups that promotes both our own development and the development of individuals from diverse groups with whom we interact.

Educators who truly appreciate diversity transform attitude into action by seeking out interaction with members of diverse groups, collaborating with them, and learning from them (Smith, 1997, 2015). In so doing, they help realize an important objective of multicultural education: self-transformation (Gorski, 1995-2019).

When educators attain cultural competence, they are positioned to deliver culturally inclusive education that recognizes and capitalizes on student differences, using these differences to advance the level of learning achieved by all students (Ety et al., 1995). Culturally competent educators engage in such practices as:

- ▶ Communicating high expectations to students from all cultural backgrounds
- ▶ Allowing students opportunities to become acquainted with one another and learn about each other's cultural experiences
- ▶ Encouraging students from different cultures to work collaboratively, enabling them to encounter new perspectives and experience multicultural perspectives
- ▶ Participating in community meetings and activities to gain a deeper understanding of their students' cultural backgrounds
- ▶ Soliciting input from family and community members of students with diverse backgrounds and being mindful of that input when making educational decisions
- ▶ Offering families a variety of ways to participate in their students' education
- ▶ Becoming an advocate for diverse students at school and in the local community

In summary, we attain cultural competence by advancing through successive steps or stages which involve increasingly higher levels of cultural sensitivity and appreciation—as depicted in Box 4.1.

Box 4.1 Progressive Steps to Cultural Competence

▶ **Cultural Competence:** being proficient at relating to, learning from, and collaborating with people from diverse cultural backgrounds.

⇧

▶ **Cultural Action:** moving beyond recognizing and valuing diversity to actually seeking it out and experiencing its benefits.

⇧

▶ **Cultural Acknowledgement:** acknowledging that differences exist between individuals, races, and cultures, and viewing these differences as assets rather than liabilities.

⇧

▶ **Cultural Acceptance:** tolerating and accommodating cultural differences (rather than resisting and rejecting them)

⇧

▶ **Cultural Awareness:** awareness of personal biases toward different cultural groups and their effect on oneself and others

PERSONAL INSIGHT

The courses I teach, the workshops I give, and the life I live are dedicated to valuing diversity. I am committed to recognizing and appreciating the variety of characteristics that contribute to our uniqueness and promote our individual and collective achievement. I have learned not just to be tolerant of people and their differences but to value them as contributing to the richness of our society. I want to be a person who isn't just "politically correct," but a person who continually self-checks and self-corrects my beliefs about human differences. I will continue to challenge myself to move beyond diversity tolerance and continually strive to attain a higher level of cultural competence.

Aaron Thompson

If moving toward cultural competence were to take place at a *societal* level, it could be visualized as an ascending stairway of 12 steps (see **Figure 4.3**). Throughout history, human societies have held beliefs about different social groups that remained (and continue to remain) on the lower steps of this stairway. It should be the goal of humankind to ascend these steps, progress to their pinnacle, and never again regress to descend them.

Figure 4.3

Staircase to Cultural
Competence

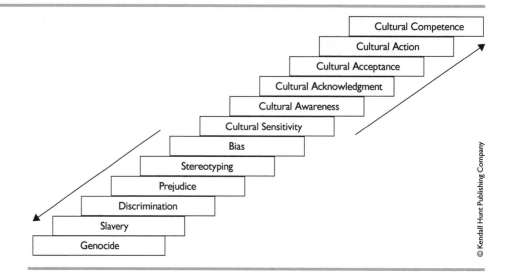

Specific Strategies for Developing & Demonstrating Cultural Competence

The following practices can be used by educators for their personal and professional development, and they may also be shared with and modeled for students to help them develop cultural competence.

Be intentional about perceiving others on a person-to-person basis, not their group membership. Research shows that humans tend to perceive individuals from less familiar groups as being more alike than individuals of their own group (Taylor, Peplau, & Sears, 2006). We need to consciously combat this tendency and make an intentional effort to perceive and judge people from other cultural groups as unique individuals, not according to some general (stereotypical) rule of thumb, and not by the familiarity of their outer features but by the quality of their inner attributes.

Take a stand against prejudice and discrimination by constructively disagreeing with others who make stereotypical statements and prejudicial remarks. By saying or doing nothing, we can avoid conflict, but silence can send others the message that we tacitly agree with the person making the prejudicial remark. Studies show that when members of a social group hear one of its own members make a prejudicial remark about a member belonging to another group, prejudice increases among other members belonging to the same group as the person who made the prejudicial remark—likely due to the pressure of group conformity (Stangor, Sechrist, & Jost, 2001). However, if the person's prejudicial remark is challenged by another member of his or her own social group, particularly a member who is liked and respected by other group members, it reduces the prejudice of the person making the remark as well as any such prejudice held by other members of the group (Baron, Branscombe, & Byrne, 2008). Thus, when we resist peer pressure and take and challenging

"You can't judge a book by the cover."

—1962 hit song by Ellas McDaniel, a.k.a. Bo Diddley (Note: a "bo diddley" is a one-stringed African guitar)

"In the end, we will remember not the words of our enemies, but the silence of our friends."

—Martin Luther King, Jr.

"In a racist society, it is not enough to be non-racist; we must be anti-racist."

—Angela Davis, political activist, professor, and author

peers who make prejudicial comments, we not only reduce the prejudice of those making the comments, but also reduce the prejudice of others who witness prejudicial comments.

> **Consider this ...**
> By actively opposing prejudice in class and on campus, educators serve as role models for students and colleagues, and they send a clear message to other members of the school community that valuing diversity is not just the "politically correct" thing to do; it is the morally responsible thing to do.

> "I grew up in a very racist family. Even a year ago, I could honestly say, 'I hate Asians' with a straight face and mean it. My senior AP teacher taught me not to be so judgmental. He got me to open up to others, so much so that my current boyfriend is half Chinese."
>
> —First-year college student

Take a leadership role with respect to diversity. Research on leadership suggests that one distinguishing feature of effective leaders is their ability to enable diverse individuals to feel that they are all members of the same community, and by advancing the community's interest, they advance their own interests (Bass & Riggio, 2005). Similarly, educational research shows that when students see themselves as members of a community that is open and welcoming to students from diverse groups, both white students and students of color perceive and experience a stronger sense of belonging (Locks et al., 2008).

Educators can demonstrate diversity leadership by: (a) modeling responsible ethical social behavior, (b) making others feel welcome—particularly members of minority groups, (c) drawing out people who may be shy and including them in their conversations and activities, and (d) being an empathic listener who provides an emotional sounding board for others—especially for members of groups who may feel marginalized or disenfranchised.

Promote positive intercultural relationships by applying principles of social intelligence and using effective human relations skills. Human intelligence was once considered to be a general intellectual trait that could be measured by a single intelligence test (IQ). Scholars have since discovered that the singular word "intelligence" is incomplete and should be replaced by the more inclusive term "intelligences" to reflect the fact that humans demonstrate intelligence in multiple forms that cannot be captured by an intelligence test score. One of these multiple forms of intelligences is *social intelligence* (a.k.a. "interpersonal intelligence")—the ability to effectively communicate with, and relate to, other people (Gardner, 1993, 1999; Goleman, 2006).

© Monkey Business Images/Shutterstock.com

Interpersonal communication and human relations skills provide the foundation for social intelligence. Educators with these skills are better able to establish positive relationships with students, gain their interest and trust, and increase their receptivity to educational efforts designed to promote their learning and development. (For further details and specific strategies, see chapter 6.) Interpersonal skills are especially important when communicating with students from diverse cultures because if the educator's message is unclear or culturally insensitive, it can lead to serious communication breakdown and possible termination of a potentially fruitful relationship. As Du Praw and Axner (1997) note when people attempt to communicate with others from different cultures, they're often so concerned about saying the "right thing" (what to say), they forget about saying it the "right way" (how to say it).

> "I have a dream that my four little children will one day live in a nation where they will not be judged by the color of their skin, but by the content of their character."
>
> —Martin Luther King, Jr., civil rights leader and winner of the Nobel Peace Prize

It is well documented that human relations skills are critical to effective leadership (Avolio, Walumbwa, & Weber, 2009; Zaccaro et al. 1991). So when educators exhibit these skills when interacting with diverse students, they not only exhibit both cultural competence and intercultural leadership. Described below are human relations practices supported by research indicating that they are effective ways to enhance the quality of interpersonal relationships in general, and intercultural relationships in particular.

Social Intelligence and Human Relations Skills

Interpersonal relationship skills, also referred to as human relations skills, represent another key component of social intelligence (Goleman, 2006). These skills involve relating harmoniously to others and building positive relationships with them. How can educators encourage students from diverse groups to view them as approachable and amenable to forming positive relationships? The first steps are to learn (and remember) students' names and get to know them not just as students, but as persons, learn about. Listed below are specific strategies for taking these initial steps.

Learn and remember *names*. One practice of effective leaders is that they learn and remember the names and interests of their constituents (Hogan, Curphy, & Hogan, 1994). When educators learn and remember students' names, and refer to students by name, it affirms their individuality and uniqueness.

People often say they have a good memory for faces but not names, which seems to suggest that they are not good at remembering names and never will be. The truth is that the ability to retain and recall names isn't an innate talent or inherited ability. Instead, it's a skill developed through intentional effort and effective use of memory-improvement strategies, such as those discussed below.

> ▶ When meeting someone, pay close attention to the person's name when you first hear it. The crucial initial step to remembering a name is to get the name into your brain in the first place. As obvious as this may seem, when we first meet someone, instead of listening actively and closely for the person's name, we're often more concerned about the first impression we're making on the person or what they're going to say next (Demarais & White, 2004). Consequently, we often *forget* a person's name because we never did *get* the person's name into our brain in the first place. In other words, we were absentminded—our mind was literally "absent" (off somewhere else, thinking about something else), instead of being present and attentive.

> ▶ Say the person's name soon after you first hear it. For example, if your friend Gertrude just introduced you to Geraldine, you might say: "Geraldine, how long have you known Gertrude?" Stating the person's name shortly after first hearing it combats forgetting at a time when forgetting is most likely to occur—during the first moments after the brain takes in new information (Averell & Heathcote, 2011). Besides improving memory for names, there's another benefit of saying a

person's name right after you've heard it: It makes the person feel immediately acknowledged and welcomed.

▶ Associate the person's name with something else you've learned about or know about the person. For instance, a person's name can be remembered by associating it with: (a) some physical characteristic of the person (e.g., "tall Paul"), (b) the place where you first met the person, or (c) your topic of conversation. Making a mental connection between the person's name and something else you know about the person capitalizes on the brain's natural tendency to store (retain) information as part of an interconnected network of related information (Zull, 2011).

▶ Keep a name journal that includes the names of people you meet along with some information about them (e.g., where you met, what you talked about, or what their interests are). When we want to be sure not to forget something, we write it down, such as tasks we need to complete or items to buy at the store, so why not use this same memory-improvement strategy not to forget the names of people who we want to remember?

> "When I joined the bank, I started keeping a record of the people I met and put them on little cards, and I would indicate on the cards when I met them, and under what circumstances, and sometimes [make] a little notation which would help me remember a conversation."
>
> —David Rockefeller, prominent American banker, philanthropist, and former CEO of the Chase Manhattan Bank

Refer to people by name when you see them and interact with them. Once you learn someone's name, be sure to continue referring to that person by name. If you happen to see Waldo, saying, "Hi, Waldo" will mean a lot more to him than simply saying "Hi" or "Hi, there"—which sounds like you've just encountered an unidentifiable object floating around "out there" in public space, like you're or addressing a personal correspondence to someone you know as "to whom it may concern." Continuing to use people's names after first learning their names serves to strengthen your memory of their names; it also shows them that you remember who they are (and that they're important to you). Remembering students' names provides all students with a sense of personal validation, and it's especially important way to provide personal validation for minority students who may feel marginalized or disenfranchised.

Show interest in others, remember what they share with you, and refer to what they previously shared with you in subsequent conversations. Listen closely to and make a concerted effort to retain what people share with you, especially to what seems important to them or they really care about. For one person that may be sports, for another it may be family matters, and for another it may be peer relationships. Remember the topics of interest or concern and bring up those topics in future conversations. Try to move beyond the mindless routine of asking the standard generic questions that everyone asks anyone (e.g., "How are you?" What's new?"). Instead, ask personalized questions about something specific the person shared with you previously (e.g., "How did things go on that math test you told me about?").

Studies of underrepresented college students indicate they're more likely to succeed if they experience *personal validation*—feel recognized as individuals and that they matter to school representatives, who care about their success (Rendón-Linares & Muñoz, 2011). Educators can provide students with personal validation by knowing and referring to them by name, showing interest

© Pressmaster/Shutterstock.com

> "You can make more friends in 2 months by becoming interested in other people than you can in 2 years by trying to get other people interested in you."
>
> —Dale Carnegie, *How to Win Friends and Influence People*

in them, and remembering what interests them. By remembering what students share with us, we show them that they matter to us, and by showing interest in students' lives and talking about their interests, they become more interested in us and what we talk about, including what we're trying to teach them.

Be an active and empathic listener. When people answer survey questions that ask them to identify the characteristics of a good friend, "good listener" ranks among the top characteristics cited (Berndt, 1992). Effective listening skills also characterize effective problem solvers (Steil & Bommelje, 2007) and effective leaders (Johnson & Bechler, 1998), and it ranks among the top skills sought by employers (Gabric & McFadden, 2001; Wolvin, 2010).

Despite the well-documented importance of listening skills, scholars in the field of interpersonal communications and human relations report that most people spend too much time talking and not enough time listening or listening actively and empathically (Nichols, 1995; Nichols & Stevens, 1957; Wolvin, 2010).

We can understand spoken words at a rate more than twice as fast as the rate at which others can speak them (Barker & Watson, 2000; Headlee, 2016). This leaves plenty of time for our mind to wander and slip into *passive listening*—hearing the words spoken to us, but not really listening closely to those words. *Active listening* is a human relations strategy for minimizing this attention drift; it involves: (a) focusing our *full attention* on the speaker's message—as opposed to "half-listening" and waiting for our turn to talk or thinking about what we're going to say next; (b) listening *empathically*—paying close attention not only to what the speaker is communicating verbally but also to the speaker's nonverbal communication; and (c) listening with *engagement*—expressing interest in the speaker, checking our understanding of the speaker's words and feelings, and encouraging the speaker to elaborate.

> "We have been given two ears and but a single mouth in order that we may hear more and talk less."
>
> —Zeno of Citium, ancient Greek philosopher

> "Most people do not listen with the intent to understand; they listen with the intent to reply."
>
> —Stephen Covey, author, *The 7 Habits of Highly Effective People*

Consider this ...

Listening actively and empathically to others from diverse backgrounds enables us to give their thoughts and feelings our undivided attention, sending them an undeniable message that we respect and appreciate them.

Active and empathic listening doesn't happen automatically; it's a skill developed through disciplined effort and deliberate practice until it eventually becomes a natural habit. Engaging in the following practices can develop active and empathic listening into a regular habit.

►   **Monitor your understanding of what the speaker is saying.** Good listeners take personal responsibility for following the speaker's message. In contrast, poor listeners put all the responsibility on the speaker to make the message clear and interesting. To check if you're understanding the speaker's message, occasionally paraphrase what you hear the speaker saying in your own words (e.g., "Let me make sure I understand …" or "What I hear you saying is …"). Check-in statements ensure that you're following what's being said; they also assure the speaker that you're listening closely to what's being said and taking the message seriously.

► **In addition to checking your understanding of what the speaker is saying, check your understanding of what the speaker is feeling.** Pay particularly close attention to nonverbal messages—such as tone of voice and body language—which often provide clues to the emotions behind the words. For example, speaking at a faster rate and at higher volume often indicate that strong emotions underlie the words being spoken.

► **Avoid the urge to interrupt the speaker when you think you have something important to say.** Wait for a prolonged pause to be sure that the speaker's point has been completed; otherwise, you may send the off-putting message that you're interrupting or disrupting the speaker's train of thought.

► **If the speaker pauses and you start to say something at the same time the speaker starts to speak again, let the person continue before expressing your thought.** It's more socially sensitive (and socially intelligent) to listen first and speak second.

► **When posing questions, allow the speaker sufficient time to answer.** Silent spots may feel uncomfortable, but are desirable because they give the speaker time to formulate thoughts and figure out how to express them. Such pause time may be is especially necessary for speakers who may be communicating cross-culturally or cross-linguistically (e.g., speakers whose first language isn't English).

► **Use active listening "body language" to send a clear message of interest and acceptance.** It's that more than two-thirds of all human communication is nonverbal, and it sends a stronger and truer message than verbal communication (Driver, 2010; Navarro, 2008). When a speaker perceives inconsistency between a listener's verbal and nonverbal messages (e.g., one signals interest and the other disinterest), the nonverbal message is more likely to be perceived as the true message (Ekman, 2009). Consequently, body language may be the most powerful way a listener can communicate genuine interest in what is being said and convey respect for the speaker. (See **Box 4.1** for a summary of effective nonverbal messages to send while listening.)

Box 4.2 Nonverbal Signals Associated with Active Listening

Good listeners listen not only with their ears but with other parts of their body. They use their whole body to communicate that they're paying full attention to, and are fully interested in, the speaker.

Communication experts have created the acronym "SOFTEN" to summarize and help us remember all the key body-language signals that should be sent while listening. Listed below are the effective nonverbal signals associated with each letter of the SOFTEN acronym.

S = Smile. Smiling sends signals of acceptance and interest. However, it should be done periodically, not continuously. (A continuous, non-stop smile can come across as inauthentic or artificial.)

   Sit Still. Fidgeting or squirming sends the message that you're bored or growing inpatient (and can't wait to get out of there).

O = Open Posture. Avoid closed-posture positions, such as crossing your arms or folding your hands—such nonverbal signals can send a message that you're not open to what the speaker is saying or passing judgment on what's being said.

F = Forward Lean. Leaning *forward* sends the message that you're looking forward to what the speaker is going to say next. In contrast, leaning back can send a signal that you're backing off from (losing interest in) what's being said or, worse yet, that you're evaluating or psychoanalyzing the speaker.

Face the Speaker Directly. Try to line up your shoulders directly or squarely with the speaker's shoulders—as opposed to turning one shoulder toward the speaker and one shoulder away—which may send the message that you want to get away or are giving the speaker the "cold shoulder."

T = Touch. A light touch on the arm or hand once in a while, particularly to reassure a person who's speaking about something they're worried about or uncomfortable with, can be a good way to communicate warmth. However, touch sparingly and make it more like a pat rather than a sustained touch or stroke, which could be interpreted as inappropriate intimacy (or sexual harassment).

E = Eye Contact. Lack of eye contact with the speaker can send the message that you're looking elsewhere to find something more interesting or stimulating to do than continue listening to what's being said (e.g., looking to check your text messages). However, eye contact shouldn't be continuous or relentless because it could be perceived as staring or glaring. Instead, strike a happy medium by making periodic eye contact—occasionally look away and then return your eye contact to the speaker. (Temporarily taking your eyes off the speaker can also send the message that you're taking time to think about what's being said.)

N = Nod Your Head. Nodding slowly and periodically while listening sends the signal that you're following what's being said and affirming the person saying it. However, avoid rapid and repeated head nodding because it can send a signal that you want the speaker to hurry up so you can start talking (or that you want to end to the conversation as soon as possible).

Sources: Barker & Watson (2000); Nichols, (2009); Purdy & Borisoff (1996)

▶ **Listen with an open mind.** Avoid close-mindedness or selective listening—selecting or tuning into only what appeals to your own personal interests or affirms your personal viewpoints, and tuning out or turning off everything else. Even if others express ideas we don't agree with, we still owe them the courtesy of listening to what they have to say, rather than immediately shaking our head, frowning, or interrupting them.

Ignoring or blocking out information and ideas that we don't immediately find interesting or don't support our viewpoint is not only a poor social skill, it's also a poor critical thinking skill. As discussed in Chapter 2, our thinking becomes deeper and more complex when we're exposed to perspectives that don't duplicate or replicate our own.

> "Listening well is as important to critical thinking as is contributing brilliantly."
>
> —Stephen Brookfield, author, *Developing Critical Thinkers*

Consider this . . .
Here are five keys to building positive interpersonal and intercultural relationships: (1) know and refer to people by name; (2) show interest in them by asking about their interests; (3) listen to them actively and empathically; (4) remember what they share with you, and (5) show them that you remembered (and cared about) what they shared by bringing it up in future conversations.

Strategies for Increasing Personal Contact and Interpersonal Interaction among Members of Diverse Groups

Some scholars prefer the term *intercultural* education to multicultural education because the former suggests that diversity appreciation involves meaningful *interaction* between members of different cultures and the ability to communicate cross-culturally (Banks, 2016). When students listen to presentations on diversity, they and engage in reading about diversity, they are learning vicariously *about* diversity. In contrast, when students interact with others from diverse backgrounds, they are learning directly *from* diversity. The difference is comparable to the difference between students acquiring knowledge about a country by reading about it or hearing a teacher talk about it, as opposed to actually traveling to that country and interacting with its natives. Interpersonal interaction among students from different cultural groups takes students beyond multicultural awareness to intercultural interaction, transforming diversity appreciation from a tacit attitude to an explicit action.

The need for intentional intercultural interaction is underscored by research in social psychology, which indicates that humans are strongly predisposed to associate with others who share the same cultural backgrounds, beliefs, and interests. Scholars refer to this phenomenon as the "self-similarity principle" (Uzzi & Dunlap, 2005). Thus, to resist succumbing to the self-similarity principle, we need to make a very conscious, intentional attempt to step outside our cultural comfort zone and seek out opportunities to interact with people from different cultural backgrounds. Failing to do so is likely to result in our reverting to the default human tendency of distancing ourselves from diversity and denying ourselves the opportunity to experience it and benefit from it.

One way in which teachers can effectively promote intercultural interaction between students is by intentionally forming collaborative learning teams composed of students from different cultural backgrounds. When members of a work group collaborate to pursue a common goal, it creates positive interdependence and a sense of camaraderie among teammates that can continue after the work task has been completed and in other social settings. The power of teamwork for promoting positive intercultural interaction and relationships is evidenced by the frequency and durability of interracial friendships that are formed among athletes who play together on the same team and among soldiers who fight together in the same military unit (Putnam, 2007).

Research in classroom settings indicates that the intercultural impact of student learning is maximized when it's infused with the following features of *cooperative learning* (Cuseo, 1992; Johnson & Johnson, 1989; Slavin, 1990):

▶ Intentionally forming of learning teams composed of students from diverse cultural backgrounds to maximize intercultural interaction and exposure to multicultural perspectives. (As opposed to forming groups by random selection or student self-selection.)

- Prior to having students engage in the group-learning task, they are provided with explicit instruction on how to collaborate, engage in constructive dialogue, and negotiate group decisions.
- The group pursues a common goal, culimating in the creation of a single work product that represents the collective and unified work of the entire team.
- Each group member has a specific, indispensable role to play, ensuring that all members have equal status, have equal opportunity to participate, and develop a mutually-supportive sense of positive inter-dependence—the feeling that they must rely on each other to reach their common goal.

Research indicates when group learning takes place under the above conditions, students are more likely to develop positive attitudes toward other racial groups and are more likely to develop interracial friendships (Banks, 2016). These conditions have also been found to elevate the academic achievement of Hispanic and African American students (Slavin, 2012). (More specific and detailed strategies for implementing the key features of cooperative learning are provided in **Chapter 7, pp. 134** .)

In addition to forming cooperative learning teams, educators may share the following practices with students to promote intercultural interaction and friendship formation. These same practices may be used by educators themselves to increase their access to, and interaction with, members of diverse cultural groups.

Place yourself in situations or locations on campus where you're most likely to encounter and experience diversity. Research in social psychology provides hard evidence for what we know to be true anecdotally: find themselves in the same place at the same time are more likely to communicate with one another and form relationships (Latané et al., 1995). Research also shows that when ongoing contact takes place between members of different racial or ethnic groups, stereotyping is sharply reduced and intercultural friendships are more likely to form (Pettigrew, 1997, 1998; Pettigrew & Tropp, 2006). Students can be encouraged to create these conditions by: (a) making intentional attempts to place themselves in situations where they will have opportunities to interact with others from different cultural backgrounds (e.g., in the library, in the cafeteria, and in class), (b) teaming up with diverse for group discussions, study groups, and group projects. Students can also be encouraged to join school clubs or organizations whose mission is to promote diversity awareness, interaction, and appreciation (e.g., multicultural clubs or international student organizations). By intentionally placing themselves in these social contexts, students become positioned to engage in regular contact with members of different cultural groups, providing them with the opportunity to learn with them and from them.

Take advantage of social media to "chat" virtually with students from diverse groups. Electronic communication can be a convenient and comfortable way to initiate contact with members of groups with whom we've had little prior experience. Interacting *online* can also serve to "break the ice" and lead to future interaction *in person*. (Students can also engage in online exchanges with students from other countries by encouraging them to visit http://www.epals.com.)

Engage in extracurricular programs relating to diversity. When students from different cultures participate in the same club, campus organization, or athletic team, their joint membership that cuts across their different cultural backgrounds and creates a "superordinate group identity" which transcends their cultural differences and unites them (Banks, 2016). Studies show that participation in out-of-class experiences relating to diversity reduces unconscious prejudice (Blair, 2002) and elevates critical thinking (Pascarella & Terenzini, 2005).

Sponsor a school club or organization that is devoted to diversity awareness. When educators interact with students in such contexts, it sends a message to students from diverse cultural backgrounds that they value spending time with them, above and beyond the time required by their formal position, and are willing to interaction with students outside the classroom.

Helping students form clubs and organizations that support and celebrate their cultural background is not encouraging separatism. Smith (2015) reminds us that when members of minority racial or ethnic groups form their own support groups, they are not attempting to self-segregate or distance themselves from members of other groups; they are simply creating one social place where they are not the minority. There is a difference between separatism and segregation. The latter is an attempt by a dominant majority group to reduce contact and maintain its dominance of minority groups; the former is an attempt on the part of members of a minority group to value their own culture while, at the same time, welcoming and valuing interaction with members of the majority group (Banks, 2016). In a major study of college campuses where Hispanic students formed their own club or organization *and* socialized with White students, students on those campuses reported less racial tension and a more welcoming campus climate (Hurtado, 2002).

Encourage students to participate in volunteer experiences that allow them to interact with people in diverse communities or neighborhoods. Better yet, organize these experiences for your students and participate with them. Research indicates that students who engage in volunteer service experience gains in self-esteem and sense of purpose (Astin et al., 2000; Vogelgesang et al., 2002). Studies also show that people who devote time and energy to be of service to others are more likely to report higher levels of personal happiness and life satisfaction (Myers, 1993).

Volunteer experiences also provide students with experiential learning opportunities that allow them to develop career-relevant skills, such as teamwork, problem-solving, decision-making, intercultural competence, and leadership (Astin et al., 2000; National Association of Colleges & Employers, 2019).

Internet Resources

Becoming aware of implicit bias: https://www.youtube.com/watch?v=kKHSJHkPeLY

Valuing diverse people and organizations: https://managementhelp.org/interpersonal/multicultural-diversity.htm

Cross-cultural communication challenges & strategies: http://www.pbs.org/ampu/crosscult.html

Intercultural interaction and conflict resolution: https://www.coursera.org/lecture/intercultural-communication/dimensions-of-intercultural-interactions-and-conflict-lesson-1-dICLc

Cultural competence for educators: http://www.nea.org/tools/30402.htm

Teaching Tolerance (https://www.tolerance.org)
Provides free resources to educators (teachers, administrators, counselors, and other practitioners) who work with children from kindergarten through high school. Educators can use materials housed at this site to supplement the curriculum, inform their practices, and create civil and inclusive school communities where children are welcomed, respected, and valued.

References

Astin, A.W., Vogelgesang, L.J., Ikeda, E.K. & Yee, J.A. (2000). *How service learning affects students.* Los Angeles: University of California Los Angeles, Higher Education Research Institute.

Averell, L., & Heatchote, A. (2011). The form of the forgetting curve and the fate of memories. *Journal of Mathematical Psychology, 55*(1), 25–35.

Avolio, B. J., Walumbwa, F. O., &. Weber, T. J. (2009). *Leadership: Current theories, research, and future directions. Annual Review of Psychology, 60,* 421–449.

Banks, J. A. (2016). *Cultural diversity and education: Foundations, curriculum, and teaching* (6ᵗʰ ed.). New York: Routledge.

Baron, R. A., Branscombe, N. R., & Byrne, D. R. (2008). *Social psychology* (12ᵗʰ ed.). Hoboken, NJ: Pearson.

Baron, R. A., Byrne, D., & Brauscombe, N. R. (2006). *Social psychology* (11ᵗʰ ed.). Boston: Pearson.

Barker, L., & Watson, K. W. (2000). *Listen up: How to improve relationships, reduce stress, and be more productive by using the power of listening.* New York: St. Martin's Press.

Bass, B. M., & Riggio, R. E. (2005). *Transformational leadership* (2nd ed). Mahwah, NJ: Lawrence Erlbaum Associates.

Berndt, T. J. (1992). Friendship and friends' influence in adolescence. *Current Directions in Psychological Science, 1*(5), 156–159.

Blair, I. V. (2002). The malleability of automatic stereotypes and prejudice. *Personality and Social Psychology Review, 6*(3), 242–261.

Bowman, B. T. (1995). *Cultural diversity and academic achievement.* Retrieved from http://www.ncrel.org/sdrs/areas/issues/educatrs/leadrshp/le0bow.htm#author

Butler, J. E. (1993).Transforming the curriculum: Teaching about women of color. In J. A. Banks & C. Banks (Eds.), *Multicultural education: Issues and perspectives.* Needham Heights, MA: Allyn & Bacon.

Byrnes, D. A., & Kiger, G. (1990). The effect of a prejudice-reduction simulation on attitude change. *Journal of Applied Social Psychology, 20,* 341–356.

Clewell, B. C., Anderson, B. T., & Thorpe, M. E. (1992). *Breaking the barriers: Helping female and minority students succeed in mathematics and science.* San Francisco, CA: Jossey-Bass.

Cochran-Smith, M. (2012). Teacher preparation for diversity. In J. A. Banks (Ed.), *Encyclopedia of diversity in education* (Volume4) (pp. 2127–2130). Thousand Oaks, CA: Sage Publications

Cooley, C. H. (1922). *Human nature and the social order.* New York: Scribner's.

Demarais, A., & White, V. (2004). *First impressions: What you don't know about how others see you.* New York Bantam.

Driver, J. (2010). *You say more than you think: A 7-day plan for using the new body language to get what you want.* New York: Crown Publishers.

Du Praw, M. & Axner, M. (1997). *Toward a more perfect union in an age of diversity: Working on common cross-cultural communication challenges* Retrieved from http://www.pbs.org/ampu/crosscult.html.

Ekman, P. (2009). *Telling lies: Clues to deceit in the marketplace, politics, and marriage* (revised ed.). New York: W. W. Norton.

Etsy, K., Griffin, R., & Hirsch, M. S. (1995). *Workplace diversity.* Holbrook, NA: Adams Media Corporation.

Fiarman, S. E. (2016). Unconscious bias: When good intentions aren't enough. *Educational Leadership, 74*(3), 10–15.

Gabric, D., McFadden, K. L. (2001). Student and employer perceptions of desirable entry-level operations management skills. *American Business Law Journal, 16*(1), 50–59.

Gardner, H. (1993). *Multiple intelligences: The theory of multiple intelligences* (2nd ed.). New York: Basic Books.

Gardner, H. (1999). *Intelligence reframed: Multiple intelligences for the 21st century.* New York: Basic Books.

Ginsberg, M. B., & Wlodkowski, R. J. (2009). *Diversity and motivation: Culturally responsive teaching in college.* San Francisco: Jossey-Bass.

Goleman, D. (1995). *Emotional intelligence: Why it can matter more than IQ.* New York: Random House.

Goleman, D. (2006). *Social intelligence: The new science of human relationships.* New York: Dell.

Gorski, P. C. (1995-2018). *Key characteristics of a multicultural curriculum.* Critical Multicultural Pavilion: Multicultural Curriculum Reform (An EdChange Project). Retrieved from www.edchange.org/multicultural/curriculum/characteristics.html

Green, R. L. (2012). Teacher expectations. In J. A. Banks (Eds.), *Encyclopedia of diversity in education* (vol. 4, pp. 2126–2127). Thousand Oaks, CA: Sage Publications.

Headlee, C. (2016, February 16). *Ten ways to have a better conversation* [TED talk]. Retrieved from https://www.ted.com/talks/celeste_headlee_10_ways_to_have_a_better_conversation

Hogan, R., Curphy, G. J., & Hogan, J. (1994). What we know about leadership: Effectiveness and personality. *American Psychologist, 49,* 493–504.

Huffpost (2018). *The daring racism experiment that people talk about 20 years later.* Retrieved from https://www.huffingtonpost.com/2015/01/02/jane-elliott-race-experiment-oprah-show_n_6396980.html

Hurtado, S. (2002). Creating a climate of inclusion: Understanding Latina(o) college students. In W. A. Smith, P. T. Altbach, & K. Lometey (Eds.), *The racial crisis in American higher education: Continuing challenges for the twenty-first century* (pp. 121–136). Albany, NY: State University of New York Press.

Johnson, S., & Bechler, C. (1998). Examining the relationships between listening effectiveness and leadership emergence: Perceptions, behaviors, and recall. *Small Group Research, 29*(4), 452–471.

Latané, B., Liu, J. H., Nowak, A., Bonevento, N., & Zheng, L. (1995). Distance matters: Physical space and social impact. *Personality and Social Psychology Bulletin, 21,* 795–805.

Locks, A. M., Hurtado, S., Bowman, N. & Osequera, L. (2008). Extending notions of campus climate and diversity to students' transition to college. *Review of Higher Education, 31*(3), 257–285.

Myers, D. G. (1993). *The pursuit of happiness: Who is happy—and why?* New York: Morrow.

National Association of Colleges & Employers (NACE). (2019). *Career readiness defined.* Retrieved from http://www.naceweb.org/career-readiness/competencies/career-readiness-defined/

Navarro, J. (2008). *What every BODY is saying.* New York: Harper Collins.

Nichols, M. P. (1995). *The lost art of listening.* New York: Guilford Press.

Nichols, M. P (2009). *The lost art of listening: How learning to listen can improve relationships.* New York, NY : The Guilford Press.

Nichols, M. P., & Stevens, L. A. (1957). *Are you listening?* New York: McGraw-Hill.

Pascarella, E. T., & Terenzini, P. T. (2005). *How college affects students: A third decade of research* (Vol. 2) San Francisco: Jossey-Bass.

Peters, W. A (1987). *Class divided: Then and now.* New Haven: Yale University Press.

Pettigrew, T. F. (1997). Generalized intergroup contact effects on prejudice. *Personality and Social Psychology Bulletin, 23,* 173–185.

Pettigrew, T. F. (1998). Intergroup contact theory. *Annual Review of Psychology, 49,* 65–85.

Pettigrew, T. F. & Tropp, L. R. (2006). A meta-analytic test of intergroup contact theory. *Journal of Personality and Social Psychology, 90*(5), 751–783.

Purdy, M., & Borisoff, D. (Eds.) (1996). *Listening in everyday life: A personal and professional approach.* Lanham, MD: University Press of America.

Rendón-Linares, L. I., & Muñoz, S. M. (2011). Revisiting validation theory: Theoretical foundations, applications, and extensions. *Enrollment Management Journal, 5*(2), 12–33.

Slavin, R. E. (2012). Cooperative learning. In J. A. Banks (Ed.), *Encyclopedia of diversity in education* (Volume 1, pp. 453-456). Thousand Oaks, CA: Sage Publications.

Smith, D. (1997). How diversity influences learning. *Liberal Education, 83*(2), 42–48.

Smith, D. (2015). *Diversity's promise for higher education: Making it work* (2nd ed.). Baltimore, MD: Johns Hopkins University Press.

Steil, L. L., & Bommelje, R. (2007). *Listening leaders: The ten golden rules to listen: Lead and succeed.* Edina, MN: Beaver Pond Press.

Stangor, C., Sechrist, G. B., & Jost, J. T. (2001). Changing racial beliefs by providing consensus information. *Personality and Social Psychology Bulletin, 27,* 484–494.

Taylor, S. E., Peplau, L. A., & Sears, D. O. (2006). *Social psychology* (12th ed.). Upper Saddle River, NJ: Pearson/Prentice-Hall.

Tobias, S. (1978). *Overcoming math anxiety.* New York: Norton.

Uzzi, B., & Dunlap, S. (2005). How to build your network. *Harvard Business Review, 83*(12), 53–60.

Vogelgesang, L. J., Ikeda, E. K., Gilmartin, S. K., & Keup, J. R. (2002). *Service-learning and the first-year experience: Outcomes related to learning and persistence. In E. Zlotkowsky (Ed.), Service-learning and the first-year experience: Preparing students for personal success and civic responsibility* (pp. 27–36). (Monograph No. 34) Columbia, SC: University of South Carolina, National Resource Center for the First-Year Experience and Students in Transition.

Wolvin, A. D. (2010). *Listening and communication in the 21st century.* Malden, MA: Blackwell.

Zaccaro, S. J., Gilbert, J., Thor, K. K., & Mumford, M. D. (1991). Leadership and social intelligence: Linking social perceptiveness and behavioral flexibility to leader effectiveness. *Leadership Quarterly, 2,* 317–331.

Zull, J. E. (2011). *From brain to mind: Using neuroscience to guide change in education.* Sterling, VA: Stylus.

Reflections and Applications

4.1 Review the sidebar quotes contained in this chapter and select two that you think are particularly meaningful or inspirational. For each quote you selected, provide an explanation of why you chose it.

4.2 Review the strategies for *increasing personal contact and interpersonal interaction with members of diverse groups* on **pp. 69–71**. Select three you think are most important and intend to put into practice.

4.3 **Diversity Comfort Zones**

Racial bias can be subtle and may only begin to surface when the social or emotional distance between members of different groups grows closer. Honestly rate your level of comfort with the following situations.

Someone from another racial group:

1. going to your school	High	Moderate	Low
2. working in your place of employment	High	Moderate	Low
3. living on your street as a next-door neighbor	High	Moderate	Low
4. living with you as a roommate	High	Moderate	Low
5. socializing with you as a personal friend	High	Moderate	Low
6. being an intimate friend or romantic partner	High	Moderate	Low
7. being your partner in marriage.	High	Moderate	Low

For items you rated "high," why would you feel comfortable?

For items you rated "low," why would you feel uncomfortable?

4.4 Self-Assessment of Cultural Competence

Go to the following site: https://nccc.georgetown.edu/documents/ChecklistEIEC.pdf

Follow the directions provided and respond to each of the statements contained in the self-assessment instrument by noting what you already do—if you are already teaching—or what you intend to do if you are preparing to be a teacher.

After completing the instrument, review your responses and honestly answer the following questions:

* Do your responses suggest that you practice culturally competent teaching:
   a) frequently,
   b) occasionally, or
   c) rarely?

* What practices could you adopt to become a more culturally competent teacher?

4.5 Look at the levels of the staircase to cultural competence in (Figure 4.3, **p. 62**).
   a) Which step would you say our society is at right now? Why?
   b) In order for our society to reach the highest step of cultural competence, what still needs to be done or overcome?

4.6 What would you say are the two most powerful and universal principles of effective cross-cultural communication (verbal or nonverbal)? Why?

4.7 What intercultural skills have you already developed that are or could be useful to you as an educator? What intercultural skills do you need to develop further in order to maximize your effectiveness as a teacher and educational leader?

4.8 Would you say the campus climate or culture of the schools you have attended was conducive to intercultural interaction among students from different racial and cultural groups? Was there anything that school administrators or teachers could have done to improve the school climate so that it better supported and promoted intercultural interaction?

The Societal Context for Diversity Education: Family, School, and Community

Chapter Purpose and Preview

This chapter examines how family, school, and community exert an intersectional influence on students' academic achievement. Specific strategies are suggested for building productive partnerships with parents and for strengthening school-community relations. The chapter documents the pivotal role that teachers and school leaders play in promoting the educational achievement and success of diverse students. Lastly, practices are identified for creating an inclusive multicultural curriculum and a school climate conducive to culturally competent teaching and educational leadership.

Introduction

Certainly, the academic achievement of students in general and underrepresented students in particular is affected by their classroom experiences, but it's also affected by their experiences outside the classroom. As illustrated in **Figure 5.1**, student success is co-created by the overlapping influences of student diversity, and the diversity of the student's family, school, and community. The important interplay of these factors in promoting student

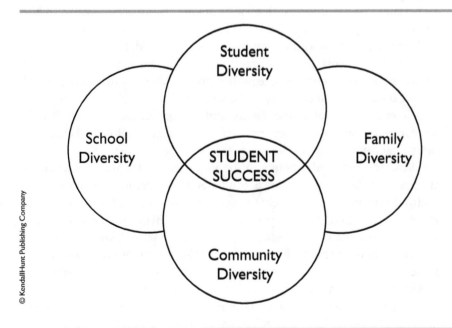

Figure 5.1

Key Spheres of Influence Affecting Student Success

success is underscored by a seven-year analysis of 400 elementary schools, which revealed that the higher the level of relational trust there was among parents, teachers, and principals, the higher were students' scores on standardized achievement tests (Bryk & Schneider, 2002).

As Figure 5.1 suggests, when these sources of influences intersect and reinforce one another, students are more likely to experience academic success. Support for this conclusion this conclusion is supplied by research demonstrating that the educational achievement of African American students is influenced strongly by the quality of: (a) the students' relationship with their parents, (b) the parents' relationship with the school's teachers and officials, and (c) the parents' relationships with the parents of other students attending the same school. When these three relationships are mutually supportive and focus on improving student learning, higher levels of student achievement take place (Yan, 1999). Research also indicates that students of all races and ethnicities attain higher levels of academic performance when they have positive perceptions of both their family and school environments (Chang, McBride-Chang, Stewart, & Au, 2003; Ireson & Hallam, 2005).

Additional studies demonstrate that when schools acknowledge student diversity and family diversity, and encourage family interaction with school officials, the academic achievement of minority students is enhanced (Epstein, 1995; Lareau and Horvat, 1999; Yan, 1999). Conversely, when parents of African American students perceive racism taking place in their children's school, they are more likely to report that their children dislike school and that the school's teachers do not hold high expectations for their children (Thompson, 2003).

Role of the *Family*

To appreciate the influence of the family on today's students requires appreciation of the diversity that exists among family arrangements in the United States. American families are diverse with respect to such characteristics as the number of wage-earning parents in the household, the marital status of the student's parents or guardians, the primary language spoken by the student's parents or guardians, as well as the number of other children and extended family members living in the student's home. Culturally competent educators are mindful of the variety and distinctiveness of today's family arrangements and how they can impact students' self-perceptions and behavioral patterns.

Research repeatedly points to the importance of family influence on students' academic performance. Students whose parents are involved in their education are more likely to succeed in school (DeWitt, 2018). For example, children whose parents read to them at home—in any language—are more successful in elementary school, which in turn increases their prospects for success in middle school and high school (Tracey & Morrow, 2012). Engagement of parents in their children's education has been found to have an effect size on student achievement of more than .50—which represents more than a year's worth of academic growth (Hattie, 2012). This relationship between parental involvement

© vystekimages/Shutterstock.com

and student success exists for parents of all races and ethnicities, level of educations, and income level (Thompson & Luhman, 1997).

The stereotype that African American families do not value education as highly as white families is contradicted by a national survey of tenth-grade students, which revealed that compared to students from white families, black students were more likely to report that getting a good education is important (80% vs. 90%) and getting good grades is very important (47% vs. 62%); 77% of Black tenth graders also reported that they want to earn a college degree (U.S. Department of Education, 2008).

PERSONAL INSIGHT

My mother was a direct descendent of slaves and moved with her parents from the deep South at the age of seventeen. My father lived in an all-black coal mining camp, into which my mother and her family moved in 1938. Because blacks were not allowed to attend public schools in eastern Kentucky, my father was illiterate.

In the early 1960s, I was integrated into the white public schools along with my brother and sister. Physical violence and constant verbal harassment caused many other blacks to quit school at an early age and opt for jobs in the coal mines. But my father remained steadfast in his advice to me: "It doesn't matter if they call you n_____; don't you ever let them beat you by walking out on your education." He would say to me, "Son, you will have opportunities that I never had. Many people, white and black alike, will tell you that you are no good and that education can never help you. Don't listen to them, because soon they will not be able to keep you from getting an education like they did me. Just remember, when you do get that education, you'll never have to go into those coal mines and have them break your back. You can choose what you want to do, and then you can be a free man."

Being poor, black, and Appalachian did not offer me great odds for success, but constant reminders from my parents that I was capable and that education was the key to my future freedom and happiness enabled me to beat the odds. My parents, who weren't able to provide me with monetary wealth, provided me with the gifts of self-worth, educational motivation, and aspiration for academic achievement.

Aaron Thompson

Although national surveys show that black families value education as much or more than white families (U.S. Department of Education, 2008), African American parents have been found to be less engaged with their children's school compared to white parents (Abdul-Adil & Farmer, 2006). The lower level of engagement of African American parents has often been interpreted (or misinterpreted) to mean that they are less interested in, or committed to, their children's education (Smith, 2005). Before that conclusion can be drawn, however, it's important to remember that a variety of factors can influence and have a significant impact on parental involvement, such as the number of parents and students in the household, as well as the parents' income level and work responsibilities. For example, being a single parent, a parent holding more than one job, and being a non-English-speaking parent are all factors that have been found to reduce the level of parents' involvement in their children's education (Kohl, Lengua, & McMahon, 2000).

Culturally competent teachers and school administrators make an earnest attempt to communicate with students' families, and gain knowledge about circumstances at home that may affect parents' involvement with their children's education, and they use this knowledge to make scheduling and procedural adjustments to facilitate parental involvement (Archer-Banks, 2008). Research on effective schools indicates that two of their distinguishing characteristics are that they: (a) regularly communicate with parents about their children's performance and (b) encourage parental participation in decision-making about their children's education (Comer, 2012; Marzano, 2003). In a study of 79 elementary, middle, and high schools, large differences between schools existed in the level of trust that parents expressed toward their children's school, and these differences had no relationship to the characteristics of the school's external (local) community, but to the internal characteristics of the school environment. Schools that provided parents with authentic opportunities to influence school decisions were perceived as more trustworthy (Adams, Forsyth, & Mitchell, 2009).

> "The wider the gap between school and community cultures, the more important it is for teachers to make these connections."
>
> —Vivian Robinson, author, *Student-Centered Leadership*

The ability to build trust in racially and ethnically homogenous communities is easier than to build trust in more heterogeneous (diverse) communities because humans are more inclined to trust others whom they see as similar to themselves (Tschannen-Moran & Hoy, 2000). Consequently, schools that serve culturally diverse communities have to make more intentional attempts to reach out and build relationships with their students' families (Robinson, 2011). Studies show that schools with stronger parent-school ties have safer school environments, higher rates of school attendance, and higher levels of parent-school trust (Bryk et al., 2010; Epstein & Sheldon, 2002).

Specific strategies that effective schools have used to build parental trust and partnerships are identified in **Box 5.1**.

Box 5.1 Practices for Promoting Parental Partnerships Used by Effective Schools

▶ **Parent Newsletter:** A family newsletter is sent home periodically throughout the school year, providing information on school activities and encouraging parents' participation in upcoming school events.

▶ **School Hotline:** Parents have a designated phone line through which they are able to call the school (including after-school hours) and speak with a school representative. The school uses the telephone hotline not only to give parents a voice, but also to track patterns of parental concerns and suggestions (e.g., keeping a log of hotline calls, reviewing it to identify recurrent issues and suggestions, and using the information received as feedback to drive school-improvement initiatives).

▶ **Home Visits:** For parents unable to make school visits to discuss their student's learning or behavioral issues, the teacher or principal makes home visits. Such visits demonstrate the school's commitment to the student, enable the school to gain insight into the student's family situation, and increase parents' willingness to partner with the school to advance their student's success.

▶ **Welcoming New Students:** When a family with school-age children moves into the local community, information about the school is sent to the student's home and family members are invited to upcoming school functions. The teacher or principal may also make a home visit to welcome family members and encourage their involvement with the school.

▶ **Parent Interviews:** Students are given an assignment to interview their parents about their views of public education in general and their school in particular.

▶ **Parent Surveys:** Parents complete surveys designed to assess their expectations of the school and engagement with the school (e.g., https://www.surveymonkey.com/mp/harvard-education-surveys).

- ▶ **Parent Workshops:** Parents are provided with educational materials they can use at home for educational training (e.g., how to encourage and tutor reading).
- ▶ **Summer School Reading Programs:** Parents engage in reading and literacy activities during the summer to combat the sharper drop in student achievement that typically takes place during summer break among students from disadvantaged families relative to students from more privileged families (Cooper et al., 1996).
- ▶ **Family Guest Speakers:** Students' parents or other relatives are invited to school as guest speakers and panelists.
- ▶ **Family Use of School Facilities:** Family members are allowed to use the school's educational and recreational resources and, if possible, space and personnel are provided for after-school daycare.

Role of the *Community*

The community plays a key role in the socialization of children and can have significant impact on students' personal development and educational motivation. The local community serves as a source of "community cultural wealth" for low-income students and students of color, and can supply them with the social capital needed to persist in school despite disadvantaged or oppressive conditions (Yosso, 2005). Culturally competent educators are knowledgeable about their students' community and capitalize on this knowledge to bridge the gap between what they are teaching students in school and what their students are experiencing outside of school (Gay, 2010).

When a school builds a strong base of community support, it not only benefits students; it also generates significant benefits for the school itself, such as political support from community organizations for after-school programs and school funding. When schools reach out to members of the community with whom students can identify, recognizes role models in the community, and honors those role models on campus (e.g., inviting them to be guest speakers), it simultaneously swells student pride in their school and their community.

The local community can also supply students with opportunities for meaningful volunteer experiences. Students who engage in community service may also be asked to invite members from the community to visit class as guest speakers or panelists. When students reflect on their volunteer experiences (e.g., via reaction papers or focused discussions), volunteerism is transformed into service learning. Research strongly supports the positive impact of service learning on multiple student learning outcomes, particularly when the service involves interaction with diverse groups of people (Astin et al., 2000; Gurin et al., 2002; Vogelgesang & Astin, 2000).

By gaining knowledge about students' communities, and the cultural diversity represented in those communities, teachers and school administrators are able to use that knowledge to strengthen school-community relations by adopting programs and practices such as those cited in **Box 5.2**.

"A community may be defined as a group of people who share the same environment, interests, beliefs, and values. To ignore the school's local community is to ignore the everyday world in which students live."

—National Council for the Social Studies

"Culturally responsive instructional strategies ... use community members and parents as resources."

—James Banks, in *Cultural Diversity and Education*

"The multicultural curriculum should make maximum use of experiential learning, especially community resources."

—National Council for the Social Studies, *Curricular Guidelines for Multicultural Education*

▶ The school surveys community needs (e.g., need for child daycare), community opinions (e.g., about school dress codes), and community practices (e.g., languages spoken and ethnic traditions), and uses the results to inform school policies and educational planning.

▶ School newsletters are sent to board members, business leaders, and other key decision makers in the community to keep them apprised of school developments.

▶ News releases about the school are prepared for the local news media.

▶ Local media are informed about students' outstanding academic achievements and service to the community.

▶ Local media are asked to publicly recognize school and community members who have made special contributions to improving school-community relations.

▶ Students are regularly assigned articles to read in the local newspaper.

▶ Students write reports about their community and what their school is doing to meet the community's needs (and vice versa).

▶ Students take field trips to local museums and attend community events (e.g., outdoor markets or festivals).

▶ Student groups engage in community fundraisers to raise money for class trips or educational resources.

▶ Community businesses and organizations collaborate with student clubs (e.g., students involved with the school newspaper or journalism club work with an editor of a local newspaper).

▶ The school and community organizations share resources (e.g., share facilities, equipment, and fundraising or grant-writing ventures).

▶ Local businesses offer discounts to students who achieve academic excellence (e.g., reduced prices on store-bought items or home services).

▶ Community members from different cultural groups are invited to class to share their experiences as guest speakers or panelists.

▶ Successful members of the community serve as tutors or mentors to students.

▶ Students visit community businesses and nonprofit organizations to explore career fields (e.g., observe professionals at work and ask questions about their work).

▶ Local businesses and organizations provide part-time employment or internship opportunities for students.

Sources: Mitrofanova (2004); U.S. Department of Health & Human Services (2003)

Role of the *School*

In addition to the school's surrounding (local) community, both the classroom and the school itself are communities where students' citizenship skills and civic character can be developed. The school environment "offers students a place to question, to participate, to develop civic skills, and to respect and understand the pluralistic world in which they live" (Morse, 1989, p. 3). Development of citizenship skills starts in school when students practice civility—being respectful of, and sensitive to, the rights of other members (citizens) of their school community. Being part of a civil and mutually respectful school community benefits students of all races and ethnicities. Both white students and students of color report experiencing a greater sense of belonging and a stronger social connection with classmates when they perceive their school climate to be civil and hospitable (Locks, Hurtado, Bowman, & Osequera, 2008). In contrast, higher education research reveals that campus communities that minority students perceive to be unwelcoming or hostile have lower overall levels of student satisfaction and lower graduation rates—for both minority and majority students (Cabrera et al., 1999; Eimers & Pike, 1997; Nora & Cabrera, 1996).

The powerful role that schools can play in promoting students' long-term success is highlighted by findings that indicate the best predictor of a person's later-life wealth, health, and longevity is the number of years that person has spent in school; for example, compared to high school dropouts, high school graduates earn 50% higher income, are less likely to be on welfare, are healthier, and live six-to-nine years longer than dropouts (Levin et al., 2006). However, not all schools are created equal; a wide range of differences exist among them in terms of their culture, student-body composition, curriculum, resources, and facilities. In fact, one major goal of multicultural education is to reform schools so that students from diverse racial, ethnic, and socioeconomic groups experience equitable educational opportunities (Banks, 2016).

America has a highly decentralized system of education, with more than 15,000 local school districts making separate and independent decisions about their own instructional policies, programs, and practices. The advantage of decentralization is that it allows different schools the freedom to be responsive to the unique needs of their local community. The disadvantage of decentralization is that it creates wide disparities across schools in terms of the resources available to them because schools are funded by local property taxes. This means that the amount of financial support a school receives for educating its children varies dramatically depending on the wealth of the local community in which the school is located. Two neighborhoods adjacent to one another can provide vastly different fiscal support for their public schools based on differences in their respective property values and tax rates. Although some states have less funding gaps than others because they provide substantially more funding to their highest poverty districts than do other states, gaps exist in all states. Nationally, the highest poverty districts average about $1,200 less in per-student funding than the lowest poverty districts (The Education Trust, 2015).

The bottom line: The wealthier the community surrounding the school, the more tax dollars available to the school to support its students' education. Consequently, students attending schools in poor communities are educated in school environments that are supported with fewer educational resources and poorer physical facilities.

Because a disproportionate number of students of color are from low-income families and attend racially segregated schools (Arum & Roska, 2011), inequities relating to school-funding formulas disproportionately impact the quality of education received by students from minority racial and ethnic

> "Many of the schools that our nation's most vulnerable children attend, especially those in economically strapped urban areas, are dilapidated and segregated."
>
> —C. Talbert-Johnson, "Structural Inequalities and the Achievement Gap in Urban Schools"

groups. A significantly higher percentage of children from very poor families enroll in segregated African American and Hispanic schools, where lower funding for school resources compromises the rigor of the curriculum and the quality of student support services (Orfield & Eaton, 1996). Funding gap differences between school districts is even larger for districts that serve the most students of color and districts that serve the least students of color—averaging about $2,000 less per student in districts that serve the most students of color (The Education Trust, 2015). Such inequities exacerbate the achievement gap between white students and students of color (Ladson-Billings, 2006; The Education Trust, 2008), and raises the risk that students of color will drop out of school altogether. About 12% of America's public high schools account for one-half of the nation's high school student dropouts; in these "dropout factories," only 40% of ninth graders are enrolled as twelfth graders four years later (compared to 90% of students enrolled in other high schools around the country). Disturbingly, these dropout factories are high schools that enroll very high percentages of low-income, minority students (Balfanz & Legters, 2004), the very students for whom education is the only ticket to upward socioeconomic mobility—for themselves and their future families.

Originating with the work of Horace Mann in the mid-1800s, America's public school system was designed with the goal of providing all its citizens with equal opportunity for upward social mobility (Groen, 2008). Our nation's schools are still viewed as the primary vehicle for reducing inequality, promoting social justice, and transforming society. However, America's schools are characterized by similar inequalities that exist in its larger society; in fact, they mirror them (Gorski, 1995–2019). Instead of serving as a launching pad for propelling poor students to higher levels of socioeconomic status, our school-funding formulas reduce the likelihood of upward social mobility and perpetuate existing societal inequities (Kozol, 1991).

"No child left behind" and "every student succeeds" are political policies that will be nothing more than political platitudes unless longstanding school-funding formulas are changed to ensure that all students are given the same educational opportunities and resources to compete in the achievement race. In fact, these political policies can be demoralizing and punitive for schools and educators serving socioeconomically disadvantaged communities (Mintrop & Sunderman, 2009). Fortunately, political leaders in some states have begun to reallocate their fiscal resources to reduce the equity gap in educational funding for schools serving their poorer communities (The Education Trust, 2008).

Role of the *Curriculum*

An essential element of diversity education is exposing students to an inclusive curriculum that embraces multiple cultural perspectives. A curriculum that acknowledges and appreciates cultural diversity has been found to be one distinguishing feature of high-performing schools in low-income school districts (Wang, 1998). Transforming the traditional curriculum into a genuine multicultural curriculum—one that authentically represents the diverse

"Education ... is the great equalizer. It does better than to disarm the poor of their hostility towards the rich: it prevents being poor."

—Horace Mann, abolitionist, educational reformer, and "Father of the Common (Public) School"

"School districts with the greatest needs often receive the least funding. In too many communities, students who are poor, minority, or English learners do not get their fair share of education funds. With the right leadership, inequitable funding patterns can be changed. We can unstack the deck."

—The Education Trust

"Democratic education is a process where teachers and students work collaboratively to reconstruct curriculum to include everyone."

—Amy Guttman, author of *Democratic Education*

histories and cultures of multiple ethnic groups—typically evolves through the following of five stages of development (Banks, 1993, 2016; McIntosh, 2000).

1. Mainstream Curriculum

This is the traditional Eurocentric, male-centered curriculum that has largely ignored the contributions and perspective of non-dominant groups. When minority students see the curriculum as relevant to their culture, it increases their motivation to learn. Because there is a strong relationship between motivation and achievement (Ginsberg, 2005), a culturally relevant curriculum increases students' level of engagement in the learning process and, ultimately, their level of academic achievement. For example, research shows that students are more likely to become engaged readers when they see their cultural history and experiences reflected in the material they are reading (Gay, 2010). Thus, a culturally relevant curriculum should be responsive to the cultural characteristics and backgrounds that students bring with them to the classroom—such as their racial and ethnic identity, socioeconomic status, and gender (Ginsberg, 2005). In contrast, if the curriculum fails to validate the culture of minority groups, it can further alienate minority students from a school culture that in other ways is already likely to differ sharply from their home culture (Kitayama & Markus, 1994).

A strictly Eurocentric curriculum not only disadvantages minority students, it also disadvantages majority students by giving them a "false sense of superiority and denying them the opportunity to benefit from the knowledge, perspectives, and frames of reference that can be gained from studying other cultures and groups" (Banks, 1993, p. 195).

> "I want to study Asian history and women's history. I'm tired of studying about white people and men."
>
> —Overheard comment being made by a female high school student to a friend at a coffee shop in California

2. The Contributions Approach

This curricular approach involves supplementing the mainstream curriculum by celebrating ethnic-minority holidays (e.g., Black History Month) and the contributions of ethnic-minority heroes selected by using criteria similar to those used to select mainstream curriculum heroes. Typically, teachers involve students in classroom experiences or lessons at the time of these celebrations, but not at other times during the academic year.

The contributions approach represents a more advanced stage of curricular reform than the traditional mainstream curriculum, but it has two major weaknesses: (a) it covers non-dominant groups outside the context of the required curriculum, thus suggesting that learning about these "other" groups is not central to the curriculum, but supplemental or peripheral to it—a "side show" to the "main event"; (b) it focuses exclusively on the achievement of heroes or extraordinary people, and it fails to cover (or glosses over) the struggles, victimization, and oppression of non-dominant groups (Gorski, 1995–2019).

> "A national culture or school curriculum that does not reflect the voices, struggles, hopes, and dreams of its many peoples is neither democratic nor cohesive."
>
> —National Council for the Social Studies, *Curricular Guidelines for Multicultural Education*

3. The Additive Approach

This approach creates a more inclusive curriculum by adding a diversity book, unit, or course to the curriculum. However, its limitations are: (a) no substantive change to (or restructuring of) the curriculum takes place, and (b) the added diversity material is covered from the perspective of the mainstream curriculum. Banks (2016) illustrates how this curricular approach to teaching fifth-grade history might add a unit on the Lakota (Sioux) Indians, but cover it as part of "The Western Movement"—the movement of European Americans from eastern to western regions of the United States. However, since the Lakota Sioux Indians were already in the West and not moving anywhere, from their perspective this unit would be more aptly called "The Invasion of the East." Instead of taking this additive approach to creating an inclusive curriculum, a more integrated approach would be to include Native American content in the unit, but title it and cover it as: "Two Cultures Meet in the Americas."

An additive approach to curricular reform might also involve adding new courses to the curriculum that relate specifically to minority groups (e.g., a course on African American or Mexican American history). This represents a major advance in curricular reform because it actually infuses diversity-related content into the mainstream curriculum. Its major weakness, however, is that it covers diversity as a segregated, stand-alone topic rather than as core content that's integrated into the textbooks (Banks, 1993).

4. The Transformation Approach

This stage of curricular reform moves beyond appending or tacking on diversity-related content to the existing curriculum by integrating that content into the curriculum. Its educational objective is to expand understanding of the content covered in the curriculum by enabling students to view it from multiple cultural perspectives. For example, when students study the American Revolution, they study it from the perspectives of British loyalists, American revolutionaries, and Native Americans.

Traditionally, school textbooks covered historical events from the perspective of groups that have been politically and economically dominant, without including the perspective of groups that have been victimized or marginalized (Loewen, 2010). If students exposed to this curriculum eventually become school teachers, they will come to the classroom with an incomplete and ethnocentric view of our nation's history (Sensoy & DiAngelo, 2012). The transformation approach to the curricular reform attempts to rectify this shortcoming of the traditional curriculum by raising consciousness of how American culture has emerged from interaction between, and integration of, groups that dominated and groups that dominated. According to Banks (2016), the aim of this approach to the multicultural curriculum is to (a) raise student awareness of how the history that becomes institutionalized in the dominant culture reflects the experiences of the victors, not the vanquished; and (b) help students understand that "one irony of conquest is that those who are conquered often deeply influence the cultures of the conquerors" (p. 62). The transformational approach to curricular reform encourages students to consider the diversity implications of all topics covered in the traditional curriculum. Teachers are prepared to use diversity-related examples to support and illustrate their points; and when students conduct research a topic, they examine it from a multicultural perspective.

The transformation approach represents the most advanced stage of curricular reform because diversity is woven seamlessly into the mainstream curriculum and is examined from multiple perspectives, enabling students to view major ideas and events through a multicultural lens. For example, an American

History textbook used in the transformation curriculum would incorporate the history and perspectives of women, African Americans, Hispanics, and Asian Americans (Gorski, 1995–2019). Each American ethnic group has a unique historical experience that contributed to the development of our nation's culture. Thus, by incorporating ethnic diversity into students' historical perspective, they gain insight into the multicultural histories layered within our national history, including the unique struggles that different groups of Americans endured to secure personal freedoms, human rights, and social justice.

Shor (1992) notes that a multicultural perspective can be readily infused into the existing curriculum "as long as existing knowledge is not presented as facts and doctrines to be absorbed without question, as long as existing bodies of knowledge are critiqued and balanced from a multicultural perspective, and as long as the students' own themes and idioms are valued along with standard usage" (p. 35). Science education researchers have demonstrated that diversity material can be infused seamlessly into the science curriculum by intentionally including in each lesson plan both a Western scientific value (e.g., control over nature) and a non-Western value (e.g., harmony with nature) (Aikenhead, 1997, 2001; Lee & Buxton, 2008).

An interesting example of how concepts of diversity and social inequality can be weaved seamlessly (and critically) into the social science curriculum is provided in a junior high school textbook that examines the American Revolution from the broader concept of what defines a "revolution." In this textbook, students compare the American Revolution to the civil rights movement and women's movements of the 1960s and critically assess the ways in which these movements meet (or fail to meet) the criteria that define a revolution. Diversity can also be effectively weaved into coverage of U.S. history by highlighting discrepancies between democratic ideals and national realities. For example, coverage of American history in a transformative multicultural curriculum would include coverage of the Indian Removal Act in 1830 that forced Native Americans to leave their reservations and move west. It would also include the forced internment of Japanese Americans during World War II (Banks, with Sebesta, 1982).

If the curriculum fails to acknowledge the injustices that have taken place as America pursued its economic and political self-interests, that curriculum not only fails to provide a complete and accurate history of the United States, it can also foment cynicism and alienation among minority youth who currently see (and experience) gaps between our national ideals and their personal realities (NCSS, 1991).

5. The Decision-Making and Social-Action Approach

A powerful curriculum equips students with learning experiences that not only serve to better themselves, but also to better the society in which they live. Thus, a powerful multicultural curriculum should enable students to understand societal inequalities and advance social justice.

When students build on their knowledge of different cultural groups to analyzing power relationships and inequalities between groups, they are engaging in "critical multiculturalism" (May, 2009). By applying critical multiculturalism to American history, students unearth and analyze the roots of current-day

"For optimum effectiveness, the study of ethnic and cultural group experiences must be interwoven into the total curriculum. It should not be reserved for special occasions, units, or courses, nor should it be considered supplementary to the existing curriculum or relegated to a marginal position in the curriculum."

—National Council for the Social Sciences, *Curricular Guidelines for Multicultural Education*

"The curriculum should help students understand the significant historical experiences of ethnic groups [and] the critical contemporary issues and social problems confronting each of them."

—National Council for the Social Sciences, *Multicultural Curriculum Standards*

"It is your responsibility to change society if you think of yourself as an educated person."

—James Baldwin, African American author and activist, in a "Talk to Teachers" concepts of race and racism. For example, students would become critically aware that the term "white race" didn't even exist until it was introduced by Americans in the eighteenth and nineteenth centuries, and that it was previously used anywhere else in the world. America coined the term and became the first race-conscious nation, in large part because the young nation's expanding cotton industry needed: (a) more land—which was confiscated from land that Native Americans had already settled, and (b) a large labor force—which was obtained inexpensively by importing and enslaving African Americans. To meet their needs for land and labor, the Anglo-Protestant upper class created and disseminated the idea of a privileged "white race" that was entitled to the land and labor of "non-whites." Thus, the concept of a white race was socially constructed by English settlers for the purpose of gaining socioeconomic advantages and to justify (rationalize) enslavement of blacks—who were deemed to be "subhuman" (Hund, Mills, & Sebastiani, 2015) and enslavement of Native Americans—who were deemed to be "uncivilized savages" (Eiselein, 1996).

The decision-making and social-action approach to curriculum reform moves beyond teaching historical facts and promoting patriotism to developing critical thinking skills and addressing social inequities. Such a curriculum helps engage students in critical analysis of how knowledge is socially constructed and may be biased by the cultural group reporting it, and how the same historical event may be viewed differently from the position or perspective of different cultural groups. It's noteworthy that the term *positionality* has crept into scholars' vocabulary to convey the point that knowledge is constructed and can be strongly influenced by the cultural position of the person constructing and reporting it (Banks, 2016). In the decision-making and social-action curriculum, the issue of positionality would be addressed by having students read, compare and contrast different authors' accounts of the same event.

PERSONAL EXPERIENCE

"I'm an undocumented teacher who came to the United States with my family from Guadalajara, Mexico. I arrived at 9 months of age and attended public schools in the Los Angeles Unified School District, where my U.S. history teacher, Dr. Daniel Alamo, inspired me to find empowerment through activism. As an ethnic studies and world history teacher in a Los Angeles public school, I reframe deficit narratives, which have presented marginalized people as passive and ignore their contributions to history. I teach students about valuing their own roots and recognizing their power" (Reyes, 2019, p. A16).

The decision-making and social-action approach to curricular reform also prepares students to make decisions and take action to redress societal inequalities. It equips students with decision-making and action-taking skills that promote their political self-efficacy—the belief that participation in their nation's governance can make a difference in the quality of their lives, family, and community (Bernstein, 1986). As James Banks notes, "A curriculum designed to empower students must be transformative in nature and must help students develop the knowledge, skills, and values needed to become social critics who can make reflective decisions and can implement their decisions in effective personal, social and civic action" (Banks, 2016, p. 190). This is a particularly important curricular outcome for racial minority students because, historically, people of color have felt powerless about being able to influence political policies and institutions; as a result, many have developed a sense of helplessness with respect to effecting political change that could improve their collective future (Ogbu, 1990). A decision-making and social-action curriculum helps to combat political helplessness and cultivate political efficacy that students need to become engaged citizens in a pluralistic democratic nation (National Council for the Social Studies, 1991). Such a curriculum also increases the likelihood that students themselves will become future equality advocates, social activists, and political leaders.

To increase their sense of social and political efficacy, students could be given an assignment that asks them to develop a personal or collective action plan for making their community more inclusive and socially just. The plan could include community opinion surveys, needs assessments, personal

> "The underlying goal of multicultural education is to effect social change [which] incorporates three strands of transformation: the transformation of self, the transformation of schools, and the transformation of society."
>
> —Paul Gorski, founder of EdChange and the Multicultural Pavilion, an award-winning website on multicultural education research and practice

Box 5.3 Checklist for Evaluating the Quality of a School's Multicultural Program

- ☐ Does the curriculum reflect ethnic and cultural diversity?
- ☐ Are ethnic content and perspectives incorporated into all aspects of the curriculum?
- ☐ Do instructional materials treat racial and ethnic differences and groups realistically and sensitively?
- ☐ Does the curriculum examine the total experiences of groups instead of focusing exclusively on "heroes"?
- ☐ Does the curriculum include the study of societal problems that different ethnic and racial groups have experienced, such as racism, prejudice, discrimination, and exploitation?
- ☐ Does the curriculum help students develop a sense of efficacy—the belief that they can take action to influence the outcomes of their life and society?
- ☐ Does the curriculum assist students in developing skills needed for effective interpersonal and intercultural group interactions?
- ☐ Does the curriculum help students participate in cross-ethnic and cross-cultural experiences and reflect on those experiences? (Specific strategies for addressing the above-two questions are provided in chapters 6 and 7.)
- ☐ Does the school library and resource center offer a variety of materials on the histories, experiences, and cultures of diverse racial and ethnic groups?
- ☐ Do school assemblies, decorations, speakers, holidays, and heroes reflect racial and ethnic group differences?
- ☐ Are extracurricular activities multiethnic and multicultural in nature?
- ☐ Is the school staff (administrators, instructors, counselors, and support personnel) multiethnic and multiracial?
- ☐ Does the school have systematic, comprehensive, mandatory, and continuing multicultural staff development programs?
- ☐ Do staff development programs provide opportunities for teachers to learn how to select and create multiethnic instructional materials and how to incorporate multicultural content into the curriculum?

Source: National Council for the Social Studies (1991), *Curricular Guidelines for Multicultural Education*

© Syda Productions/Shutterstock.com

interviews with members of the community, Internet-based research about the community's history, and neighborhood walking tours in which students identify places where social action needs to be taken (Scharf, 2018).

To help schools assess the quality of their multicultural curriculum and extracurricular programs, the National Council for Social Sciences has developed self-evaluation checklist. **Box 5.3.** contains a synthesis of key questions included on this checklist.

Infusing Learning Skills and Academic Success Strategies into the Multicultural Curriculum

When students acquire effective learning strategies in addition to subject-matter knowledge, they acquire strategies with two powerful qualities:

1. *Transferability*—portable strategies that "travel well" and can be used across multiple subject areas;
2. *Durability*—enduring strategies that can be used across all levels of education and throughout life.

Classroom-observation studies show that students receive little direct instruction on *how* to learn and how to use effective learning strategies (Moseley et al., 2004; Ornstein et al., 2010). This is a disappointing finding, particularly in light of research showing that schools which promote the greatest gains in academic achievement of both minority and majority students are schools whose curriculum includes coverage of learning strategies, such as teaching students how to take notes on what they are learning and how to effectively summarize what they have learned (Marzano, Pickering, and Pollock, 2001). Additional research shows that high-performing schools which educate significant numbers of language-minority students are typically adopt a curriculum that integrates content coverage with academic-success strategies (Pierce, 1991). It is particularly critical for students from linguistically and educationally disadvantaged backgrounds to be equipped with effective academic learning strategies because they are less likely to have family members at home who can teach and model these skills for them.

Ensuring that the Multicultural Curriculum Promotes Students' Educational Advancement

An effective multicultural curriculum prepares students from all cultural groups to advance and succeed at the next level of education. Thus, an effective multicultural high school curriculum should prepare both minority and majority students to succeed in college. Following World War II, it became a national expectation that all of America's youth would graduate from high school; however, two different education tracks (curricula) were offered: one for "brighter" and more "motivated" students that prepared them for college, the other for students who were expected to enter the workforce after high school graduation (Alliance for Excellent Education, 2009). Today, the national expectation is that all young people should continue their formal education beyond high school so that they may find gainful employment in today's knowledge-based economy and to address the current workforce challenges facing our nation (College Board & National Commission on Community Colleges, 2008; McCabe, 2000). A generation ago, nearly 75% of Americans could find employment without a postsecondary credential; by 2007, that figure dropped to less than 40% and will continue to drop further (Carnevale, Smith, & Strohl, 2010; Georgetown Center for Education & the Workforce, 2014). The number of jobs held by workers with a high school diploma or less declined by 6.3 million during the Great Recession of 2008 and very few of these jobs have come back. In contrast, there are now 700,000 more jobs available for Americans with a postsecondary certificate or associated degree, and 8.1 million jobs for Americans with a bachelor's degree or higher (Lumina Foundation, 2016). By 2020, almost two-thirds of jobs in the United States will require education beyond high school (Carnevale & Smith, 2012).

Unfortunately, less-privileged high school students often experience a pre-college curriculum that leaves them unprepared for college entry and college success. By age 24, 75% of students whose family income ranks among the top quarter of American families go on to higher education and earn a bachelor's degree; in contrast, approximately 26% of children whose family income lies in the bottom quarter will graduate from college (Mortenson, 2017).

These findings suggest that the high school curriculum experienced by low-income students (and other student groups that have been historically underrepresented in college) needs to be carefully crafted and closely monitored to ensure that they are enrolling in courses that will prepare them for college entry (Conley, 2005). Because the average student-counselor ratio in American schools is 460 to 1 (American School Counselor Association, 2010), other members of the school community may need to take an active role in monitoring the course-taking patterns of underrepresented students to ensure they enroll in courses that lead to college access and success. Teachers can play a particularly influential role in this process, and school administrators can empower teachers for this role by supplying them with accurate, updated information on admission requirements to local colleges and state universities (Conley, 2005).

> "To close the gap between those who understand how to prepare to succeed in college and those who do not, high schools will have to make sustained efforts to redesign their instructional programs and their information systems."
>
> —David Conley, *College Knowledge: What It Really Takes for Students to Succeed and What We Can Do Get Them Ready*

The Role of *School Leaders*

It is well documented that the quality of educational leadership has substantial impact on school improvement (Hallinger & Heck, 1996; Leithwood et al., 2004) and student achievement (Robinson, Lloyd, & Rowe, 2008). Research on effective leaders reveals that one of their distinguishing characteristics is their ability to enable constituents from diverse groups to see themselves as members of the same community, and by advancing the community's interests, they advance their own interests (Bass & Riggio, 2006).

Multicultural education has been viewed primarily, if not exclusively, in terms of curriculum reform; other dimensions or components of the diversity experience have received considerably less attention (Banks, 2016). Effective multicultural education certainly should include a major focus on curricular reform, but it also requires systemic and holistic reform that permeates the total educational environment, including the school's learning resource center and library, classroom teaching strategies, students' out-of-class experiences, testing practices, and counseling programs. School leaders are those who are in the best position to ensure that diversity education pervades the entire school climate and culture. They can make certain that diversity is reflected outside the formal curriculum, including academic support services, extracurricular programs (e.g., honor societies and athletic teams), school assemblies, hallway decorations, and cafeteria menus.

School administrators also provide leadership for multicultural education by equipping teachers with the tools needed to accommodate and incorporate diversity in their classrooms. They can furnish teachers with instructional resources (e.g., supplies and materials), professional development opportunities (e.g., in-service development), and personal support (encouragement and recognition). Research strongly suggests that culturally responsive teaching takes place in schools whose culture has been shaped by school leaders who: (a) recruit and hire qualified minority teachers and staff members, (b) empower teachers to infuse diversity into their instructional practices by providing them with needed support and professional development opportunities, and (c) seek input from teachers and collaborate with them to close achievement gaps (DeWitt, 2018; Holmes & Wynne, 1989; Reyes, 1990; Sashkin, & Walberg, 1993).

Schools that have been found to promote the greatest gains in learning among students from all cultural backgrounds have three characteristics in common—all of which are influenced primarily by the school leader:

> *Clear School Mission*: All members of the school community have a shared understanding of and commitment to instructional goals, school priorities, and professional accountability.
> *Instructional Leadership*: the school leader articulates the school's mission and communicates it clearly and consistently to teachers, support staff, and parents.
> *Safe and Orderly Environment*: the school's atmosphere is free from threat of physical harm and the campus climate is disciplined, but not oppressive, and conducive to teaching and learning (Association for Effective Schools, 1996).

It should be noted that while the racial and ethnic background of America's school children is growing more diverse, this increasing student diversity is not being matched by increasing diversity among school leaders. For example, during the 2011–2012 school year, the vast majority of public school principals were white (80 percent), 10 percent were black, and 7 percent were Hispanic. In the 2003–2004 school year, the proportion was 82 percent white,

"The role of leadership cannot be underestimated in creating change for diversity ... Building institutional capacity for diversity is a multidimensional effort and exists in many different locations in the institution—all requiring leadership."

—Daryl Smith, author, *Making a Real Difference with Diversity: A Guide to Institutional Change*

11 percent black, and 5 percent Hispanic (U.S. Department of Education, 2016).

The shortage of minority administrators (as well minority teachers) leaves minority students with a shortage of visible role models at school with whom they can identify and they can emulate. This shortage of visible role model can lead minority students to view their school culture as different or "foreign," especially if other elements of the school's culture do not reflect the cultural characteristics of the student's family and community (Salinas, 2002). Thus, another important way in which school leaders can help create a diversity-sensitive and diversity-responsive school culture is to do all they can to recruit qualified minority teachers and staff.

Lastly, school leaders play a pivotal role in shaping *school climate*— defined as the "personality of the school, expressing the collective perception of teachers of school routine and thereby influencing their attitudes and behaviors" (Berkowitz et al., 2017, p. 425). One particularly important component of school climate that school leaders can influence is their teachers' sense of *collective efficacy*—"the collective self-perception that teachers in a given school make an educational difference to their students over and above the educational impact of their homes and communities" (Tschannen-Moran & Barr, 2004, p. 190). When teachers share a sense of collective efficacy, the school culture gravitates toward the belief that (a) students' learning successes and failures reflect what the school did or did not do, and (b) faculty and administrators can work together to solve problems of practice (Hattie & Zierer, 2018). Research consistently shows that a culture of collective efficacy outweighs all other school factors which influence student achievement, including students' socioeconomic status, home environment, parental involvement, and prior level of academic achievement (Donohoo, 2017; Hattie, 2016).

The Role of *Teachers*

Research demonstrates that students in classes taught by effective teachers outperform students with similar demographic characteristics in other class on standardized tests of reading and math achievement (Rivkin, Hanushek, & Kain, 2005). The powerful influence that teachers can have on student learning is highlighted further by a nationwide meta-analysis of studies of high-and low-impact teachers on students' academic achievement, which revealed that students in classes taught by high-impact teachers had almost a full year's advantage over students taught by low-impact teachers (Slater, Davies, & Burgess, 2009). Furthermore, the effects of high-quality teaching are cumulative: they provide students with educational advantages that persist over time. In contrast, students who experience low-quality teaching fall behind initially and often struggle to eventually catch up (Konsantopoulos & Chung, 2010).

Effective, culturally competent teachers can reduce the achievement gap significantly or eliminate it altogether. Supporting this conclusion is research indicating that effective teachers increase the math achievement scores of African American ninth graders by 50% beyond the usual gains which take place during that year of school (Aaronson, Barrow, & Sander (2007). In fact, effective teaching has been found to be a better predictor of African American

> "I have always felt that the true textbook for the pupil is his teacher."
>
> —Mahatma Gandhi, political and spiritual leader of India during the Indian independence movement

students' educational progress and academic achievement than any other factor (Wiggan, 2008). (For an extensive discussion of effective teaching practices, see chapters 6 and 7.)

Research on economically disadvantaged students also shows that when they are exposed to effective teachers for 4–5 consecutive years, their achievement gap is completely eliminated (Hanushek, 2005). Additional research demonstrates that students who have effective teachers for three years in a row experience academic gains that are almost triple those made by students taught by ineffective teachers during the same three-year period (Haycock, 1998).

Teacher expectations alone have been found to exert powerful influence on student achievement (Hattie, 2012; Rosenthal & Jacobson, 1963, 1968). Research shows that if students detect that their teacher has higher expectations for some students than others (Weinstein, 2002), or if teachers set different targets for students' expected level of achievement at the end of the year (e.g., high, moderate, or low), students typically rise or fall to the level of expectations that teachers set for them (Rubie-Davis 2007; Rubie-Davies, Hattie, & Hamilton, 2006).

Effective, culturally competent teachers: (a) view diversity as a strength and an opportunity, rather than a problem or liability; (b) believe that the teacher is primarily responsible for promoting student learning; and (c) set high expectations for all students (Cawelti, 2004; Rubie-Davies, Hattie, & Hamilton, 2006; Scharf, 2018). Research shows that effective, culturally competent teachers: (a) believe in themselves, (b) believe that all children can and will succeed, (c) view themselves as engaged members of their school community, and (d) are intrinsically interested in inspiring their students to learn and to become engaged members of their own communities (Meaney et al., 2008).

> "We need to make sure that we find a balance between knowing when our students are at risk and putting them at risk because of our expectations of them. We have to maintain high expectations for them at the same time we empathize with their situation."
>
> —Peter DeWitt, author, *School Climate: Leading with Collective Efficacy*

> "In the effective school, there is a climate of expectation in which the staff believe and demonstrate that all students can attain mastery of the essential content and school skills, and the staff also believe that they have the capability to help all students achieve that mastery."
>
> —Association for Effective Schools

PERSONAL INSIGHT

I learned early in life that I was different, not only by race but also by income and geography. I was a poor, rural, black kid from a share cropper's farm who did not live within the city limits, wore blue jeans, and had holes in my shoes. I attended elementary school in the South at a time when many schools were still strictly segregated. My first experience with the public education system was a four-room, K–8 school attended only by African American students who were taught only by African American teachers. After my education at that K–8 school, I never had another teacher of color until I was in graduate school. I was fortunate to have teachers, many of whom were white, who appreciated my uniqueness and contributed mightily to my educational achievement (e.g., Ms. Ruby Lois Hibbard). These are the teachers who inspired me to write this book.

Aaron Thompson

Internet Resources

Increasing parental involvement in promoting student success:
https://www.waterford.org/education/how-parent-involvment-leads-to-student-success/

Family-school-community partnerships:
https://safesupportivelearning.ed.gov/training-technical-assistance/education-level/early-learning/family-school-community-partnerships

Understanding teachers' impact on student achievement:
https://www.rand.org/pubs/corporate_pubs/CP693z1-2012-09.html

How principals influence student achievement:
https://consortium.uchicago.edu/publications/how-do-principals-influence-student-achievement

Key characteristics of a multicultural curriculum:
http://www.edchange.org/multicultural/curriculum/characteristics.html

Multicultural curricular reform:
http://www.edchange.org/multicultural/curriculum.html

Are attempts to ban ethnic studies racist?
https://www.youtube.com/watch?v=TgvOdD5bVsg

References

Aaronson, D., Barrow, L., & Sander, W. (2007). Teachers and student achievement in the Chicago public high schools. *Journal of Labor Economics, 25*(1), 95–136.

Abdul-Adil, J. K., & Farmer, A. D. (2006). Inner-city African American parental involvement in elementary schools: Getting beyond urban legends of apathy. *School Psychology Quarterly, 21*, 1–12.

Adams, C M., Forsyth, P. B., & Mitchell, R. M. (2009). The formation of parent-school trust: A multilevel analysis. *Educational Administration Quarterly, 45*(1), 4-33.

Aikenhead, G. S. (1997). Toward a First Nations cross-cultural science and technology curriculum. *Science Education, 81*, 217–238.

Aikenhead, G. S. (2001). Integrating Western and Aboriginal sciences: Cross-cultural science teaching. *Research in Science Education, 31*, 337–335.

Alliance for Excellent Education (2009, November). *Teaching for a new world: Preparing high school educators to deliver college- and career-ready instruction.* Policy Brief. Retrieved from http://ea.niusileadscape.org/docs/FINAL_PRODUCTS/LearningCarousel/TeachingForANewWorld.pdf

American School Counselor Association. (2010). 2008–2009 *Student to counselor ratios*. Retrieved from http://www.schoolcounselor.org/content.asp?contentid=460.

APWA Diversity Committee (2013). *American public works association diversity resource guide* (2nd ed.). Retrieved from https://www.apwa.net/Library/Diversity%20 Resource%20Guide.pdf

Archer-Banks, D. M. (2008). African American parental involvement in their children's middle school experience. *Journal of Negro Education, 77*, 143–156.

Arum, R., & Roska, J. (2011). *Academically adrift: Limited learning on college campuses*. Chicago, IL: University of Chicago Press.

Association for Effective Schools. (1996). *Correlates of effective schools*. Retrieved from http://www.mes.org/correlates.html.

Astin, A. W., Vogelgesang, L.J., Ikeda, E. K., & Yee, J. A. (2000). *How service learning affects students*. Los Angeles: Higher Education Research Institute, UCLA.

Balfanz, R., & Legters, N. (2004). *Locating the dropout crisis*. Baltimore: Johns Hopkins University Center for Social Organization of Schools.

Bandura, A. (1997). *Self-efficacy: The exercise of control*. New York: Freeman.

Banks, J. A. (1993). Approaches to multicultural curriculum reform. In J. Banks & C. Banks (Eds.), *Multicultural education: Issues and perspectives*. Boston: Allyn & Bacon.

Banks, J. A. (2016). *Cultural diversity and education: Foundations, curriculum, and teaching* (6th ed.). New York: Routledge.

Banks, J. A., with Sebesta, S. (1982). *We Americans: Our history and people* (Vols. 1 & 2). Boston: Allyn and Bacon.

Bass, B. M., & Riggio, R. E. (2006). *Transformational leadership* (2nd ed.). Mahwah, NJ: Lawrence Erlbaum Associates.

Berkowitz, R., Moore, H., Avi Astor, R., & Benbenishty, R. (2016). A research synthesis of the associations between socioeconomic background, inequality, school climate, and academic achievement. *Review of Educational Research, 87*(2), 425–469.

Bernstein, C. (1986). *Teaching about ethnic diversity*. Retrieved from http://www.ericdigests. org/pre-924/ethnic.htm.

Bowman, B. T. (1995). *Cultural diversity and academic achievement*. Retrieved from http:// www.ncrel.org/sdrs/areas/issues/educatrs/leadrshp/le0bow.htm#author

Bryk, A. S., & Schneider, B. L. (2002). *Trust in schools: A core resource for improvement*. New York: Russell Sage Foundation.

Bryk, A. S., Sebring, P. B., Allensworth, E., Luppescu, S., & Easton, J. Q. (2010). *Organizing schools for improvement*. Chicago: University of Chicago Press.

Cabrera, A., Nora, A., Terenzini, P., Pascarella, E., & Hagedorn, L. S. (1999). Campus racial climate and the adjustment of students to college: A comparison between White students and African American students. *The Journal of Higher Education, 70*(2), 134–160.

Carnevale, A. P., & Smith, N. (2012). *A decade behind: Breaking out of the low-skill trap in the southern economy*. Washington, DC: Georgetown University, Center on Education and the Workforce.

Carnevale, A. P., Smith, N., & Strohl, J. (2010). *Help wanted: Projections of jobs and education requirements*. Washington, DC: Georgetown University, Center on Education and the Workforce.

Cawelti, G. (Ed.) (2004). *Handbook of research on improving student achievement*. Arlington, VA: Educational Research Service.

Chang, L., McBride-Chang, C. M., Stewart, S. M., & Au, E. (2003). Life satisfaction, self-concept, and family relations in Chinese adolescents and children. *International Journal of Behavioral Development, 33*, 421–429.

Comer, J. P. (2012). Comer school development program. In J. A. Banks (Ed.), *Encyclopedia of diversity in education* (volume 1, pp. 411–414). Thousand Oaks: Sage Publications.

Conley, D. (2005). *The pecking order: A bold new look and how family and society determine who we become.* New York: Random House.

Cooper, H., Nye, B., Charlton, K., Lindsay, J., & Greathouse, S. (1996). The effects of summer vacation on achievement test scores: A narrative and meta-analytic review. *Review of Educational Research, 66*(3), 227–268.

DeWitt, P. M. (2018). *School climate: Leading with collective efficacy.* Thousand Oaks: Corwin.

Donohoo, J. (2017). *Collective efficacy: How educators' beliefs impact student learning.* Thousand Oaks, CA: Corwin.

Eimers, M. T., & Pike, G. R. (1997). Minority and nonminority adjustment to college: Differences or similarities. *Research in Higher Education, 38* (1), 77–97.

Eiselein, G. (1996). *Literature and humanitarian reform in the Civil War era.* Bloomington, IN: Indiana University Press.

Epstein, J. L. (1995). School/family/community partnerships: Caring for the children we share. *Phi Delta Kapplan, 76,* 701–712.

Epstein, J. L., & Sheldon, S. (2002). Present and accounted for: Improving student attendance through family and community involvement. *Journal of Educational Research, 95*(5), 308–318.

Gay, G. (2010). *Culturally responsive teaching: Theory, research, and practice* (2nd ed.). New York, NY: Teachers College Press.

Georgetown Center for Education & the Workforce. (2014). *Recovery: Job growth and education requirements through 2020.* Retrieved from https://cew.georgetown.edu/wp-content/uploads/2014/Recovery2020.ES_.Web_.pdf

Ginsberg, M. B. (2005). Motivation, cultural diversity, and differentiation. *Theory into Practice, 44*(3), 218–225.

Gorski, P. C. (1995–2019). *EdChange, Multicultural Pavilion.* Retrieved from http://www.edchange.org/multicultural/index.html.

Groen, M. (2008). The Whig party and the rise of common schools, 1837–1854. *American Educational History Journal, 35*(1/2), 251–260.

Gurin, P., Dey, E. L., Hurtado, S., & Gurin, G. (2002). Diversity and higher education: Theory and impact on educational outcomes. *Harvard Educational Review, 72,* 330-67.

Hallinger, P., & Heck, R. H. (1996). Leadership for learning: Does collaborative leadership make a difference in school improvement? *Educational Management Administration & Leadership, 38*(6), 654–678.

Hanushek, E. (2005). *Some U.S. evidence on how the distribution of educational outcomes can be changed.* Paper prepared for Schooling and Human Capital in the Global Economy: Revisiting the Equity-Efficiency Quandary, Munich, Germany.

Hattie, J. (2012). *Visible learning for teachers: Maximizing impact on learning.* London: Routledge.

Hattie, J. (2016, July). *Mindframes and maximizers.* 3rd Annual Visible Learning Conference held in Washington, DC.

Hattie, J. A. C., & Zierer, K. (2018). *Ten Mindframes for Visible Learning: Teaching for Success.* Routledge.

Haycock, K. (1998). *Good teaching matters … a lot.* Washington, DC: Education Trust.

Holmes, M., & Wynne, E. A. (1989). *Making the school an effective community: Belief, practice, and theory in school administration.* Philadelphia, PA: Falmer Press.

Hund, W.D., Mills, C. W., & Sebastiani, S. (Eds.) (2015) *Simianization: Apes, gender, class, and race.* (Racism Analysis - Series B: Yearbooks). Zurich: Lit Verlag.

Ireson, J., & Hallam, S. (2005). Pupils' liking for school: Ability grouping, self-concept and perceptions of teaching. *British Journal of Educational Psychology, 75,* 297–311.

Kitayama, S., & Markus, H. (1994). Introduction to cultural psychology and emotion research. In S. Kitayama & H. Markus (Eds.), *Emotion and culture.* Washington, DC: American Psychological Association.

Kohl, G. O., Lengua, L. J., & McMahon, R. L. (2000). Parent involvement in school conceptualizing multiple dimensions and their relations with family and demographic risk factors. *Journal of School Psychology, 38*(6), 501–523.

Konstantopoulos, S., & Chung, V. (2010). The persistence of teacher effects in elementary grades. *American Educational Research Journal, 48*(2), 361–386

Kozol, J. (1991). *Savage inequalities: Children in America's schools*. New York: Harper Collins.

Ladson-Billings, G. (2006). From the achievement gap to the education debt: Understanding achievement in U. S. schools. *Educational Researcher, 35*(7), 3–12.

Lareau, A., & Horvat, E. N. (1999). Moments of social inclusion and exclusion: Race, class, and cultural capital in family-school relationships. *Sociology of Education, 72*, 37–53.

Lee, O., & Buxton, C. (2008). Science curriculum and student diversity: Culture, language, and socioeconomic status. *The Elementary School Journal, 109*(2), 123–137.

Leithwood, K., Jantzi, D., Earl, L., Watson, N., Levin, B., & Fullan, M. (2004). Strategic leadership for large-scale reform: The case of England's national literacy and numeracy strategy. *School Leadership & Management, 24*(1), 57–79.

Levin, H., Belfield, C., Muennig, P., & Rouse, C. (2006). *The costs and benefits of an excellent education for all of America's children*. New York: Teachers College.

Locks, A. M., Hurtado, S., Bowman, N. A., & Oseguera, L. (2008). Extending notions of campus climate and diversity to students' transition to college. *The Review of Higher Education, 31*, 257–285.

Loewen, J. W. (2010). *Teaching what really happened: How to avoid the tyranny of textbooks and get students excited about doing history*. New York, NY: Teachers College Press.

Lumina Foundation (2016). *A stronger nation through higher education*. Indianapolis, IN: Author. Available at https://www.luminafoundation.org/files/publications/stronger_nation/2016/A_Stronger_Nation-2016-Full.pdf

Marzano, R. J. (2003). *What works in schools*. Alexandria, VA: Association for Supervision and Curriculum Development.

Marzano, R. J., Pickering, D.J., & Pollock, J. (2001). *Classroom instruction that works: Research-based strategies for increasing student achievement*. Alexandria, VA: Association for Supervision and Curriculum Development.

May, S. (2009). Critical multiculturalism and education. In J. A. Banks (Ed.), *The Routledge international companion to multicultural education* (pp. 33–48). New York, NY & London, England: Routledge.

McCabe, R. H. (2000). *No one to waste: A report to public decision-makers and community college leaders*. Washington, DC: American Association of Community Colleges.

McIntosh, P. (2000). Interactive phases of personal and curricular revision with regard to race. In G. Shin & P. Gorski (Eds.), *Multicultural resource series: Professional development for educators*. Washington, D.C.: National Education Association.

Meaney, K. S., Bohler, H. R., Kopf, K., Hernandez, L., & Scott, L. S. (2008). Service-learning and pre-service educators' cultural competence for teaching: An exploratory study. *Journal of Experiential Education, 31*(2), 189–208.

Mintrop, H., & Sunderman, G. L. (2009). Predictable failure of federal sanctions-driven accountability for school improvement—and why we may retain it anyway. *Educational Researcher, 38*(5), 353–364.

Mitrofanova, H. (2004). *Building community-schools relations*. Retrieved from http://lancaster.unl.edu/community/articles/communityschools.shtml.

Morse, S. W. (1989). *Renewing civic capacity: Preparing college students for service and citizenship. ASHE-ERIC Higher Education Report No. 8*. Washington, DC: The George Washington University, School of Education and Human Development.

Mortenson, T. (2017). *Unequal family income and unequal opportunity for higher education*. Seattle, WA: National Scholarship Providing Association. Retrieved from https://c.ymcdn.com/sites/www.scholarshipproviders.org/resource/collection/D39D3812-B15F-4B4D-AC7C-B45A04A66820/4.04.P.UnequalFamilyIncomeUnequal.pdf

Moseley, D., Baumfield, V., Higgins, S., Lin, M., Miller, J., Newton, D., Robson, S., Elliot, J., & Gregson, M. (2004). *Thinking skills framework for post-16 learners: An evaluation*. London: Learning Skills Research Centre.

National Council for the Social Studies. (1991). *Curriculum guidelines for multicultural education*. Retrieved from http://www.socialstudies.org/positions/multicultural.

Nora, A., & Cabrera, A. (1996). The role of perceptions of prejudice and discrimination on the adjustment of minority college students. *The Journal of Higher Education, 67* (2), 119–148.

Ogbu, J. (1990). Overcoming racial barriers to equal access. In J. Goodlad & P. Keating (Eds.), *Access to knowledge: An agenda for our nation's schools* (pp. 59–89). New York: The College Board.

Orfield, G., & Eaton, S. E. (1996). *Dismantling desegregation: The quiet reversal of Brown v. Board of Education*. New York: The New Press.

Ornstein, P., Coffman, J., McCall, L., Grammer, J., & san Souci, P. (2010). Linking the classroom context and the development of children's memory skills. In J. L. Meece & J. S. Eccles (Eds.), *Handbook on research on schools, schooling, and human development* (pp. 42–59). New York: Routledge.

Pierce, L. (1991). *Effective schools for national origin language minority students*. Washington, DC: The Mid-Atlantic Equity Center.

Reyes, A. (2019, July 2018). How DACA enriches public education. *Los Angeles Times*, p. A16.

Reyes, P. (Ed.). (1990). *Teachers and their workplace: Commitment, performance and productivity*. San Francisco: Sage Publications.

Rivkin, S. G., Hanushek, E. A., & Kain, J. F. (2005). Teachers, schools, and academic achievement. *Econometrica, 72*(2), 417–458.

Robinson, V. (2011). *Student-centered leadership*. San Francisco: Jossey-Bass.

Robinson, V. M. J., Lloyd, C. A., & Rowe, K. J. (2008). The impact of leadership on student outcomes: An analysis of the differential effects of leadership types. *Educational Administration Quarterly, 44*(5), 635–674.

Rosenthal, R., & Jacobson, L. (1963). Teacher's expectancies: Determinants of pupils' IQ gains. *Psychological Reports, 19*, 115–118.

Rosenthal, R., & Jacobson, L. (1968). *Pygmalion in the classroom: Teacher expectation and pupils' intellectual development*. New York, NY: Holt, Rinehart and Winston.

Rubie-Davies, C. (2007). Classroom interactions: Exploring the practices of high- and low- expectation teachers. *British Journal of Educational Psychology, 77*, 289–306.

Rubie-Davies, C., Hattie, J. A. C., & Hamilton, R. (2006). Expecting the best for students: Teacher expectations and academic outcomes. *British Journal of Educational Psychology, 76*, 429–444.

Salinas, J. P. (2002). *The effectiveness of minority teachers on minority student success. National Association of African American Studies & National Association of Hispanic and Latino Studies: 2000 Literature Monograph Series*. Proceedings (Education Section) (Houston, TX, February 21–26, 2000).

Sashkin, M., & Walberg, H. J. (Eds.). (1993). *Educational leadership and school culture*. Berkeley, CA: McCutchan.

Scharf, A. (2018). *Critical practices for anti-bias education*. Teaching Tolerance: A Project of the Southern Poverty Law Center. Retrieved from https://www.tolerance.org/.../2019-04/TT-Critical-Practices-for-Anti-bias-Education.pdf

Sensoy, O., & DiAngelo, R. (2012). *Is everyone really equal? An introduction to key concepts in social justice education*. New York, NY: Teachers College Press.

Shor, I. (1992). *Empowering education: Critical teaching for social change*. Chicago: University of Chicago Press.

Slater, H., Davies, N., & Burgess, S. (2009). *Do teachers matter? Measuring the variation in teacher effectiveness in England*. Centre for Market and Public Organisation Working Series No. 09/212. Retrieved from www.bristol.ac.uk/cnpo/publications/papers/2009/wp212.pdf

Smith, R. (2005). Saving black boys: Unimaginable outcomes for the most vulnerable students require imaginable leadership. *School Administrator*, 62(1), 1–7.

The Education Trust. (2008). *Funding gaps 2008*. Washington, DC: Author.

The Education Trust (2015). *Funding gaps 2015*. Washington, DC: Author.

Thompson, A., & Luhman, R. (1997). Familial predictors of educational attainment: Regional and racial variations. In P. Hall (Ed.), *Race, ethnicity, and multiculturalism* (pp. 63–88). New York: Garland Publishing.

Thompson, G. L. (2003). Predicting African American parents and guardians satisfaction with teachers and public schools. *The Journal of Educational Research*, 96, 277–285.

Tracey, D. H., & Morrow, L. M. (2012). *Lenses on reading*. New York, NY: Guilford Press.

Tschannen-Moran, M., & Barr, M. (2004). Fostering student learning: The relationship of collective teacher efficacy and student achievement. *Leadership and Policy in Schools*, 3(3), 189–209.

Tschannen-Moran, M., & Hoy, W. K. (2000). A multidisciplinary analysis of the nature, meaning, and measurement of trust. *Review of Educational Research*, 70(4), 547–593.

U.S. Department of Education. (2008). *Public school principal, BIE school principal, and private school principal data files, 2007–2008*. Washington, DC: National Center for Education Statistics, Schools and Staffing Survey (SASS).

U.S. Department of Education. (2016). *The state of racial diversity in the educator workforce*. Retrieved from https://www2.ed.gov/rschstat/eval/highered/racial-diversity/state-racial-diversity-workforce.pdf

U.S. Department of Health & Human Services (2003). *School-community partnerships: A guide*. Washington, DC: Author.

Vogelgesang. L. J., & Astin, A. W. (2000). Comparing the effects of community service and service-learning. *Michigan Journal of Community Service Learning*, 7, 24–34.

Wang, J. (1998). Opportunity to learn: The impacts and policy implications. *Educational Evaluation and Policy Analysis*, 20(3), 137–156.

Weinstein, R. S. (2002). *Reaching higher: The power of expectations in schooling*. Cambridge, MA: Harvard University Press.

Wieman, C. E. (2007). Why not try a scientific approach to science education? *Change*, 39(5).

Wiggan, G. (2008). From opposition to engagement: Lessons from high achieving African American students. *Urban Review*, 40(4), 317–349.

Yan, W. (1999). Successful African American students: The role of parental involvement. *The Journal of Negro Education*, 68, 5–22.

Yosso, T. J. (2005). Whose culture has capital? A critical race theory discussion of community cultural wealth. *Race Ethnicity and Education*, 8(1), 69–91.

Reflections and Applications

5.1 Review the sidebar quotes contained in this chapter and select two that you think are particularly meaningful or inspirational. For each quote you selected, provide an explanation of why you chose it.

5.2 Review the checklist *for evaluating the quality of a school's multicultural program* on p. 87. Select three practices you think are most important and intend to put into practice.

5.3 What was your family arrangement as a child (two parents or single parent, nuclear or extended, etc.)? In what way(s) do you think this arrangement affected your educational achievement and personal development?

5.4 Family Ties

Ask yourself (and your students) the following questions:
- What is the race or ethnicity of your father, mother, and grandparents?
- How strongly do your family members identify with their race or ethnicity?
- How strongly do you identify with your race or ethnicity?
- How do your views of other racial or ethnic groups differ from those of your parents and grandparents?

Adapted from APWA Diversity Committee (2013). *American Public Works Association Diversity Resource Guide*, 2nd ed.

5.5 Community Ties

Ask yourself (and your students) the following questions:
- What was the majority ethnic group in the neighborhood where you grew up?
- If you had contact with other racial ethnic or racial groups in your community, where did this contact typically take place?

5.6 School Ties

Answer the following questions about yourself:
- What was the majority ethnic group in the elementary and high school you attended?
- How much exposure did you have to other racial or ethnic groups during your elementary and high school years?

5.7 Privilege Walk: Uncovering Sources of Advantage and Disadvantage

Steps:
1. Have students line up in a straight line across the middle of the room, leaving them space to move forward or backward as the exercise proceeds.
2. Ask students to take a step forward or backward in response to each of the following statements it applies to them. (Teachers can add or subtract statements that they deem appropriate for their class, and may participate in the exercise along with their students.)
   - If English is your first language, take one step forward.
   - If one or both of your parents have a college degree, take one step forward.
   - If you rely, or have relied, primarily on public transportation, take one step back.
   - If you have attended previous schools with people you felt were like yourself, take one step forward.
   - If you constantly feel unsafe walking alone at night, take one step back.
   - If your household employs help as servants, gardeners, etc., take one step forward.
   - If you studied the culture of your ancestors in elementary school, take one step forward.

- If you were ever made fun of or bullied for something you could not change or that was beyond your control, take one step back.
- If your family has ever left your homeland or entered another country not of their own free will, take one step back.
- If you would never think twice about calling the police when trouble occurs, take one step forward.
- If your family owns a computer, take one step forward.
- If you ever had to skip a meal or were hungry because you didn't have enough money to buy food, take one step back.
- If you have a visible physically disability, take one step back.
- If you have an invisible illness or disability, take one step back.
- If you were ever discouraged from participating in an activity because of your race, class, ethnicity, gender, disability, or sexual orientation, take one step back.
- If you ever tried to change your appearance, mannerisms, or behavior to fit into a more dominant group, take one step back.
- If you have ever been profiled by someone else who stereotyped you, take one step back.
- If you feel good about how your group identities are portrayed by the media, take one step forward.
- If you ever applied to something and were accepted because of your association with a friend or family member, take one step forward.
- If your family has health insurance, take one step forward.
- If you come from a single-parent household, take one step back.
- If you live in an area with crime and drug activity, take one step back.
- If you ever felt uncomfortable about a joke people made about your race, religion, ethnicity, gender, disability, or sexual orientation but felt unsafe to confront those people, take one step back.
- If you can make mistakes and not have people attribute your mistake to a flaw in related to your race or gender, take one step forward.
- If you have always assumed that you would go to college, take one step forward.
- If you have more than fifty books in your household, take one step forward.

3. Exercise Debrief:
   Point out that the point of the Privilege Walk was to promote awareness of how people are advantaged (privileged) and disadvantaged (marginalized) in different ways. Becoming aware of and acknowledging these differences increases self-knowledge and appreciation of diversity.

4. Pose follow-up questions to students, such as:

- As the exercise proceeded and you started moving farther away from people beside you, how did you feel?
- Was there a question you responded to by stepping back that you wish others better understood or acknowledged about you? (If yes, what question was it?)
- Was there a question you responded to by taking a step forward that you didn't realize was a privilege or advantage not experienced by others? (If yes, what question was it?)
- When the exercise ended, and you found yourself standing in the front, middle, or back of the room, what thought(s) ran through your mind?
- Did this exercise increase your awareness of ways in which you have been advantaged or disadvantaged? If yes, in what ways?
- Can you think of any other factors that may advantage or disadvantage people which should be added to the list of questions asked during this exercise?

Adapted from *Peace Learner: Cultivating Peace and Nonviolence in the Field of Education* (https://peacelearner.org/2016/03/14/privilege-walk-lesson-plan/)

Student-Centered Teaching, Part I: Culturally Inclusive Strategies for Motivating and Engaging Students with the Subject Matter

6

Chapter Purpose and Preview

This chapter supplies a detailed set of student-centered, culturally inclusive teaching strategies for motivating and engaging students with the subject matter. The instructional strategies identified in this chapter elevate the academic achievement of all students but have particularly positive impact on closing the achievement gap, and give disadvantaged students equal opportunity to participate in and benefit from the classroom learning experience.

Introduction

A core component of diversity education is exposing students to an inclusive curriculum with subject matter that represents and recognizes multiple cultures. While inclusive subject matter is a necessary condition for multicultural education, it is not a sufficient condition or the sole condition. Comprehensive diversity education addresses both the subject matter (content) of the curriculum and the *process* through which that subject matter is delivered—the teaching methods used to convey the content.

Numerous studies show that the academic achievement of low-income students and students of color increases when they are taught by teachers who not only possess subject-matter knowledge, but also use effective, culturally-inclusive pedagogical practices (Darling-Hammond, 2010). Inclusive pedagogy may be defined as a student-centered teaching process that motivates and engages students from all cultural backgrounds, allowing their voices to be heard and creating opportunities for them to engage in intercultural interaction. As the term "student-centered teaching" suggests, it's a process of teaching that centers on the student by: (a) connecting the content being taught to students' life experiences, (b) empowering students to play an active role in the learning process, and (c) focusing on learning outcomes that develop the student as a "whole person" (Angelo, 1997; Barr & Tagg, 1995; Johnson, 2003). Meta-analyses of multiple studies indicate that student-centered teaching has a sizable effect on student gains in academic achievement (Hattie, 2012).

> "All aspects of teaching and learning in school must be refocused on, and rededicated to, the students themselves."
>
> —EdChange Multicultural Pavilion

A Model for Implementing Student-Centered Teaching

Student-centered instruction can be systematically implemented through lesson plans that are intentionally designed to make three key student connections:

1. the student-*subject* connection: connecting students to the subject matter with teaching strategies that actively engage students with the material they are learning;
2. the student-*teacher* connection: connecting students with the instructor by cultivating positive student-teacher relationships; and
3. the student-*student* connection: connecting students with one another to create an inclusive learning community.

Instructional strategies that promote these three student-centered connections benefit all students, and have a particularly positive impact on minority students, thus serving to narrow the achievement gap (Schmid et al., 2016).

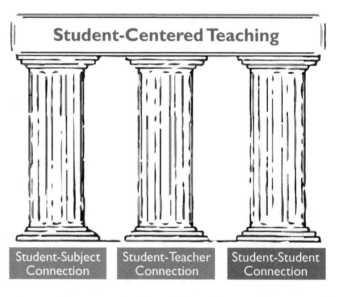

This chapter focuses on the first of these three student-centered connections: the student-*subject* connection. The next two chapters focus on the student-*teacher* and student-*student* (classmate) connections, respectively.

The Student-*Subject* Connection
Connecting Students to the Subject Matter with Engaging Teaching Strategies

Effective teachers spend less time telling (or showing) students what they know and more time connecting students with the subject matter being taught. Deep learning doesn't take place through a process of osmosis whereby students passively soak up information and simply store it in their brain in the exact way it appears in a textbook or in a teacher's presentation. Instead, deep and meaningful learning takes place when students actively engage with the subject matter and transform it into a form that connects it to what they already know or have previously experienced (Bransford, Brown, & Cocking, 2000; Mayer, 2002; Nuthall, 2000). Effective, culturally competent teaching capitalizes on students' cultural backgrounds and current life experiences to bridge the gap between the unfamiliar—the material students are expected to learn—and the familiar—the prior knowledge they already possess (Gay, 2010; Ladson-Billings, 2009).

> " They [students] are much less motivated by classes where they are cast in the role of passive recipients of knowledge to be delivered by the teacher."
>
> —Anthony Bryk, in *Organizing Schools for Improvement*

Consider This . . .

Deep learning is not a passive process of information *transmission* from teacher to students; it's a process of active *transformation* of information into knowledge on the part of the learners—who "construct" knowledge by building it onto what they already know.

Motivational Strategies for Engaging Students with the Subject Matter

Motivation is a prerequisite or necessary pre-condition for both student engagement and deep learning. Simply stated, without motivation students will neither engage actively nor learn deeply. As Stanford Ericksen puts it in *The Essence of Good Teaching*: "In whatever instructional setting, the first charge of the teacher is to get and to hold the attention of students because interest (motivation) is a prerequisite condition for effective learning" (1984, p. 39). High-impact teachers strive to make their classes interesting because they know that by capturing student interest, they capture student attention—the critical first step in the learning process. The need to capture increase students' interest in material they're expected to learn is strongly suggested by a Gallup survey of over 900,000 fifth- through twelfth-grade students, which revealed that only 43 percent of the responding students agreed with the statement: "In the last seven days, I have learned something interesting at school" (Gallup, 2016).

The following instructional strategies may be used to engage students' attention by stimulating their interest in the subject matter and increasing their intrinsic motivation—"the drive to do something because it is interesting, challenging, and absorbing" (Pink, 2009, p. 246).

Before launching into a lesson, take time to highlight *why* the lesson is worth learning. Educators cannot assume that students will automatically appreciate the purpose or value of academic learning. The relevance or usefulness of academic subject matter needs to be articulated intentionally and proactively. If students see the importance or significance of what they are learning, they're more likely to invest the time and effort needed to learn it. Classroom-based research repeatedly shows that students' academic motivation, depth of thinking, and educational achievement increase significantly when teachers make intentional efforts to increase students' awareness of the relevance or usefulness of academic concepts presented to them in class, in the textbook they're required to read, and in the homework they're expected to complete (Hulleman & Harackiewicz, 2009; Hyungshim, 2008; Roueche & Comstock, 1981). This relationship holds true for all students, but is particularly true for minority students (Winkelmes, 2013). As Amy Scharf notes in *Critical Practices for Anti-bias Education*: "Students should consider why the texts are important, not just what they mean. What does this material have to do with their lives? How does it help them understand their families or communities? How does their learning connect to events in the news? And how can they use it to take action?" (2018, p. 6).

PERSONAL INSIGHT

One of the first courses I taught was a course on educational psychology taken by students in a teacher-education program. As I was about to begin a unit on child development, I announced to the class that the first topic would focus on children's imitation behavior. As soon as I made that announcement, one student raised his hand and said: "So kids imitate. So what?" I never forgot that student's comment and referred to it thereafter as the "So What" Question. Throughout the remaining years of my teaching career, I always kept that question in mind whenever I introduced a new topic in class. That student's "so what" question made me aware that before I attempted to teach anything, I needed to be sure my students knew *why* it was worth learning.

Joe Cuseo

Identify student-centered learning outcomes at the beginning of an instructional unit. Research on effective classroom instruction reveals that this is a classroom practice that's associated with greater gains in student achievement (Dean et al., 2012; Marzano, Pickering, & Pollock, 2001). Articulating learning goals at the outset of a lesson increases students' motivation by enabling them to see the point of what they're about to learn, which creates a positive "anticipatory mindset" (Ginsberg & Wlodkowski, 2009).

Illustrate academic concepts with examples from popular media (TV, movies, etc.). Students could be asked to identify their favorite programs, movies, or what they like to read (either online or in print). Teachers might then use this information might to connect academic concepts to ideas they're acquiring through the media. Popular media may also be used to motivate and engage students in diversity-related topics; for example, students could write letters of protest to popular media outlets that they think are promoting racial or cultural stereotypes.

Be on the lookout for newsworthy events occurring at school and in the local community that relate to concepts being covered in class (e.g., events reported in the local or school newspaper). Headlines and stories from the daily newspaper relating to the day's lesson may be conveniently shared with the class by means of a document camera (a.k.a. ELMO). Using late-breaking, news-making information in class serves to highlight the contemporary relevance of academic subjects. It also models for students the value of keeping up with current events and connecting what they're learning in school to life in the "real world."

When presenting concepts in class, ask students to provide examples from their own experiences, or ask them to apply the concepts to situations or scenarios that are currently taking place in their life. For example, students could be asked: "How might you apply this idea to your personal experiences in school, at home, or in your local community?"

As topics arise in the curriculum, pay close attention to the ideas that students share, the comments they make, the questions they ask, and what they choose to write about in their papers or journals. Questions that students raise in class and topics they elect to write about in their assignments may be tracked in a "teaching journal." Teachers can periodically review their journal to detect recurrent themes—ideas, issues, and examples that reveal patterns in students' in student interests and curiosities. What students choose to talk about or write about can help teachers identify relevant examples and illustrations they can use in future lessons (e.g., as focal points for stimulating class discussions).

After finishing a class topic or instructional unit, seek feedback from students about its perceived relevance and usefulness. For example, students could be asked: "In what ways (if any) did you see the ideas discussed in this unit relating to, or being relevant to your life, either currently or in the future?"

At the start of a lesson, present an attention-grabbing prompt to ignite student interest in topic to be covered. An evocative stimulus can generate student motivation at the outset of a new instructional unit by creating a positive "anticipatory set"—a state of heightened curiosity and sense of positive anticipation about the upcoming learning experience (Hunter, 1994). The following prompts may be used for this purpose:

- ▶ a powerful *picture* or *image* (e.g., of a hate crime)
- ▶ an intriguing *artifact* (e.g., a relevant historical or cultural object)
- ▶ a thought-provoking *quote* (e.g., a "classic quote" chosen from a famous or influential person)
- ▶ a provocative *passage* (e.g., a poignant paragraph or short poem)
- ▶ an engaging *video vignette* (e.g., from a popular movie)
- ▶ a topic-relevant *cartoon* (e.g., one that visually and humorously depicts or drives home a point about the upcoming topic).

Using visual images not only can stimulate student interest in the subject matter, it also enhances retention of the concept associated with the image. Studies show that concepts presented verbally are better remembered if they are accompanied by a visual image (Paivio, 1990). One characteristic of K–12 teachers who have been found to generate the have been found to greatest gains in student achievement is that they make frequent use of "nonlinguistic representations"—visual representations of concepts presented verbally in class (Dean, 2012; Marzano, Pickering, & Pollock, 2001).

The power of visual learning and visual memory is likely rooted in the critical role that the sense of vision originally played in the early survival of the human species. Our distant ancestors could neither read nor write, so in order to survive, they had to rely on nonverbal (visual) cues to learn and remember where food and shelter were located. Since the human species has such a long history of relying on the sense or survival, the human brain is naturally equipped or "hard-wired" to learn and retain visual information (Milner & Goodale, 1998). This may account for why it's so common to hear people say: "I have a great memory for faces, but not for names." (The former involves visual memory; the latter requires verbal memory.)

Confront students with paradoxes, incongruities, controversial ideas, and counterintuitive findings that create a sense of surprise or incredulity. For example, a lesson on diversity could start with a paradoxical quote such as: "We are all the same, and we are all unique" (Georgia Dunston, African-American biologist), or: "Every human is, at the same time, like all other humans, like some humans, and like no other human" (Clyde Kluckholn, anthropologist).

Erickson and Strommer report that highly engaging teacher presentations: "Open with a problem, question, quandary, or dilemma. Or they start with something students take for granted and confront them with information or observations indicating things are not so obvious or certain as they initially appear. Or they present a list of incongruous facts or statistics and ask, 'How can this be'?" (1991, p. 98).

End class sessions with an unanswered question, unresolved issue, or puzzling dilemma that builds student curiosity about, and anticipatory interest in, the next class session. This instructional strategy can whet student interest in learning the same way that a TV series concludes an episode with an uncertain ending to motivate viewers to tune into the next episode.

Change it up: expose students to a variety of instructional methods and learning activities. Student motivation for, and attention to, information presented in class can be enhanced by using:

(a) different instructional *formats*—alternating teacher presentations with such practices as: whole-class discussions, small-group work, paired peer interactions, self-reflection exercises, cases, role plays, simulations, panels, or guest speakers;

(b) different instructional *modalities* and *media*—accompanying verbal information with visual images (e.g., pictures and photos), visual movement (e.g., short films or online videos), and kinesthetic ("hands-on") experiences (e.g., manipulating objects, building models, or using technology).

Studies show that variations in sensory experiences combat attention loss which typically takes place when we are repeatedly exposed to the same stimulus conditions over an extended period of time (Bunzeck & Duzel, 2006). Periodic changes in learning formats and modalities supply a variety of sensory experiences in the classroom, which helps sustain students' attention that otherwise would be lost if they were repeatedly exposed to the same instructional routine.

Diversifying instructional methods and formats also enables teachers to accommodate individual differences in the way students prefer to learn, which is consistent with the principle of "differentiated instruction" (Tomlinson, 1999)—an instructional strategy designed to increase the academic success of culturally diverse students (Hitchcock et al., 2002). (For a summary of the key differences between traditional and differentiated instruction, see Table 6.1) It's unrealistic or impossible for teachers to accommodate the learning preferences of all students at all times; however, if teachers are mindful about periodically varying or rotating instructional formats (e.g., individualized and

"Differentiated instruction actively honors and addresses student diversity ... and highlights diversity as a positive aspect of the learning process."

—*Critical Practices for Anti-bias Education*, Southern Poverty Law Center collaborative learning) and sensory modalities (e.g., aural and visual), then students with different learning preferences will at least have the opportunity to periodically experience an instructional format that aligns most closely their preferred way of learning (Erickson, Peters, & Strommer, 2006).

Table 6.1 Key Differences between Traditional and Differentiated Instruction		
Traditional Classroom	**Differentiated Classroom**	**Differentiated Classroom Incorporating Cultural Competence**
Assessment takes place at the end of a unit of study	Assessment is ongoing, diagnostic, and has an influence on instruction	Assessment, instruction, classroom climate, and curricula use the strengths, interests, cultural background, home life, and real-life experiences of students to validate their individual identities
Whole class instruction	Variety of instructional strategies	Recognizes the influence of culture and utilizes cultural resources to mediate instruction
Adapted textbooks serve as the primary instructional resource	Multiple types of materials are utilized as instructional resources	Utilizes instructional resources that provide the viewpoints of all cultural and ethnic groups
Teacher is the problem solver and knowledge holder who "deposits" their knowledge to students	Students engage in problem solving, inquiry, and critical thinking	Students have an active role in all aspects of teaching and learning
Assignments have a quantitative focus	Assignments have a qualitative focus	Assignments are meaningful and purposeful to students, families and teachers

Source: Huber, J. (2010). Culturally responsive differentiated instruction. AEMP 2010 Education Forum, Los Angeles, CA. Retrieved from http://www.equityallianceatasu.org/sites/default/files/9.pdf.

There is some educational research which suggests that students from different cultural groups favor different approaches to learning and different instructional methods (Gay, 2010; Valenzuela, 1999). Such findings point to another potential advantage of varying learning modalities and instructional formats: It may be one way to put "equity pedagogy" into practice (Banks, 2016).

Give students opportunities to make *educational choices*. When students are given the opportunity to make their own educational decisions, it gives them some sense of autonomy and personal ownership of the learning process, which increases their intrinsic motivation to learn (Pink, 2009; Ryan & Deci, 2000). Thus, whenever possible, teachers should give students decision-making opportunities about what they will learn and how they will learn it. For instance, they could be given a "menu" of topics from which to choose what they will to read or write about. If members of different cultural groups happen to choose the same topic, they could be grouped into diversified learning teams with a unified learning interest. This grouping practice has been found to promote gains in learning and critical thinking, while reducing prejudice and stereotyping. (For supporting evidence and more detailed information pertaining to the formation of diverse learning teams, see Chapter 7, p. 129.)

Engaging Pedagogy: Active Learning Strategies

Culturally inclusive teachers use student-centered instructional methods that provide students from all sociocultural backgrounds with equal opportunity to become actively involved in the learning process. Research consistently shows that when students are exposed to engaging pedagogy in the classroom, they learn more deeply and make more significant gains in academic achievement (Creekmore & Deaton, 2015; Mayhew et al., 2016); this is particularly true for students from ethnic minority groups (Wiggan, 2008). Engaging teaching strategies promote deeper learning by implementing two powerful learning principles: (a) "time on task" (McLeod, Fisher, & Hoover, 2003) and (b) active involvement (Astin, 1984; 1993). These principles stipulate that the more time and energy, respectively, that students invest in the learning process, the more learning takes place.

Engaging pedagogy is also an effective vehicle through which to achieve one of the most important outcomes of multicultural education: cultivating positive student attitudes toward, and appreciation of, human diversity. Research has repeatedly shown that class lectures (teacher presentations) are not the most effective way to influence student attitudes and viewpoints. After reviewing over 100 years of research on the effectiveness of different instructional methods for promoting attitude change, Bligh (2000) reached the following conclusion: "Lectures are relatively ineffective for teaching values associated with subject matter. Sermons rarely convince agnostics, but they give solidarity to the faithful. Similarly, lectures are ineffective in changing people's values, but they may reinforce those that are already accepted" (p. 12).

Not only is overreliance on teacher-centered presentations or lectures ineffective for changing student attitudes toward diversity, it also fails to model the democratic process in the classroom. A class may be viewed as a community composed of followers (students) and a leader (teacher). Prominent educational scholars and multicultural advocates have argued that teaching predominantly with lectures is analogous to autocratic political ship that relegates citizens (students) to a non-participatory role in the democratic (learning) process. The famous Brazilian educator, Paulo Freire, make this point poignantly in his classic work, *Pedagogy of the Oppressed*:

> *Narration (with the teacher as narrator) leads the students to memorize mechanically the narrated content. Worse yet, it turns them into 'containers,' into 'receptacles' to be "filled" by the teacher. The more completely [s]he fills the receptacles, the better a teacher [s]he is. The more meekly the receptacles permit themselves to be filled, the better students they are. Education thus becomes an act of depositing, in which the students are to memorize mechanically the narrated content. This is the "banking" concept of education, in which the scope of action allowed to the students extends only as far as receiving, filing, and storing the deposits. The banking concept maintains attitudes and practices, which mirror oppressive society as a whole: the teacher is the subject of the learning process, while the pupils are mere objects (1970, pp. 71-73).*

Similarly, African American author and educator bell hooks (a.k.a. Gloria Jean Watkins) argues that when teachers use engaging, student-centered pedagogy they are practicing "liberating pedagogy." As she puts it: "Our educational institutions are so deeply invested in the banking system, *engaged* [pedagogy] is a great way to talk about liberatory classroom practice" (*Teaching to Transgress: Education as the Practice of Freedom*, 1994, p. 5).

Engaging teaching practices implement principles of both democratic education and culturally inclusive pedagogy by empowering students to: (a) play an active and participative role in the learning process, (b) take personal ownership and responsibility for their own learning, (c) engage in interaction with members of diverse groups, and (d) contribute to the learning of other students (Curren, 2007; Gutmann, 1999).

The following research-based instructional practices serve to actively engage students in the classroom and enable them to play a more central and responsible role in the learning process. In so doing, these practices enact the principles of democratic, student-centered education.

> "Democracy and freedom ought to be both the end result of education as well as the means through which education takes place."
>
> —Dana Bennis & Isaac Graves, *Democratic Education*

Intersperse teacher-centered presentations with thought-provoking questions to elicit student involvement. Frequently asking questions of students in class is one distinguishing characteristic of teachers whose students make significant gains in academic achievement (Rosenshine, 1971; Rosenshine, 2012). Additional studies show that when students are asked and respond to questions about ideas a teacher presents in class, the more likely they are to retain those ideas than are students who simply listen to a teacher presenting those ideas (Karpicke & Roediger, 2007, 2008; Ruhl, Hughes, & Schloss, 1987). These findings strongly suggest that a lesson plan which calls for a formal teacher presentation should be accompanied by the intentional preparation of questions that will be asked of students during the presentation.

> "You must highlight [questions] in your outline. You should know *exactly* what questions, word for word, you are going to ask."
>
> —William Welty, "Discussion method teaching: How to make it work"

Well-prepared teacher questions not only promote student learning, they also increase student motivation to learn by inducing a state of productive puzzlement in the mind of the learner that stimulates curiosity to discover the answers to those questions. Furthermore, when teachers ask thought-provoking questions in class, they model a contemplative process of reflective inquiry that students can observe and emulate.

Naturally, not all questions are created equal or are equally effective. How a question is focused, framed or phrased can determine how (or if) it elicits student responses. Characteristics of questions that most effectively elicit student engagement are described in Box 6.1 below.

Box 6.1 Characteristics of Questions that Most Effectively Elicit Student Involvement

▶ **Open-ended** questions that allow for more than one correct or acceptable answer. Such questions invite a variety of interpretations, welcome a diversity of perspectives (including multicultural perspectives), and encourage *divergent* thinking—expansive thinking that does not force students to converge on one (and only one) correct answer (Cuseo, 2005). For example, asking students, "Which rights in the Universal

Declaration of Human Rights focus on economic issues?" is a closed-ended question calling for just one correct answer. In contrast, the following is an open-ended question: "Which rights in the Universal Declaration of Human Rights do you think are most important?" (Scharf, 2018).

When students are asked factual questions to which there is only one correct answer, the number of possible incorrect answers is limitless. Consequently, they may be reluctant to answer such questions because there's a good chance they will give the wrong answer and be embarrassed. In contrast, open-ended questions encourage students to think freely and creatively without the fearing they will fail to supply "the" correct answer that the teacher (authority figure) is "looking for." Although there may be occasions when teachers need to "test" students for their knowledge of correct answers, these occasions should be complemented or augmented by more engaging, open-ended questions.

▶ **Conditionally-phrased** questions (e.g., "What *might* be …?" "What *could* be …?" or "What *may* be …?"). Questions phrased in this way send a clear verbal signal to students that a diversity of answers is possible and acceptable.

▶ **Higher-order thinking** questions that call for a higher level of thought than rote recall. Such questions include those that solicit:

(a) Critical thinking (e.g., "What would you say are the strengths and weakness of _____?")

(b) Creative thinking (e.g., "What may be a new way to look at or approach this _____?"),

(c) Application (e.g., "What purpose or function could _____ serve?")

(d) Analysis (e.g., "What are the key ideas contained or embedded in _____?")

(e) Synthesis (e.g., "How can this idea be combined or integrated with _____?")

▶ **Focused** questions that are clearly tied to (focus on) a specific concept or issue.

An unfocused question would be a question such as: "Does anybody have any questions or comments at this time?" Questions like this aren't tied to a particular point or idea. In contrast, here's a focused question: "What might be possible causes of prejudice?" This question guides students to a specific issue, and in so doing, gives them a clear target at which to aim and deliver an answer.

▶ **Personalized** questions that situate students in a relevant, real-life setting and ask them to make a personal decision or choose a course of action. For example, if a teacher is discussing prejudice and discrimination, students could be asked: "Suppose you overheard a student tell a racist joke and other students laughing it. What would you do?" Questions like this implement the principle of *situated learning*, which posits that deep learning is more likely to take place when it is "situated" (placed) in a real-life context and encourages students to personally apply the concept being learned (Bransford, Brown, & Cocking, 1999; Ewell, 1997).

▶ Questions that call for *all* students to respond *nonverbally*. Instead of asking individual students to respond verbally to a question, one student at a time, all students in class could be asked to respond nonverbally (with "body language") at the same time. For example, the whole class could respond with a show of hands to a question like: "How many of you agree with the following statement …?" or "How many of you have had an experience similar to …?" In addition to a show of hands, the following practices could also be used to have the whole class engage in a nonverbal response to a teacher-posed question:

(a) Students *vote with their feet* in response to a question about whether they agree or disagree with a statement by moving to one of the four *corners* of the room, with each corner representing one of four positions: "strongly agree," "agree," "disagree," or "strongly disagree."

(b) Creating a space down the middle of the room and asking students to *move to either side of the room* depending on where they stand on an issue. For example, students could be asked where they stand on whether or not schools should have a dress code by moving to the right side of the room if they agree, or the left side of the room if they disagree. (The center aisle may be used as "middle ground" where students can stand if they are undecided or think they need more information about the issue before making a firm decision.)

(c) Equip students with "clickers"—a technology-mediated classroom response system that enables students to answer teacher-posed questions nonverbally (and anonymously) by submitting their answers electronically. The computer system then amalgamates their submitted answers and displays the percentage of students choosing each of the response options.

When students are asked to respond a question nonverbally, all students get involved, not just verbally assertive students who tend to answer more frequently, more rapidly, or more impulsively than their more reticent and reflective classmates. Having students respond nonverbally to a question can also be used as a "foot in the door" technique to engage them verbally with follow-up questions. For example, if students are first asked to take a position by moving to a particular place or space in the room, they could then be asked to explain *why* they chose that position. After students share their reason for the position they took and listen to the reasons shared by their classmates, they could then be given an opportunity to change their initial position nonverbally—by moving to a different place in the room. Those students who choose to change their position (nonverbally) could then be asked to explain (verbally) why they changed their mind.

> "Participation does not have to be verbal; gender, culture, and ability may affect student comfort levels with verbal communication. Modeling equity and inclusiveness calls for a broader definition of participation."
>
> —*Critical Practices for Anti-bias Education,* Southern Poverty Law Center

Pose questions that intentionally seek out the views and opinions of students from diverse groups. Research suggests that when members of different racial and ethnic groups come together to discuss ideas, intergroup prejudice decreases and intercultural appreciation increases—but only if each member's cultural identity and perspective is sought out and valued by other members of the discussion group (Baron, Branscombe, & Byrne, 2008). Consequently, when questions are posed in class to promote discussion, it's important that teachers ensure that the ideas of students from diverse backgrounds are invited and heard. If the views and opinions of minority students do not emerge naturally during class discussions, then the teacher may need to explicitly seek them out by explicitly directing questions to student groups whose thoughts have not been shared. For example, a teacher might say: "I haven't heard the perspective of Hispanic students on this issue. May I ask you to share your thoughts on the subject?"

If certain minority ethnic or racial groups are not represented among the students in the classroom, the class could be asked how members of these groups might respond to the topic or issue under discussion if they were there. For example, the teacher might ask: "If there were Native American students in class today, what might they have said during our discussion?"

Lastly, during class discussions, it's important that the teacher first seek out the views of all student groups before expressing his or her own ideas; otherwise, students are more likely to give socially acceptable or "politically correct" answers they think their teacher wants to hear (Hess, 2009).

When teaching factual information, consider using game formats to stimulate students' interest in, and engagement with, the information they are expected to learn. Games can make acquiring factual knowledge more engaging than hearing it from stand-and-deliver teacher presentations. Using a TV game format like *Jeopardy* could make fact-based learning more stimulating, and a game like *Family Feud* may be used to create team-learning tournaments promote friendly competition between teams.

The *Who Wants to Be a Millionaire?* game format is ideal for involving all students in class. Students could volunteer to be contestants or compete to be contestants by correctly answering a "toss-up" question. Incentives may be given to students to serve as a contestants by awarding them with prizes that increase in value in proportion to the number or complexity of questions they answer correctly. The student who serves as the contestant can involve other students in class by using the game's "lifeline" supports, such as "polling the audience" for their thoughts about the correct answers (via a show of hands) or "phoning a friend" (asking another student in class). The teacher would assume the role of game-show moderator and could occasionally interject elaborative or explanatory comments after students give correct or incorrect answers thus providing collateral instruction as the game proceeds.

Use role-playing exercises to engage students with the subject matter. An educational role play may be described as learning experience that engages students in dramatic enactments involving characters with whom they can identify. Drama can serve as a powerful vehicle for actively involving students in the learning process—both as actors in the drama and as reactors to it. Students can play themselves or assume the role of another person to gain that person's perspective (e.g., a majority student plays the role of a minority student). Student actors could also be asked to reverse roles during the dramatic skit to gain a more balanced perspective.

The entire class can be engaged in a role play at the same time by having all students assume the same role while the teacher assumes a different role. For instance, the teacher could assume the role of a student who has just immigrated to the U.S. while the class serves as an advisory committee of American citizens whose role is to help the recent immigrant transition to America and learn about our country's key cultural norms, values, and priorities (and cultural biases).

If the intended learning outcome of a diversity lesson is to promote empathy for others, role plays are much more likely to achieve that outcome than teacher-centered presentations. For example, if students assume the role of a blind person by wearing a blindfold for a certain period of time, or the role of a deaf person by wearing soundproof earmuffs, they will develop a stronger sense of empathy for the blind and the deaf than they would by listening to a teacher's lecture on the importance of being sensitive to the needs of people with disabilities. Studies show that when white students engage in role-playing experiences that involve taking on the role of members of minority racial groups, it reduces prejudice and fosters development of more positive attitudes toward people of color (Baron, Branscombe, & Byrne, 2008; Stephan, 1985).

Scripts. Similar to role plays, scripts actively involve students in dramatic scenarios; the only difference being that instead of acting out their parts, students *read* the parts (lines) of different characters in the script. Students may also be allowed to go beyond the script and improvise, or they may be asked to complete an unfinished script as if they were one of the characters. For instance, students could be given a script that depicts a scenario in which

"Role playing of various ethnic and cultural experiences should be interspersed throughout the curriculum to encourage understanding of what it means to belong to various ethnic groups."

—NCSS Task Force

a student someone makes a racist remark in the presence of other students, and the reading the script could finish it by adding statements describing what they would do after hearing the remark.

Simulations. These are exercises that engage students in the learning process by immersing them in an environment that simulates (approximates) a real-life experience. *BaFa'-BaFa'* is a popular intercultural simulation in which students are assigned membership in either the Alpha culture or Beta culture, each of which has its own set of cultural values, expectations, customs and language. Students learn the rules and customs of their assigned culture separately, then visit each other's culture and try to interact with members of the other ("foreign") culture, thus simulating the experience of immigrants trying to assimilate into a culture that differs radically from their own. The intended learning outcome of this simulation is to reduce ethnocentrism and promote empathy for people who must adapt to an unfamiliar culture.

Case Studies. A "case" is an actual event, or a close approximation an actual event, that requires students to make a decision about a problem or issue for that there is no one "correct" answer or clear-cut solution (Christensen & Hansen, 1987). Cases are typically presented in written form and students read them individually before joining teams to reach a decision about the best way to solve the problem or resolve the issue presented in the case.

> "By providing students with opportunities to use decision-making abilities and social action skills in the resolution of problems affecting ethnic, racial and cultural groups, schools can contribute to more effective education for democratic citizenship."
>
> —NCSS Task Force

Cases actively engage students in the learning process by requiring them to make action-based decisions about concepts they are learning. Exposing students to cases also helps them realize that solving real-life problems can be a "messy" or ambiguous process that involves considering multiple perspectives, weighing various alternatives, and prioritizing different solution strategies.

Cases relevant to diversity education may be drawn from:

- ▶ News items relating to human rights issues that are featured in the national media (TV, movies, or newspaper articles). (For example, see the anti-Semitism case on p. 106.)
- ▶ Instances of intergroup conflict that have taken place on campus or in the local community
- ▶ Educational documentaries that poignantly capture the personal experiences of people who have encountered prejudice and discrimination
- ▶ Actual events that the teacher has experienced or observed, either personally or professionally
- ▶ Experiences solicited from students in class, such as prejudicial incidents they have witnessed at school, or that friends and family members have encountered in their home community.

Teachers can supply students with some structure or scaffolding for tackling the problem presented in the case by supplying them with open-ended questions that prompt them to think about:

- ▶ the likely cause(s) of the incident
- ▶ if and how the incident could have been prevented

▶ whether they've had personal experiences similar to those being depicted in the case

▶ whether students can identify with any characters involved in the case.

Based on their research and teaching experiences, Meyers & Jones (1993) suggest that the following types of questions can effectively promote higher-level thinking in response to cases and other problem-based tasks:

▶ *Analytical/Evaluative* Questions—e.g., "What particular action is at the root of this problem? Which action played the most pivotal role?"

▶ *Implication* Questions—e.g., "If events like this continue, what might be the consequences?"

▶ *Predictive/Hypothetical* Questions—e.g., "If the roles of the main characters were switched, what would have happened?" Note: Providing students with opportunities to predict and test hypotheses about causes and effects is a K–12 teaching practice associated with significant gains in student achievement (Dean et al., 2012; Marzano, Pickering, & Pollock, 2001).

When making extended an presentation, engaging learning activities should be inserted at three key junctures: *before*, *during*, and *after* **the presentation.** An instructional presentation may be viewed as unfolding in three major stages: beginning, middle, and end. By intentionally planning a lesson with these three stages in mind, an effective *learning sequence* can be created that engages students:

1. at the *start* of the presentation—serving to "warm up" and *activate* students' pre-existing ideas about the topic (e.g., "What do you already know or hope to learn about this topic?");

2. *during* the presentation—serving to "break up" or *punctuate* teacher-delivered information with engaging, student-centered learning activities (e.g., How do you think you might apply or make use of the ideas we've discussed thus far?"); and

3. *after* the presentation—serving to "wrap up" and *consolidate* the presentation and provide students with a sense of closure (e.g., "What was the most important idea you took away from this lesson?" or "What more would you like to know about this topic?").

Described below are strategies for engaging students at each of these three key stages of an instructional presentation.

Pre-Presentation Strategies. Engage students *before* the presentation by activating their pre-existing feelings, attitudes, and knowledge (or misconceptions) about the to-be-presented topic. For example, before a presentation on diversity, students could be asked to jot down the first ideas that come to mind when they hear the word "diversity." More formal practices for activating students' thoughts and feelings prior to a teacher presentation include the following:

▶ *Verbal "Whips"*: a procedure in which students, in rapid succession, take turns verbalizing a thought that comes to mind about the topic.

- ▶ *Pre-Tests*: students engage in a short, non-graded assessment of their knowledge or attitudes about the upcoming topic (e.g., by answering a short series of true-false questions).
- ▶ *Background Knowledge Probes*: students jot down what they already know, or think they know, about an upcoming topic and how they got to know it (the origin or source of their knowledge) (Angelo & Cross, 1993).
- ▶ *Background Interest Probes*: students respond to a prompt that asks them to reflect on what they would like to know about the upcoming topic or what questions they have about it (Angelo & Cross, 1993).
- ▶ *"Shared* Presentation"*: students first share what they think they know about the topic and record their ideas on the board. After all students have shared their ideas, the teacher highlights accurate and important ideas the class mentioned (e.g., by underlining them on the board) then adds additional ideas to create a composite ("master list") that represents the collaborative work of both the students and the teacher.

Any of these pre-presentation strategies can be used to initially draw students into the learning process by drawing out their prior thoughts and feelings about the topic to be presented. K–12 research indicates that activating students' background knowledge and experiences *before* beginning a lesson, and using this information *during* the lesson, is a teaching practice associated with significant gains in academic achievement (Dean et al., 2012; Marzano, Pickering, & Pollock, 2001).

Another effective pre-presentation is providing students with an outline of concepts, definitions, and the key parts (categories and subcategories) to be covered during the upcoming presentation. The outline could also be provided in the form of key questions that the presentation intends to answer. Research indicates that supplying students such outlines increases their attention to and retention of key concepts delivered during teacher presentations (Bligh, 2000). Outlines serve as an "advance organizer" (Ausubel, Novak, & Hanesian 1978) that enables students to see the whole topic (forest) before tackling the parts (trees) and reduces the risk they will get lost in the forest (and disengage). Because novice learners typically lack the background knowledge needed to distinguish between central and peripheral ideas, they often spend too much mental energy on secondary details, losing sight of primary concepts and the "big picture" (Hrepic, Zollman, & Rebello, 2007).

An additional advantage of supplying students with an outline in advance of a teacher presentation is that it ensures that all students in class have access to common background information (Bligh, 2000), which helps level the playing field for underprivileged students whose circumstances may have deprived them of information or experiences that more privileged students were able to access.

Lastly, providing students with an outline of a presentation's major ideas ahead of time reduces teacher-centered talk (lecture) time and students' note-taking time, opening up more class time for engaging, student-centered learning activities.

Within-Presentation Strategies. During a teacher presentation, inserting pauses for students to engage in short active-learning exercises serves to intercept attention loss that takes place when students process verbal information for an extended stretch of time (Bligh, 2000). Research on effective teachers indicates that one practice they share is breaking up material they're teaching into small parts, and after teaching each part, having students engage with or practice what they've just been taught (Rosenshine, 1971, 2012).

The following strategies may be used to break up teacher presentations with short, learner-centered activities that actively engage students with the material being presented.

- ▶ *Pauses for Personal Reflection*: during the presentation, pauses are made and students are asked to write a short, reflective response to a focused question about a portion of the material that was previously presented (e.g., "How would you apply what you have just learned to some aspect of your life?"). Research indicates that when students are given just a short amount of time to reflect on information that has been presented to them, they are more likely to retain the information that preceded the pause; in addition, they exhibit greater attention to and retention of information delivered after the pause (Bunce, Flens, & Neiles, 2010).
- ▶ *"Writing-to-Discuss"*: after a pause is made during the presentation for students to write a personal reflection in response to material presented to them, the teacher uses their written responses as a springboard for class discussion. This practice not only provides the attention and retention benefits associated with providing students with a pause for personal reflection, it builds on those benefits by engaging students in discussion—the quality of which is enhanced because students have been given time to gather their thoughts in writing before expressing them orally. (This is an especially effective way to engage second-language students in class discussions because it gives them time to think and record what they're going to say in advance of saying it, rather than doing having to speak extemporaneously.)
- ▶ *Problem-Solving Presentations*: students listen to a short teacher presentation (e.g., 5–10 minutes) that focuses on a particular problem, after which they discuss possible solutions to the problem (Bonwell & Eison, 1991). Teachers could use this practice at several junctures during the same lesson by making a series of "mini-presentations" targeting different problems, each of which is followed by student discussion of how best to solve or resolve that particular problem.

The three practices cited above serve to break up an extended presentation with short learner-centered exercises that actively involve students with the presented material. These practices also implement a teaching behavior that research shows is to be associated with significant gains in student achievement: Providing students with frequent opportunities to act on or practice what they're learning (Rosenshine, 1971, 2012). Effective teachers give *all* students regular opportunities to pause and check their understanding of a concept before moving on to the next concept. In contrast, less effective teachers tend to ask the class a question about what they presented, call on a student who raises his or her hand to answer it (often the correct answer, because it's likely to be volunteered by a student who "got it"), and then move on to teach the next segment of the lesson without checking to see if other students in class also "got it" (Rosenshine, 1997).

Post-Presentation Strategies. Following a teacher presentation, students engage in activities that prompt them to review and consolidate (lock in) key ideas or concepts covered during the presentation. The final step in the learning process, whether it be learning from a teacher presentation, a class discussion, or a hands-on experience, is for students to step back from the process and reflect on whey learned. Deep learning requires both active involvement during the learning process and thoughtful reflection after the learning process is completed (Bligh, 2000; Brown, Roediger, & McDaniel, 2014). The latter gives the brain time to move information it has taken in while working on the learning task (working memory) and transfer it to long-term memory storage (Rosenshine, 1997; Carey, 2015). This is also true for learning experiences related to diversity. For example, postsecondary research has demonstrated that students learn most effectively from diversity experiences when they take time to reflect on those experiences in writing (Lopez, Gurin, & Nagda, 1998; Nagda, Gurin, & Lopez, 2003).

One particularly effective and efficient reflective writing strategy is the *one-minute paper*—a short, informal writing exercise (taking one minute or less to complete) that engages all students in personal reflection on the day's lesson. The following questions may be used as one-minute paper prompts:

▶ What do you think was the major *purpose or objective* of today's lesson?
▶ What do you think was the most *important* point discussed in class today?
▶ Without looking at your notes, what *stands out in your mind* (or what do you *recall most vividly*) about today's lesson?
▶ Looking back at your notes, what would you say was the *most interesting* or *stimulating* idea you wrote down?
▶ Did you see any *connections* between what was discussed in class today and what was covered in *previous classes or units*?
▶ What was the most *surprising* or *unexpected* idea you encountered in today's class?
▶ What do you think was the most *puzzling, confusing, or disturbing* idea covered in class today?
▶ What *helped* (or *hindered*) your understanding of today's presentation?
▶ During today's class, what idea(s) struck you as ideas you could immediate *use or put into practice*?
▶ In what way(s) do you see which the material discussed in today's class *relating to your current or future life*?

One-minute papers can also be tailored for use as follow-up reflections to class discussions of diversity topics. For example, students could write a one-minute paper in response to questions such as:

▶ Were there any particular topics or issues raised during today's discussion of diversity that provoked intense reactions or emotional responses from you or your classmates? If yes, why do you think they did?
▶ Did today's discussion lead you to change your previously held attitudes or opinions? If yes, in what way?
▶ Do you think that today's discussion changed the attitudes or opinions of your classmates? If yes, why? If no, why not?

Other effective reflective-writing exercises include: (a) *freewriting*—students write freely about anything related to the topic under discussion—to stimulate their thoughts, feelings, or viewpoints on a topic (without worrying about writing mechanics, such as punctuation or spelling), and (b) *learning logs* or *learning journals*—in which students record written reflections about their learning experiences on an ongoing basis throughout the term. Written entries in students' learning log or journal could focus on (a) what they find most interesting or useful about the material they are learning, (b) their feelings or attitudes about what they are learning (e.g., their level of level of confidence, anxiety, or enthusiasm), and (c) the ways in which they are engaging in the learning process (their learning habits and strategies). These sorts of journal entries encourage students to engage in two key forms of reflection: (a) metacognition—reflecting on what they have learned or what thinking processes they are using while learning, and (b) self-regulation—reflecting on the strategies they used to learn and whether those strategies were effective (Darling-Hammond et al., 2003).

Reflective writing exercises such as the one-minute papers, freewriting, and learning logs or journals are examples of *writing-to-learn* assignments. They differ from formal writing assignments in three major ways: (a) they're shorter, requiring less time for students to complete; (b) they're written primarily for the purpose of deepening students' learning (as opposed to developing their writing skills); and (c) they don't require extensive teacher commentary, correction, or grading (Zinsser, 1993).

Writing-to-learn assignments are short and flexible, so they can be used at any time during a lesson and to engage students in thoughtful reflection about any learning experience, including multicultural learning experiences. Writing-to-learn exercises can also be used with students whose writing skills are still developing because these exercises are not designed to evaluate students' writing, but to stimulate their thinking and deepen their learning.

Consider This . . .
Students can still write to learn even if they're still learning to write.

Internet Resources

Strategies for increasing student motivation and engagement:
https://www.gettingsmart.com/2016/08/15-actionable-strategies-for-increasing-student-motivation-and-engagement/

Teaching techniques for promoting active learning:
https://activelearner.ca/free-download-active-learning-ibook/

Designing questions that effectively engage students:
https://www.edtechlens.com/blog/how-to-engage-students-with-well-designed-questions

Case studies for teaching diversity appreciation:
http://www.edchange.org/multicultural/case-studies.html

Experiential learning exercises relating to diversity:
https://ubwp.buffalo.edu/ccvillage/wp-content/uploads/sites/74/2017/06/Experiencing-Diversity.pdf

http://www.civiceducationproject.org/legacy/teachandlearn/other/bafa.html

References

Angelo, T. A. (1997). The campus as learning community: Seven promising shifts and seven powerful levers. *AAHE Bulletin, 4*(9), pp, 3–6

Angelo, T. A., & Cross, K. P. (1993). *Classroom assessment techniques: A handbook for college faculty* (3rd ed.). San Francisco: Jossey-Bass.

Astin, A. W. (1984). Student involvement: A developmental theory. *Journal of College Student Personnel, 25,* 297–308.

Astin, A. W. (1993). *What matters in college?* San Francisco: Jossey-Bass.

Ausubel, D., Novak, J., & Hanesian, H. (1978). *Educational psychology: A cognitive view* (2nd ed.). New York: Holt, Rinehart & Winston.

Banks, J. A. (2016). *Cultural diversity and education: Foundations, curriculum, and teaching* (6th ed.). New York: Routledge.

Baron, R. A., Branscombe, N. R., & Byrne, D. (2008). *Social psychology* (12th ed.). Boston: Pearson.

Barr, R. B., & Tagg, J. (1995). From teaching to learning: A new paradigm for undergraduate education. *Change, 27*(6), pp. 12–25.

Bligh, D. A. (2000). *What's the use of lectures?* San Francisco: Jossey-Bass.

Bonwell, C. C., & Eison, J. A. (1991). *Active learning: Creating excitement in the classroom.* ASHE-ERIC Higher Education Report No. 1. Washington, D.C.: The George Washington University, School of Education and Human Development.

Bransford, J., Brown, A., & Cocking, R. (2000). *How people learn: Brain, mind, experience, and school.* Washington, DC: The National Academic Press.

Brown, P.C., Roediger, H. L, & McDaniel, M.A. (2014). *Make it stick: The science of successful learning.* Cambridge, MA: Harvard University Press.

Bunce, D. M., Flens, E. A., & Neiles, K. Y. (2010). How long can students pay attention in class? A study of student attention decline using clickers. *Journal of Chemical Education, 87*(12), 138–1443.

Bunzeck, N., & Duzel, E. (2006). Absolute coding of stimulus novelty in the human substantia nigra/VTA. *Neuron, 51*(3), 369-379.

Carey, B. (2015). *How we learn.* London: Pan Macmillan.

Christensen. C. R., & Hansen. A. J. (1987). *Teaching and the case method.* Boston: Harvard Business School.

Creekmore, J., & Deaton, S. (2015). *The active learning classroom: Strategies for practical educators.* Stillwater, OK: New Forums Press.

Curren, R. (2007). *Philosophy of education: An anthology.* Malden, MA: Blackwell.

Cuseo, J. (2005). Questions that promote deeper thinking skills. *On Course Newsletter* (July), Monkton, MD.

Darling-Hammond, L. (2010). *The flat world and education: How America's commitment to equity will determine our future.* New York, NY: Teachers College Press.

Darling-Hammond, L., Austin, K., Cheung, M., & Martin, D. (2003). Thinking about thinking: Metacognition. *The learning classroom: Theory into practice.* Stanford University School of Education.

Dean, C. B., Hubbell, E. R., Pitler, H., & Stone, B. (2012). *Classroom instruction that works: Research-based strategies for increasing student achievement* (2nd ed.). Alexandria, VA: Association for Supervision and Curriculum Development.

Ericksen, S. C. (1984). *The essence of good teaching.* San Francisco: Jossey-Bass.

Erickson, B. L., Peters, C. B., & Strommer, D. W. (2006). *Teaching first-year college students.* San Francisco: Jossey-Bass.

Erickson, B. L., & Strommer, D. W. (1991). *Teaching college freshmen.* San Francisco: Jossey-Bass.

Ewell, P. T. (1997). Organizing for learning: A new imperative. *AAHE Bulletin, 50* (4), pp. 3-6.

Freire, P. (1970). *Pedagogy of the oppressed.* New York: Continuum.

Gallup. (2016). *Gallup Student Poll 2015 results.* Retrieved from https://news.gallup.com/reports/189926/student-poll-2015-results.aspx

Gay, G. (2010). *Culturally responsive teaching: Theory, research, and practice* (2nd ed.). New York, NY: Teachers College Press.

Ginsberg, M. B., & Wlodkowski, R. J. (2009). *Diversity and motivation: Culturally responsive teaching in college.* San Francisco: Jossey-Bass.

Gutmann, A. (1999). *Democratic education.* Princeton, NJ: Princeton University Press.

Hattie, J. (2012). *Visible learning for teachers: Maximizing impact on learning.* New York, NY: Routledge.

Hess, D. E. (2009). *Controversy in the classroom: The democratic power of discussion.* New York, NY: & London, England: Routledge.

Hitchcock, C., Meyer, A., Rose, D., & Jackson, R. (2002). *Access, participation, and progress in the general curriculum.* Wakefield, MA: National Center on Accessing the General Curriculum. Retrieved from http://citeseerx.ist.psu.edu/viewdoc/download;jsessionid=A82D231E271E74EA832D4D536C4A3F65?-doi=10.1.1.529.9078&rep=rep1&type=pdf

hooks, B. (1994). *Teaching to transgress: Education as the practice of freedom.* New York: Routledge.

Hrepic, Z., Zollman, D., & Rebello, S. (2007). Comparing students' and experts' understanding of the content of a lecture. *Journal of Science Education and Technology, 16*(3), 213–224.

Hulleman, C. S., & Harackiewicz, J. M. (2009). Making education relevant: Increasing interest and performance in high school science classes. *Science, 326,* 1410–1412.

Hyungshim, J. (2008). Supporting students' motivation, engagement and learning during an uninteresting activity. *Journal of Educational Psychology, 100* (No. 4), 798–811.

Johnson, B. (2003). *The student-centered classroom handbook: A guide to implementation. Volume One: Secondary social studies/history.* New York: Routledge.

Karpicke, J. D., & Roediger, H. L. (2007). Repeated retrieval during learning is the key to long-term retention. *Journal of Memory and Language, 57,* 151–162,

Karpicke, J. D., & Roediger, H. L. (2008). The critical importance of retrieval for learning. *Science, 15*(219), Issue 5865, 966–968.

Ladson-Billings, G. (2009). *The dream-keepers: Successful teachers of African American students* (2nd ed.). San Francisco: Jossey-Bass.

Lopez, G. E., Gurin, P., & Nagda, B. A. (1998). Education and understanding structural causes for group inequalities. *Journal of Political Psychology, 19*(2), 305–329.

Marzano, R., Pickering, D. J., & Pollock, J. (2001). *Classroom instruction that works: Research-based strategies for increasing student achievement.* Alexandria, VA: Association for Supervision and Curriculum Development

Mayer, R. E. (2002). Rote versus meaningful learning. *Theory into Practice, 41*(4), 226–232.

Mayhew, M. J., Rockenback, A. N., Bowman, N. A., Seifert, T. A., Wolniak, G. C., with Pascarella, E. T., & Terenzini, P. T. (2016). *How college affects students, Volume 3.* San Francisco: Jossey-Bass.

McLeod, J., Fisher, J., & Hoover, G. (2003). *The key elements of classroom management: managing time and space, student behavior and instructional strategies.* Alexandria, VA: Association for Supervision and Curriculum Development.

Meyers, C., & Jones, T. B. (1993). *Promoting active learning: Strategies for the college classroom.* San Francisco: Jossey-Bass.

Milner, D. A., & Goodale, M. A. (1998). *The visual brain in action.* Oxford: Oxford University Press.

Nagda, B. R., Gurin, P., & Lopez, G. E. (2003). Transformative pedagogy for democracy and social justice. *Race, Ethnicity, & Education, 6*(2), 165–191.

Nuthall, G. (2000). The anatomy of memory in the classroom: Understanding how students acquire memory processes from classroom activities in science and social studies units. *American Educational Research Journal, 37*(1), 274–304.

Paivio, A. (1990). *Mental representations: A dual coding approach.* New York: Oxford University Press.

Pink, D. (2009). *Drive: The surprising truth about what motivates us.* New York, NY: Penguin.

Rosenshine, B. (1971). *Teaching behaviors and student achievement.* Slough, England: National Federation for Educational Research.

Rosenshine, B. (1997). Advances in research on instruction. In J. W. Lloyd, E. J., Kameanui, & D. Chard (Eds.), *Issues in educating students with disabilities* (pp. 197–221). Mahwah, NJ: Lawrence Erlbaum.

Rosenshine, B. (2012). Principles of instruction: Research-based strategies that all teachers should know. *American Educator* (Spring), pp. 12–19, 39.

Roueche, S. D., & Comstock, V. N. (1981). *A report on theory and method for the study of literacy development in community colleges.* Technical Report NIE-400-78-0600. Austin: Program in Community College Education, The University of Texas at Austin.

Ruhl, K. L., Hughes, C. A., & Schloss, P. K. (1987). Using the pause procedure to enhance lecture recall. *Teacher Education and Special Education, 10,* 14–18.

Ryan, R. M., & Deci, E. L. (2000). Self-determination theory and the facilitation of intrinsic motivation, social development, and well-being. *American Psychologist, 55*(1), 68.

Scharf, A. (2018). *Critical practices for anti-bias education.* Teaching Tolerance: A Project of the Southern Poverty Law Center. Retrieved from https://www.tolerance.org/.../2019-04/TT-Critical-Practices-for-Anti-bias-Education.pdf

Schmid, M. E., Gillian-Daniel, D., Kramer, S., & Kueppers, M. (2016). Promoting student academic achievement through faculty development about inclusive teaching. *Change, 48*(5), 16–25.

Stephan, W. G. (1985). Intergroup relations. In G. Lindzey & E. Aronson (Eds.), *The handbook of social psychology* (3rd ed., vol. 2, pp. 599–658). Hillsdale, NJ: Erlbaum.

Tomlinson, C. A. (1999). *The differentiated classroom: Responding to the needs of all learners.* New Jersey: Pearson Education.

Valenzuela, A. (1999). *Subtractive schooling: U.S.-Mexican youth and the politics of caring.* Albany, NY: State University of New York Press.

Wiggan, G. (2008). From opposition to engagement: Lessons from high achieving African American students. *Urban Review, 40*(4), 317–349.

Winkelmes, M. A. (2013). Transparency in teaching: Faculty share data and improve students' learning. *Liberal Education, 99*(2), 48-55.

Zinsser, W. (1993). *Writing to learn.* New York: HarperCollins.

Reflections and Applications

6.1 Review the sidebar quotes contained in this chapter and select two that you think are particularly meaningful or inspirational. For each quote you selected, provide an explanation of why you chose it.

6.2 Review the *motivational strategies for engaging students with the subject matter* on pp. 99–103. Select three you think are most important and intend to put into practice.

6.3 One way in which teachers can motivate students to learn is by showing them that what they are being asked to learn is relevant to their lives. Identify a key topic in a subject are that you teach (or will teach) and describe how you would articulate or demonstrate the relevance of that topic to your students.

6.4 Diversifying instructional methods is an effective way to elevate student motivation and accommodate diverse learning styles. What diverse teaching methods do or will you use to "change things up" and infuse variety into your instructional repertoire?

6.5 Students' intrinsic motivation to learn increases when are given learning options or choices. In what ways could you provide students with more opportunities to make personal choice about what they learn or how they will learn, while still adhering to a standardized curriculum?

6.6 One way that teachers can increase student engagement in the learning process is by posing questions that effectively elicit student responses or reactions to the material they are learning. What types of questions or questioning methods do you think would be most effective for evoking responses from your students?

6.7 There are three key stages in the learning process: (a) *before*, (b) *during*, and (c) *after* a lesson. What strategies do you use or will you use you use to engage students at each of these stages?

6.8 You are planning to develop a culturally inclusive lesson plan that has the following learning outcome: At the end of this lesson, students will understand how science is a multicultural discipline.

   a) Before beginning the lesson, what will you do to increase student motivation for learning the upcoming material?

   b) During the lesson, what techniques will you use to actively engage students in the learning process?

   c) At the end of the lesson, what will you have students do to demonstrate that the lesson's intended learning outcome was achieved?

7

Student-Centered Teaching, Part II: Culturally Inclusive Strategies for Promoting Positive Student-Teacher and Student-Student (Peer-to-Peer) Relationships

Chapter Purpose and Preview

This chapter supplies instructional practices for building teacher-student rapport and for developing positive relationships with students from diverse cultural backgrounds. Specific strategies are supplied for building a sense of community among classmates, designing small-group work that fosters appreciation of both cultural differences and cross-cultural commonalities, and for intentionally forming diverse learning teams that enable students to experience multicultural perspectives and engage in intercultural teamwork.

Introduction

As noted in the previous chapter, one way to transform student-centered teaching principles into actionable practices is by designing an instructional plan that intentionally makes three key, student-focused connections:

1. the student-*subject* connection: connecting students with the subject matter by using instructional strategies that actively engage them with the content they're learning;
2. the student-*teacher* connection: connecting students with their teacher by building positive student-teacher relationships; and
3. the student-*student* connection: connecting students with their classmates by creating an inclusive classroom community.

Instructional strategies that promote these three connections benefit all students and they have particularly positive impact on students from minority groups, thus serving to narrow the achievement gap (Schmid et al., 2016).

The last chapter centered on strategies for making the first of these connections: the student-*subject* connection. This chapter focuses on research-based strategies for promoting *student-teacher* and *student-student* (*classmate*) connections.

The Student-*Teacher* Connection:
Connecting Students with their Teacher and Building Positive Student-Teacher Relationships

High-impact teachers not only use good teaching techniques; they also exhibit personal attributes and behaviors that humanize the classroom, creating a classroom atmosphere in which all students experience a sense of importance, inclusiveness, and self-worth (Jones, 1989). Establishing positive teacher-student relationships may be viewed as a precondition or prerequisite for student engagement. When students feel comfortable relating to the teacher, they become more responsive to the teacher's attempts to engage them in the learning process. In multiple studies conducted at the elementary, middle, and high school level, it has been found that when students report that their teacher likes them and cares about them, they are more engaged in class (Hattie, 2009; Shernoff, Ruzek, & Sinha, 2016). It has also been found that students exhibit greater gains in learning in classes characterized by interpersonal warmth, empathy, and positive teacher-student relationships (Cornelius-White, 2007). Furthermore, when children agree with statements such as "most of my teachers care about me" and most are "interested in what I have to say," their parents report higher trust in the school (Adams, Forsyth, & Mitchell, 2009).

How can teachers begin to build positive relationships with their students? It starts with knowing who their students are (by name) and taking a personal interest in them. It's as important for teachers to know *who* they're teaching as it is to know *what* they're teaching and *how* to teach it. Certainly, an effective teacher has subject matter knowledge and employs pedagogical methods that get students interested in the subject matter, but students are also interested in knowing that their teacher is interested in them.

Carl Rogers, eminent humanistic psychologist, artfully expresses the value of knowing our students: "I think of it as prizing the learner. It is a caring for the learner. It is an acceptance of this other individual as a separate person, a respect for him as having worth in his own right" (Rogers, 1975, p. 107). Said in another way, when students sense that their teacher knows them and cares about them, they experience *personal validation* (Rendón, 1994). When students feel personally validated, they relate more easily and openly to the teacher, are more comfortable engaging in class, and are more willing to seek out the teacher's advice and assistance. Postsecondary research indicates that personal validation is a necessary precondition for the engagement of under-represented students—when they feel personally validated, then they become actively engaged in the learning process (Rendón-Linares & Muñoz, 2011).

Listed next are specific practices that teachers may use to supply students with a genuine sense of personal validation.

> "In teaching, you can't do the Bloom stuff until you do the Maslow stuff."
>
> —Dr. Allen Beck, school teacher and educational administrator

> "People don't care how much you know until they know how much you care."
>
> —John C. Maxwell, author, *The 21 Indispensable Qualities of a Leader*

> "Learners may be disengaged because they do not feel emotionally connected with the material, with the teacher, or both."
>
> —Vivian Robinson, *Student-Centered Leadership*

Make learning students' names a top priority. Before diving into the first lesson plan of the term, student-centered teachers begin by making an intentional and effortful attempt to know their students' names. Probably the most effective way to initially establish teacher-student rapport and make a positive first impression on the class is by learning the names of students and doing so within the first week of the term.

Once students' names have been learned expeditiously, the teacher can immediately use this knowledge to solicit their personal engagement in class, sending an early message of high expectations for every student from all cultural backgrounds.

Once students' names have been learned, consistently refer to them by name. Knowing students' names is important; letting students know that their names are known is just as important. Whenever a student raises a hand to ask a question or make a contribution, that student should be called on by name. Consistently referring to students by name has three key benefits: (a) it sends an ongoing signal to students that their teacher knows them, (b) it reinforces the teacher's memory of students' names, and (c) it helps students learn and remember the names of their classmates, which helps create a stronger sense of class intimacy and community.

Tactfully seek out personal information from students and remember the information they share. Step one in building rapport with the class is for teacher to know *who* students are (their names); step two is to know something *about* them. When teachers gain knowledge about their students, they are better better positioned to connect the subject matter to students' personal interests and experiences. As Bryk et al. (2010) note: "A deep understanding of students' background represents a powerful resource for teachers as they seek to establish the interpersonal connections necessary to teach. Good teachers draw on such background knowledge as they attempt to connect seemingly abstract academic topics to student lives" (p. 58).

One effective way for teachers to can gain background knowledge about their students is by having them complete a "student information sheet" on which they answer questions about their past and current experiences, their personal interests, talents and values, and their future goals and plans (Cuseo, 2004). (See Appendix A for a sizable sample of questions that may be used for this purpose.) In addition to using a student information sheet to relate material they're to students' lives, teachers can use it to engage in conversations with students outside of class, which, in turn, is likely to increase their willingness to engage in class.

The questions included on a student information sheet can also help teachers identify forms of student diversity that are not visibly detectable (e.g., students' family arrangement, current living situation, and special circumstances). This information may be used by the teacher to intentionally form diverse learning teams composed of students with different cultural backgrounds and current life experiences. (For further details on forming diverse learning teams, see **p. 129**.)

"You never get a second chance to make a first impression."

—Will Rogers, famous Native American actor and writer, born in the Cherokee Nation, Indian Territory (now Oklahoma).

"High expectations are communicated as teachers learn students' names and call on them by name."

—Donelson Forsyth and James McMillan, in *Practical Proposals for Motivating Students*

During my first year of teaching, I had an African American student in class by the name of Lance. I knew he played on our school's basketball team, so I would always ask him something related to how the team was doing and how his game was going. The third time I asked him a question about basketball, he said to me: "Why do you always ask me about basketball? You know, I do other things and have other interests as well."

Lance's comment made me aware that I needed to know more about students in my classes before I could have meaningful interactions with them. So, on the first day of class, I began asking students in my classes to complete a "student information sheet" that included questions relating to their personal backgrounds, current experiences and future plans, personal talents, interests and values. While students wrote their answers on a sheet of paper, I responded to the same questions by writing my answers on the board. (This allowed my students to get to know me while I got to know them.) I then collected all their information sheets, called out the names individually, and asked them to raise their hand when their name was called. This gave me the opportunity to associate their name and face. After I called each student's name, I quickly jotted down a word or two next to the student's name that I reviewed later to help me remember that student's name, (e.g., something distinctive about the student's appearance or the specific area of the room where the student was seated).

I saved the students' information sheets and used the information they shared with me to engage them in informal conversations outside of class. In addition, I reviewed the interests they shared on their sheets and attempted to connect what I'm teaching in class to their personal interests or goals. I did this by recording the student's name and strongest interest on a sticky note and placing it in my class notes next to any topic or concept that related to the student's interests or to something else the student shared on the information sheet. When we got to that topic in class (which could be months later), I immediately see the students' names posted by it. As I begin to discuss the topic, I mentioned the name of the student in conjunction with the topic (e.g., "Gina, we're about to study something that really interests you," or "Paul, I'm sure you can relate to this topic."). Students really perked up when I mentioned their name in association with their topic; plus, they're amazed (and touched) by my ability to remember something they shared with me weeks or months earlier—on the first day of class. Because weren't aware of my sticky note strategy, they thought I had extraordinary social memory and social sensitivity—which was fine with me because it increased my rapport with the class and their interest in me (and what I was teaching them).

Joe Cuseo

Create opportunities for students to share their cultural background and history. It's unrealistic to expect a teacher to be able to master curricular-specific knowledge pertaining to each and every cultural group. A more reasonable expectation is for teachers to learn enough about their students' personal backgrounds and current life circumstances to be able to design classroom learning exercises and homework assignments that relate meaningfully to their cultural experiences (Mercado, 2001). As Robinson (2011) points out:

> In large multicultural schools, there may be more than fifty different ethnic groups represented in the student body. Rather than expecting teachers to have curriculum-relevant knowledge about all such groups, it is more appropriate to focus on the attitudes and inquiry skills that enable students to learn, in context and as required, about how to make effective connections between the curriculum and cultural knowledge. It is the desire to make such connections and the provision of support for doing so that are important rather than the transmission of prepackaged information about students' cultures (pp. 134–135).

Teachers can only make curricular connections with their students' cultural experiences if they know about those experiences. One of the most important tasks of teachers is to listen to their students. By listening, teachers exhibit humility and reciprocity—an understanding of the student's perspective (Parker, 2006).

Teachers can listen to their students and gain insight into their cultural experiences and perspectives by asking them to write a short, autobiographical story about their personal journey. For such an assignment, students are likely to need some structure or scaffolding, which teachers can supply by suggesting their personal stories be constructed around such topics as: (a) turning points in their life, (b) past experiences that continue to affect their life (positively or negatively), (c) their future dreams or goals, and (d) their role models or sources of inspiration. Students may share their stories in writing, with pictures, via technology, or some combination thereof. Research shows that when people learn about the personal experiences of individuals from different cultures (e.g., reading their diary entries), their feelings of "cultural distance" and prejudice decline, and they become more aware of experiences, interests, and concerns they have in common (Jackson & Gefland, 2019).

Teachers should share their personal stories with students. Human relations scholars point out that when we share experiences and feelings with others, it shows them that we trust them and increases their trust in us (Adler & Towne, 2014). When teachers share their personal stories, they model transparency and authenticity; in so doing, they increase the likelihood that students will follow their example and do the same.

By sharing their personal experiences, teachers show students that they are more than teachers—they are "real" people who students can identify with and emulate. When teachers engage in transparent self-disclosure, it increases the likelihood that students will follow suit. Teachers' self-disclosure should include sharing their personal struggles and challenges. As Peter Elbow (1986) eloquently puts it:

> We [teachers] should reveal our own position, particularly our doubts, ambivalences, and biases. We should show we are still learning, still willing to look at things in new ways, still sometimes uncertain or even stuck. We can increase the chances of our students being willing to undergo the necessary anxiety involved in change if they see we are willing to undergo it (p. 150).

Furthermore, when teachers share personal examples and anecdotes from their own life experiences that relate to the material they're teaching, it deepens students' learning by providing them with concrete and poignant "human" examples that can bring academic concepts to life (literally). Also, by relating academic material to their personal experiences, teachers model a deep-learning principle that students should apply to their own learning—"constructing knowledge" by connecting what is being learned to what you already know or have previously experienced (Bruner, 1990; David, 2015; Piaget, 1978).

"Instruction begins when you, the teacher, learn from the learner; put yourself in his place so that you understand what he learns and the way he understands."

—Søren Kierkegaard, 19th-century Danish philosopher and theologian

"Educators should be chosen not merely for their special qualifications, but more for their personality and their character, because we teach more by what we are than by what we teach."

—Will Durant, Pulitzer Prize and Presidential Medal of Freedom winner, former teacher and principal of a school for working-class children

Teachers should make an intentional attempt to interact with students in a personable and empathic manner. The following practices can be used to implement this recommendation:

► Greeting students personally when they enter class and when seeing them on campus.

► Welcoming back students after a weekend or semester break.

► Recognizing the return of an absent student ("Glad to have you back; we missed you.").

► Acknowledging emotions that students exhibit in class ("You seem excited about this topic." "I sense that you're feeling tired, so let's take a short break.").

► Wishing students luck on upcoming exams and assignments.

► Expressing concern to a student who is not performing well or seems to be disengaged ("Everything okay?" "Anything I can do to help?").

In a study of close to 1,900 different classrooms, it was found that classes exhibiting substantial year-to-year gains in academic achievement had teachers who were viewed by their students as personable and empathic. Their students said things like "My teacher wants us to share our thoughts" and "My teacher seems to know if something is bothering me" (Ferguson, as cited in Duckworth, 2016, p. 218).

Teachers should use humor to build rapport with the class. Using humor in the classroom shouldn't be viewed as "unprofessional" or feared as something that will result in the teacher "losing control" of the class. Incorporating content-relevant, socially appropriate into the teaching process can build teacher-student rapport and facilitate learning (Stambor, 2006). Being funny isn't synonymous with being frivolous. A humorous anecdote can serve as a very intentional and effective strategy for illustrating a concept, or driving home the point of a lesson. In one carefully controlled study, students were randomly assigned to learn the same material illustrated with or without humor. The students who experienced the lesson with humor scored higher on test questions about the material they had been taught (Ziv, 1988).

In addition to humorous anecdotes, concept-relevant *cartoons* can be used to increase student interest in, attention to, and retention of a concept—by illustrating it visually and evoking an emotional response to it. Cartoons may also be projected before starting a lesson to stimulate students' anticipatory interest in the upcoming topic, or they may be used to break up lengthy teacher presentations and maintain (or regain) students' attention.

Teachers can use student journals to maintain personal connections with students throughout the term. A journal may be defined as a series of written reflections on, or reactions to, personal experiences that take place over an extended period of time (e.g., an academic term). Student journals can be assigned in either of two formats: (a) *"free" journals*—in which students have complete freedom to make journal entries about any personal experience they like, or (b) *"prompted" journals*—in which students respond in writing to specific, teacher-posed prompts (e.g., "My first impression of this class is ... ").

By responding regularly (or even periodically) to student journals, teachers can engage in ongoing narrative conversations with students, enabling them to stay "in touch" with their students and to maintain a personal relationship with them throughout the term. These journaling conversations can take place on paper (e.g., in a composition notebook) or online (e.g., via an e-journal).

The Student-*Student* Connection:
Connecting Students with their Classmates and Creating an Inclusive Class Community

In addition to the student-teacher connection, another key relationship that impacts the learning process is the relationship between and among students. The classroom should be both student-centered and *community*-centered—a place where students share and learn from one another (Bransford, Brown, & Cocking, 2000). Classmates can contribute to each other's academic success by providing mutual social support, reciprocal feedback, formal or informal tutoring, or simply by making the classrroom a place where students want to be (Wilkinson et al., 2002). The important role peers can play in promoting student success is suggested by research showing that when students change schools, the best predictor of their academic performance at their new school is whether or not they make a friend within the first month (Pratt & George, 2005).

The first few days of class can shape students' first impression of their classmates, which in turn can shape their attitude toward classroom learning. By providing early opportunities for students to get to know one another and feel comfortable communicating with each another, teachers create a social environment conducive to student engagement and collaborative learning.

Moreover, when teachers take time to intentionally promote positive peer relations, they build a classroom culture in which open and honest discussion of diversity can take place. The power of multicultural education is more likely to be realized by students engage in mutually supportive interaction with diverse classmates than by listening to teachers lecture about the benefits of diversity.

> "Students are likely to learn more from classroom instruction when they feel accepted and valued by their teachers and peers."
>
> —Cheryl Bernstein Cohen, *Teaching about Ethnic Diversity*

Establish an early sense of class community by using icebreaker activities that "warm up" students to one another. Educational sociologists point out that a classroom of individual students has the potential to be be transformed into a bona fide *learning community* (Tinto, 1997). Icebreakers may be viewed as "community builders" that serve to build early connections among learners. To establish an early sense of community in a class of diverse students, students could be asked to bring to class an artifact that reflects their culture (e.g., food, clothing, music, art) and share why they chose it. A community-building exercise such as this can serve as a springboard that can "warm up" students for subsequent, more in-depth discussions of diversity.

Students might also be asked to create "identity boxes," in which they bring to class a shoebox or a box of similar size that they decorate on the outside with images or words which capture their cultural experiences. Inside the box would be objects (or pictures of the objects if they're too large to fit in

> "The classroom can provide a 'public place' where community can be practiced."
>
> —Suzanne W. Morse, *Renewing Civic Capacity: Preparing College Students for Service and Citizenship.*

the box) that they believe have shaped their personal identity. Students can share their boxes with the class as a whole or in small groups, after which the class could reflect on the experience by answering questions such as the following:

> What did you learn about your classmates that you thought was particularly interesting or surprising?
> How were your experiences different from your classmates?
> In what way(s) were your classmates' experiences different from one another?
> How were your experiences similar to your classmates?
> Did you learn anything from this exercise that changed your views about your classmates or how you might interact with them? ("Exploring Diversity," 2019).

When students from a variety of backgrounds get to hear each other's stories, they gain insight into both the differences and similarities in their personal journeys. This helps create a classroom community in which cultural differences are affirmed and cultural commonalities are acknowledged—a hallmark of effective multicultural education (National Council for the Social Studies, 1991).

Another icebreaker exercise that may be used to build an early sense of class community is the "Classmate Scavenger Hunt" (Metz, Cuseo, & Thompson, 2019). In this procedure, the teacher gathers information from individual students by asking them to complete a student information sheet on the first day of class. Drawing on the information that students provide on their individual sheets, the teacher constructs a list of statements that includes one distinctive piece of information about each student in class. Students are then given a copy of this list and asked to mill around the room and find the classmate who "matches" (is associated with) each personal statement on the list. This exercise ensures that all students in class get a chance to meet and have an early personal exchange with every one of their classmates.

Similar to the Classmate Scavenger Hunt, "Diversity Bingo" is popular icebreaker that involves giving students a bingo game card containing a grid of squares; within each square is a statement or question about a particular student in class. Students take their bingo cards, mingle around the classroom and find the person who matches the statement.

A key advantage of both the Classmate Scavenger Hunt and Diversity Bingo icebreaker is that all students are involved at all times throughout the entire exercise. Thus, both of these community-building experiences effectively address two key principles of student engagement: (a) "the *Simultaneity* Principle: What percentage of our students are overtly active at any one moment?" and (b) "The *Equality* Principle: How equal is participation among all students?" (Kagan, 1998, p. 9).

Engaging Students in Small-Group Work

A teacher-centered classroom becomes a student-centered class room when the teacher steps off stage and students learn together in small groups (2–4 students). The process begins by creating a classroom learning environment conducive to student-student dialogue and collaboration (Scharf, 2018)—e.g., arranging desks so that students make eye contact with each other and can engage in face-to-face interaction.

A large body of research indicates that students learn more deeply when learning takes place in a social context that involves interpersonal interaction and collaboration (Cuseo, 1996; 2002). As learning scholars put it, personal knowledge is "socially constructed"—built up from interpersonal interaction and dialogue with others (Bruffee, 1993). Brain-imaging studies show that when learning takes place in the context of social interaction, more areas within the thinking part of the brain are activated than when learning takes place alone (Carter, 1998). The human brain may be "hard-wired" to learn in a social context because interpersonal interaction and collaboration have played a critical role in the survival of the human species (e.g., our ancient ancestors survived by hunting and gathering in groups). Thus, learning in groups is qualifies as a "brain-based" or "brain compatible" form of learning (Jensen, 1998).

As a general rule, group size and student participation are inversely related—as the size of the group size increases, individual members' level of participation of decreases. Since a group of two is the smallest possible group size, it's the one that maximizes face-to-face interaction between members and their overall level of engagement (Cuseo, 2002). As the old adage goes, "It's hard to get lost in a group of two." In addition, pair work has the logistical advantage of allowing the teacher to form groups quickly. Rather than students having to move their desks or leave their desks, they can simply turn to a classmate seated near them.

To increase the number and diversity of students with whom students have paired interactions, after a pair of neighboring students interacts for a designated period of time, students seated in the adjacent row could slide over one seat and pair up with a new student. This practice can be repeated to create a succession of paired interactions between different students that's similar to the process of "speed dating" or "speed friending." Another way teachers can increase the number and diversity of paired interactions is by using a procedure called "Inside/Outside Discussion Circles." Students are first asked to stand in two concentric circles; the inside circle faces out and the outside circle faces in. The teacher then poses a question for the students to discuss and all students in the inside circle respond first, after which students in the outside circle respond to the same question. Once each partner takes a turn responding to the discussion question, all students in the inside circle move one step to the right and the two new partners respond to the same question or a different question (Kagan, 1994).

During pair work, each student is engaged at all times—either speaking to or listening to their partner. Thus, pair work effectively implements both of the previously mentioned principles of an effective student-engagement exercise: (a) the "equality principle"—every student in class is equally engaged, and (b) the "simultaneity principle"—all students are engaged at the same time (Kagan, 1998). In contrast, when a teacher posing a question to the whole class, it engages students *unequally* (only one student answers the question) and *sequentially* (students are called on one at a time). Moreover, when teachers pose questions to the whole class, research shows that a small percentage of students typically raise their hands to volunteer an answer (Karp & Yoels, 1976), and the students who do so are often the most confident and verbally dominant (Boyer, 1987). Those least likely to respond are (a) students who are reticent or fearful about speaking in large groups (Bowers, 1986), and (b) underrepresented students who tend to be less verbally assertive in classroom settings (Astin et al., 1972; Levitz, 1992). Use of small-group work, particularly pair work, can address these shortcomings and increase the level of engagement among less dominant students and students from underrepresented groups.

When to Use Small-Group Work

Small-group learning can be infused into the learning process at any of the following key junctures.

> ▶ At the *start* of a lesson—to activate students' ideas about the upcoming topic. For example, students could formulate questions in small groups about the topic to be covered. Or, students may engage in a group process called "*active knowledge sharing*," in which the teacher provides them with a list of questions relating to the upcoming lesson (e.g., words to define, historical figures to identify, or a pre-test of prior knowledge). Students then pair up to answer the questions as best they can, after which they dialogue with other pairs to share and compare answers.

Students may also be placed in teams to do preliminary work on problems or assignments that they subsequently complete individually. This practice supplies students with initial social scaffolding that can build their academic self-confidence and bridge their transition to independent work.

> ▶ *During* a lesson—to intercept attention loss and interject active learning after key points are presented during the lesson. For example, after the teacher explains a critical concept, students work in pairs to compare their notes and generate examples relating to the concept just presented. This practice is also an effective way to hold students accountable for taking notes in class because they know they will be sharing their notes with a classmate (Kagan, 2014).
> ▶ At the *end* of a lesson—to create a sense of "closure" (a meaningful ending to the lesson) and consolidate key concepts covered during the lesson. For example, the lesson ends with a small-group task in which students pair-up and check each other's notes for accuracy and completeness.

Strategies for Enhancing the Quality of Small-Group Work

The positive impact of small-group learning can be magnified by using the following practices.

Before **students are asked to share their thoughts with the group, they are given time to gather their thoughts individually.** This recommendation can be implemented through use of a popular procedure known as *think-pair-share* (Lyman, 1992). Students are first alloted a certain amount of think time to gather their thoughts individually (and silently), after which they join a partner to share their thoughts verbally. Providing students with time for personal reflection personal reflection prior to group discussion encourages them to think through what they're going to say before saying it, which serves to improve the quality of their subsequent verbal contributions they make to the group discussion. It also increases the likelihood that shy or verbally apprehensive students will share their ideas. Research indicates that students who are apprehensive about communicating in classroom settings are more likely to participate in class discussions if they're given time to think about what they're going to say before being asked to say it (Neer, 1987).

Notify students that any member of their group may be called on to report the group's ideas. This practice provides a strong incentive for students to listen actively to the ideas shared by their teammates because they may be called on by the teacher to report their team's ideas. Since any member of the group may be called on to report their team's ideas, it also sends the message that the teacher holds high expectations for participation by all students, including students from minority groups.

Have groups keep a visible record of the ideas they generate. Each group could be supplied with a flip chart or blank sheet on which their ideas can be recorded or projected (e.g., on an Elmo projector or document camera). Students are more likely to remain "on task" during a group discussion if they know they will be held accountable for creating a concrete "product" of their collective thinking that will be displayed publicly.

Small groups may also be asked to come to the front of class to share their work as a panel. In addition to holding students accountable for their work, this practice can also alleviate students' fear of public speaking because it allows them the opportunity to speak as a panelist along with teammates—which is a less threatening form of public speaking than delivering a stand-up, stand-alone speech.

Intentionally form discussion groups composed of students from diverse backgrounds. According to the social constructivist theory of human learning, our thinking consists largely of "internal" (mental) representations of conversations we've had with other people (Vygotsky, 1978). If our conversations take place with people from diverse backgrounds, our thinking becomes more diversified, nuanced, and complex.

By intentionally forming learning groups composed of students from diverse cultural backgrounds, students gain greater exposure to multicultural perspectives. Such heterogeneity not only diversifies the group and makes it more inclusive, it also deepens the group's learning by enabling its members to

engage in multiple perspective-taking—which implements two longstanding instructional recommendations for promoting critical thinking and attitude change: (a) teachers should give students opportunities to "collaborate and 'stretch' their understanding by encountering divergent views" (Kurfiss, 1988, p. 2) and (b) teachers should intentionally create an "atmosphere of disequilibrium [cognitive dissonance created by encountering the unfamiliar] so that students can change, rework, or reconstruct their thinking processes" (Meyers, 1986, p. 14). One large-scale educational program was once explicitly designed to generate cognitive dissonance (disequilibrium) in students' minds by having them engage in teacher-guided dialogue with peers who held conflicting views. Research on this program revealed that it had a dramatic impact—an effect size of .60+ on students' cognitive development—equivalent to more than a full-year gain in intellectual growth (Shayer, 2003).

When forming learning teams of students from different cultural backgrounds, if only a small number of students from a particular cultural group are represented in class, teams should not be constructed in such a way that only one of a minority group is represented on the team (Rosser, 1988). For example, if there are four students of color in class, it may be tempting for the teacher to place each of these students in a different learning group so a student of color is represented in as many groups as possible. Instead, these four students should be placed in only two groups, one pair per group. In subsequent small-group discussions, groups could be intentionally reconstructed so that white students who were not exposed to the perspective of students of color in their previous small-group discussion are exposed to students of color in their current group.

When at least two members of a minority group are represented on the same learning team, they are likely to feel more comfortable expressing their minority experiences and perspectives. Having more than one minority student in each learning group also combats *tokenism*—a superficial and disingenuous attempt to appear inclusive (Linkov, 2014)—which places the burden on on one individual to represent his or her entire minority group. Tokenism can be minimized by ensuring that a "critical mass" of minority students (20%–33%) is represented in any group (Kanter, 1977; Howard, 2006).

In addition to combating tokenism, a critical mass of minority students in learning groups also allows majority-group members to interact with different individuals from the same minority group, which helps combat overgeneralizing and stereotyping (Smith, 2015).

In addition to infusing diversity into learning groups in the form of, racial and cultural diversity, incorporating gender diversity in learning groups can expose students to different ways of learning and understanding concepts. Studies show that males are more likely to be "separate knowers"—they tend to "detach" themselves from the concept or issue being discussed so they can analyze it. In contrast, females are more likely to be "connected knowers"—they tend to relate personally to the concepts and connect them with their own experiences and the experiences of others. For example, when interpreting a poem, males are more likely to ask: "What techniques can I use to analyze it?" In contrast, females are more likely to ask: "What is the poet trying to say to me?" (Belenky et al., 1986). It has also been found that during group discussions females are more likely to work collaboratively, sharing their ideas with other group members and soliciting ideas from them. In contrast, males are more likely to adopt a more competitive approach, debating or disagreeing with the ideas of others (Magolda, 1992). Consistent with these findings are studies of females in leadership positions, which reveal that women are more likely to adopt a collaborative style of leadership than men (Eagly & Johnson, 1990; van Engen & Willemsen, 2004). Although these male-female approaches to learning are different, they both have merits. Teachers can help students capitalize on the merits of both male-female approaches by forming gender-diverse learning teams and discussion groups.

Establish ground rules for small-group discussions that ensure underrepresented students have an equal opportunity to participate. One strategy for ensuring equal participation among all group members is a procedure called "Talking Chips" (Kagan, 1992). This practice consists of four steps:

1. Each group member is given a symbolic "talking chip" (e.g., a checker, coin, or playing card).
2. Members are instructed to place the chip in the center of the team's workspace when they make a personal contribution to the team's discussion.
3. Members can speak in any order, but cannot speak again until all chips are in the center—indicating that every group member has spoken.
4. After all chips have been placed in the center, group members retrieve their respective chips for another round of discussion, which follows the same rules of equal participation as the initial round.

By structuring turn-taking with procedures such as this, teachers ensure that all group members participate equally in group work and all members experience the full benefits of group work experience. Structured turn-taking also minimizes the risk a group will succumb to the "cascade effect"—the tendency of the group's discussion to be unduly influenced by the person who speaks first—before others have had the opportunity to share their independent thoughts (Sunstein & Hastie, 2015). Failure to build equal participation practices into group work can also result in highly assertive, academically self-confident students doing most (if not all) of the talking. Such students are not likely to be members of underserved student populations, thus not building equal participation procedures into students' group work may have the exact opposite effect on educational equity than the teacher intended. As Kagan (2014) notes: "When we use unstructured pair and group interaction, inadvertently, we increase the achievement gap" (p. 125).

Learning teams with diverse membership should identify both *differences* **and** *commonalities* **in their experiences and perspectives.** A key advantage of forming diverse learning groups is that they can sharpen students' awareness and appreciation of cultural differences. However, focusing attention on cross-cultural differences shouldn't come at the expense of detecting and appreciating cross-cultural commonalities. If students are not mindful of the unity that co-exists along with diversity, their discussions of group differences can inadvertently magnify feelings of intergroup divisiveness or separatism (Thompson & Cuseo, 2014). In fact, research suggests that when diversity discussions focus exclusively on intergroup differences, members of disenfranchised groups can experience a heightened sense of isolation and alienation (Smith, 1997, 2015). To reduce the risk of this happening during their discussions of diversity, students should be directed to consider not only what differentiates their cultural groups, but also what unites them—common cultural denominators and cross-cultural themes of unity that traverse or transcend diversity. One way to do so is by explicitly instructing students, prior to their discussions of diversity, students to be mindful of universal experiences that crop up during their discussions which unite all cultural groups under the single umbrella of humanity. For example, while discussing cultural differences, students could be asked to identify (a) common elements or components of all cultures (see **p. 124**), (b) common needs of all humans (e.g., Maslow's need hierarchy, depicted on **p. 03**), or (c) common dimensions of the self and self-development experienced by persons in all cultures (see Box **7.1**). Students can also be asked to explore their shared experiences as citizens of the same country, members of the same gender, or cohorts of the same generation.

Each person has multiple group identities that often overlap and intersect (Carter, 2008; Dill & Zambrana, 2009). For example, students may be members of different groups with respect to one characteristic (e.g., being white or a person of color) yet share membership in another group (e.g., being a white and black females are members of the same gender group). Research indicates that when members of different racial or cultural groups are aware of their shared membership in another group, they are more likely to accept them and have positive interpersonal interactions with them (Bigler & Hughes, 2009; Gurin, Nagda, & *Zúñiga*, 2013; Stephan & Stephan, 2004).

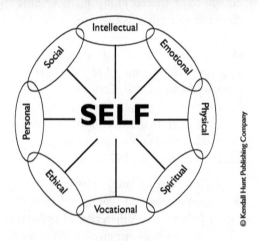

© Kendall Hunt Publishing Company

1. *Intellectual* Self: acquiring knowledge, learning how to learn, and developing thinking skills.

2. *Emotional* Self: understanding, managing, and expressing emotions.

3. *Social* Self: forming interpersonal relationships.

4. *Ethical* Self: developing moral character—making sound ethical judgments, acquiring a value system for guiding personal decision-making, and demonstrating consistency between convictions (beliefs) and commitments (actions).

5. *Physical* Self: gaining knowledge about one's body and applying that knowledge to prevent disease and promote wellness.

6. *Spiritual* Self: pondering the "big questions," such as the meaning and purpose of life, the inevitability of death, and the origins of human life and the universe.

7. *Vocational* Self: working and earning an income.

8. *Personal* Development: developing a personal identity, a sense of self-efficacy, and the capacity to effectively manage personal resources (e.g., time and money).

> "Everyone is a house with four rooms: a physical, a mental, an emotional, and a spiritual. Most of us tend to live in one room most of the time but unless we go into every room every day, even if only to keep it aired, we are not complete."
>
> —Native American proverb

Teachers can capitalize on this finding by creating learning teams composed of students who have both different and shared group memberships. For example, discussion groups could be formed among students of the same gender, but who differ with respect to race, ethnicity, or socioeconomic status. This team-formation strategy serves to increase student awareness that members of different groups can, at the same time, be members of the same group—with similar experiences, needs, and concerns. Banks (2016) points out how this group-formation practice can combat prejudice: "Making cross-cutting group memberships salient can reduce prejudice because it is hard to dislike people with whom you share important aspects of your identity" (p. 303).

> "Students should learn about the self and the other. They should experience people and events with whom they can identify and others with whom they may not identify at first glance."
>
> —James Banks, in *Cultural Diversity and Education*

Taking time during diversity discussions to raise awareness of how members of different groups share membership in other groups can help defuse feelings of divisiveness and supply students with a sense of unity that facilitates open and honest discussions of their differences. Naturally, raising awareness of their shared group memberships shouldn't come at the expense of diminishing or dismissing awareness of intergroup differences. Studies show that if members of a minority group have a strong or salient sense of group identity, that is minimized by members of the majority group, it sharpens the minority group's sense of separateness or isolation and heightens intergroup tension (Brewer, 2000; Crisp, Stone, & Hall, 2006; Hewstone, Rubin, & Willis, 2002).

To ensure that students from diverse groups remain cognizant of both their differences and commonalities during group discussions, teachers may ask them to keep the following questions in mind:

▶ What major similarities in viewpoints do all group members share? (What were the common themes?)
▶ What major differences of opinion are being expressed by diverse members of our group? (What are the variations on the themes?)
▶ Were particular topics or issues are being raised that seem to provoke intense reactions or emotional responses from different members of the group?
▶ Is the group discussion leading any members of the group to change their mind about an idea or position they originally held?

Building in time during and after group discussions for students to reflect on instances of diversity and unity that emerge during their discussions serves to implement one standard of effective multicultural education identified by the National Council for Social Studies: "Does the curriculum help students participate in cross-ethnic and cross-cultural experiences and reflect upon them?" (1991, p. 39).

Members of the discussion group could share their individual reflections with other group members, after which a representative from each discussion group could be asked to join a panel and report their group's ideas to the whole class. The teacher could follow the panel report with a synthesis that highlights key aspects of diversity and patterns of unity that emerged across the reports of different discussion groups.

Consider this . . .
Diversity education stimulates student awareness of *differences* between groups and *unity* across groups.

Small-group work should be structured so that students have opportunities to advance beyond discussion to *collaboration*. In a discussion group, group members simply share their individual ideas. The etymology of the word *discuss* means to break apart and scatter, stemming from the same root as the words *divide* and *disperse*. In contrast, members of a collaborative group "co-labor" (work together) to reach a common goal. Collaborative learning groups do not simply share their ideas with one another; they further and reach group *consensus* or make a *unified group decision* about the ideas they generate (Abercrombie, 1960; Wiener, 1986).

The instructional key that turns a discussion group into a collaborative learning group is the teacher's inclusion of an action verb in the instructions given to the group that directs them to take some joint or interdependent action on the ideas that individual members generate. For example, rather than simply asking students to "list" their ideas, the teacher might ask the group to *categorize* or *prioritize* their ideas—which requires its members to reach a collective decision about what categories should be used to classify their ideas or how their ideas should be ranked in priority order.

Research on students from from kindergarten through college indicates that when they work in well-structured collaborative learning groups, their academic performance and interpersonal skills are enhanced (Cuseo, 1996). Research also shows that when members of different racial groups work collaboratively toward the same goal, racial prejudice decreases and formation of interracial friendships increases (Allport, 1954, 1979; Amir, 1969, 1976; Brown et al., 2003; Dovidio, Eller, & Hewstone, 2011; Pettigrew & Tropp, 2000). These positive outcomes may be explained, in part, by the fact that when individuals from diverse racial and ethnic groups come together as members of the same team in pursuit of the same goal, nobody is a member of an "out" group ("them"); instead, everyone is a member of the same "in" group ("us") (Pratto et al., 2000; Sidanius et al., 2000). **Box 7.2** contains specific strategies for teachers interested in creating and facilitating diverse collaborative-learning teams.

Box 7.2 Tips for Teamwork: Creating Diverse & Effective Collaborative-Learning Teams

1. **Intentionally form learning teams of students with different cultural backgrounds and life experiences.** When students team up with friends or classmates whose backgrounds and experiences are similar to their own, it can actually interfere with the quality of their group work because like-minded teammates are more likely to get "off task" and onto topics that have nothing to do with the learning task (e.g., what they did last weekend or what they're planning to do next weekend).

   > "In life, we can't always work with others who are like-minded, nor should we want that as our goal because it limits the learning potential of the situation."
   >
   > —Peter DeWitt, in *School Climate: Leading with Collective Efficacy*

2. **Students should be given some time to interact informally with their teammates before tackling the group task.** Allowing groups some social "warm up" time prior to their collaborative work (e.g., to be sure they know each other's names and a little about one another), increases their sense of team identity and their comfort level about expressing their ideas. Creating an early foundation of familiarity and trust among group members is particularly important for learning teams composed of students from diverse (and unfamiliar) cultural backgrounds.

3. **The group's work culminate with the creation of a single work product.** When a group's goal is to complete the same "team product" (e.g., the same answer sheet, outline, or concept map), it serves to highlight the team's collaborative effort and collective achievement. Knowing that they will be creating and submitting a common final product also helps to keep individual members thinking in terms of "we" (not "me") and focused on moving together in the same direction toward the same goal.

4. **Group members should work interdependently—they should depend on one another to reach their common goal—their final work product—and all members should have equal opportunity to, and responsibility for, making an indispensable contribution to the final product.** Each teammate should contribute something distinctive and essential to completion of the team's end product, such as contributing: (a) a distinctive piece of *information* (e.g., a specific chapter from the textbook or a particular section of class notes), (b) a particular form of *thinking* (e.g., analysis, synthesis, or application), or (c) a different *perspective* (e.g., national, international, or global). Said in another way, each group member is responsible for bringing an important piece or part needed to complete the whole puzzle (final work product).

In addition to making a key cognitive contribution to the team, each team member could take on a distinctive social role, such as:

* manager—whose role is to ensure that the team stays on track, on time, and makes steady progress toward reaching its goal;

* moderator—whose role is to ensure that all teammates are being given equal opportunity to participate and contribute;

* devil's advocate (a.k.a. critical friend)—whose role is to identify limitations or oversights in the team's work;

* recorder—whose role is to keep track of the team's ideas (in writing);

* reporter—whose role is to report out the team's work to the teacher or other student groups.

5. **After group members complete their work, they should reflect on the collaborative learning experience.** The final step in any learning process, whether it be learning from a lecture or learning from group work, is to step back from the process and thoughtfully review it. As previously mentioned, deep learning requires effortful action (engagement) and reflection—thoughtful review of that action (Bligh, 2000; Roediger, Dudai, & Fitzpatrick, 2007). Students can engage in meaningful reflection on group-learning experiences, including their learning experiences in diverse groups, by responding to teacher-posed questions that prompt them to process the collaborative experience in terms of both it cognitive and social impact.

When interaction among students from diverse groups takes place under the five foregoing conditions, group work is transformed into teamwork. Research shows that when these conditions are met, it two important educational outcomes are achieved: (a) learning and thinking are strengthened, and (b) bias and prejudice are weakened (Allport, 1979; Amir, 1969; Aronson, Wilson, & Akert, 2013; Cook, 1984; Sherif et al., 1961).

To maximize the power of collaborative group work, implement the procedural principles of *cooperative learning*. Cooperative learning may be defined as a structured form of collaborative learning in which members of a learning team are intentionally assigned tasks or roles they perform individually—ensuring *individual accountability*, and interdependently—requiring individual members to rely on one another in the process of working toward a common goal, thus ensuring *collective responsibility* (Johnson & Johnson, 1989; Slavin, 1990). In a national study of K–12 teachers, one distinguishing characteristic of teachers whose students exhibited the greatest gains in academic achievement was their use of cooperative learning procedures designed with these two principles in mind (Dean et al., 2012; Marzano, Pickering, & Pollock, 2001).

More specifically, cooperative learning is an instructional methodology designed to maximize the educational impact of group work by infusing it with the following seven key procedural features (Cuseo, 1992).

1. *Intentional team formation*—rather than letting students self-select their groups or assigning students to a group randomly, the teacher forms groups intentionally with a particular educational objective in mind (e.g., students from diverse backgrounds are placed on the same team to foster student appreciation of multicultural perspectives).

2. *Intentional team building*—prior to embarking on the work task, group members engage in an icebreaker activity that gives them the opportunity to "warm up" to one another and build team spirit.

3. *Explicit instruction on collaboration and teamwork*—before beginning group work, students are given specific instruction on how to collaborate and work effectively in teams (e.g., how to engage in mutually supportive behavior, disagree constructively, resolve conflicts amicably, and reach group consensus).

4. *Positive interdependence* among team members (collective responsibility)—the group task is structured in such a way that students depend on one another for tackling different pieces of the total task, and when those pieces are integrated, it results in the completion of a single, jointly-created product.

5. *Individual accountability* (personal responsibility)—the task is structured so that each member makes a distinctive contribution to the group's work product, and if the contribution isn't made, its absence is clearly identifiable—as is the identity of the group member responsible for making that contribution.

6. The teacher assumes an active role during the group task, serving as a roving *coach and consultant* who circulates among teams to troubleshoot problems, encourage collective effort, and recognize students for exemplary teamwork.

7. After completing the group task, members "process" their work, reflecting on the quality of their collective work as a team, the quality of their personal contributions to the team (self-assessment), and the contributions of their teammates (peer assessment).

(For a more detailed description of the seven central features of *cooperative learning*, along with strategies for implementing each feature, see Appendix B.)

Research consistently shows that when the foregoing features of cooperative learning are implemented with fidelity, students experience significant gains in cognitive, social, and emotional development that exceed those produced by instructional methods that emphasize individualistic learning or competitive learning (Hattie, 2012; Johnson & Johnson, 1989; Slavin, 1990; Slavin, & Madden, 2001). Cooperative learning methods have been shown to be especially effective in promoting the academic achievement of Hispanic and

African American students (Aronson & Gonzalez, 1988; Posner & Markstein, 1994; Slavin, 2012). Research also indicates that when African American, Mexican American, and white students work together in cooperative learning teams, they develop more positive attitudes toward other racial groups and are more likely to form interracial friendships (Banks, 2016). Thus, cooperative learning may be viewed an instructional tool for converting student diversity into a social resource for advancing the goals of multicultural education (Gorski, 1995–2019).

> **Consider This . . .**
> When teachers create cooperative learning teams composed of students from different cultural backgrounds, they create opportunities for students to learn from and appreciate diversity within the context of a small, mutually supportive group of peers who interdependently toward a common goal.

Internet Resources

Building Positive Teacher-Student Relationships:
https://www.apa.org/education/k12/relationships

Icebreakers & Class Community-Building Activities:
https://www.pinterest.co.kr/amyp1302/relational-capacity-activities/

Prompts for Student Journals:
http://staff.esuhsd.org/danielle/english%20department%20lvillage/journals.html

Collaborative Learning Strategies:
https://www.edutopia.org/topic/collaborative-learning

Cooperative Learning & Teamwork:
https://www.teambonding.com/
cooperative-learning-activities-help-team-learn/

References

Abercrombie, M. L. J. (1960). *The anatomy of judgment.* New York: Hutchinson.

Adams, C. M., Forsyth, P. B., & Mitchell, R. M. (2009). The formation of parent-school trust: A multilevel analysis. *Educational Administration Quarterly, 45*(1), 4–33.

Adler, R. B., & Towne, M. (2014). *Looking out, looking in.* Boston, MA: Cengage.

Allport, G. W. (1954). *The nature of prejudice.* Cambridge, MA: Addison-Wesley.

Allport, G. W. (1979). *The nature of prejudice* (3rd ed.). Reading, MA: Addison-Wesley.

American College Personnel Association (ACPA) (1994). *The student learning imperative: Implications for student affairs.* Washington, D.C.: Author.

Amir, Y. (1969). Contact hypothesis in ethnic relations. *Psychological Bulletin, 71,* 319–342.

Amir, Y. (1976). The role of intergroup contact in change of prejudice and ethnic relations. In P. A. Katz (Ed.), *Towards the elimination of racism* (pp. 245–308). New York: Pergamon Press.

Aronson, E., & Gonzalez, A. (1988). Desegregation, jigsaw, and the Mexican-American experience. In P. A. Katz, & D. A. Taylor (Eds.), *Eliminating racism: Profiles in controversy.* New York: Plenum Press.

Aronson, E., Wilson, T. D., & Akert, R. M. (2013). *Social psychology* (8th ed.). Upper Saddle River, NJ: Pearson/Prentice Hall.

Astin, H. S., Astin, A. W., Bisconti, A. S., & Frankel, H. (1972). *Higher education and the disadvantaged student.* Washington, DC: Human Service Press.

Banks, J. A. (2016). *Cultural diversity and education: Foundations, curriculum, and teaching* (6th ed.). New York: Routledge.

Belenky, M. F., Clinchy, B., Goldberger, N. R., & Tarule, J. M. (1986). *Women's ways of knowing: The development of self, voice, and mind.* New York: Basic Books.

Bigler, R. S., & Hughes, J. M. (2009). The nature and origins of children's racial attitudes. In J. A. Banks (Ed.), *The Routledge international companion to multicultural education* (pp. 186–198). New York & London: Routledge.

Bligh, D. A. (2000). *What's the use of lectures?* San Francisco: Jossey-Bass.

Bowers, J. W. (1986). Classroom communication apprehension: A survey. *Communication Education, 35*(4), 372–378.

Boyer, E. L. (1987). *College: The undergraduate experience in America.* New York: Harper & Row.

Bransford, J. D., Brown, A. L., & Cocking, R. R. (2000). *How people learn: Brain, mind, experience and school.* Washington, D.C.: National Academy Press.

Brewer, M. B. (2000). Reducing prejudice through cross-categorization: Effects of multiple social identities. In S. Oskamp (Ed.), *Rethinking prejudice and discrimination* (pp. 165–184). Mahwah, NJ: Erlbaum.

Brown, K. T, Brown, T. N., Jackson, J. S., Sellers, R. M., & Manuel, W. J. (2003). Teammates on and off the field? Contact with Black teammates and the racial attitudes of White student athletes. *Journal of Applied Social Psychology, 33,* 1379–1403.

Bruffee, K. A. (1993). *Collaborative learning: Higher education, interdependence, and the authority of knowledge.* Baltimore: Johns Hopkins University Press.

Bruner, J. (1990). *Acts of meaning* Cambridge, MA: Harvard University Press.

Bryk, A. S., Sebring, P. B., Allensworth, E., Luppescu, S., & Easton, J. Q. (2010). *Organizing schools for improvement.* Chicago: University of Chicago Press.

Carter, R. (1998). *Mapping the mind.* Berkeley and Los Angeles: University of California Press.

Carter, R. (2008). *Multiplicity: The new science of personality, identity, and the self.* New York: Little Brown.

Cook, S. W. (1984). Cooperative interaction in multiethnic contexts. In N. Miller & M. B. Brewer (Eds.), *Groups in contact: The psychology of desegregation.* New York: Academic Press.

Cornelius-White, J. (2007). Learner-centered teacher-student relationships are effective: A meta-analysis. *Review of Educational Research, 77*(1), 113–143.

Crisp, R. J., Stone, C. H., & Hall, N. R. (2006). Categorization and subgroup identification: Predicting and preventing threats from common ingroups. *Personality and Social Psychology Bulletin, 27*(1), 76–89.

Cuseo, J. (1992). Cooperative learning: A pedagogy for diversity. *Cooperative Learning & College Teaching, 3*(1), pp. 2–6.

Cuseo, J. B. (1996). *Cooperative learning: A pedagogy for addressing contemporary challenges and critical issues in higher education.* Stillwater, OK: New Forums Press.

Cuseo, J. (2002). *Igniting involvement, peer interaction, and teamwork: A taxonomy of specific cooperative learning structures and collaborative learning strategies.* Stillwater, OK: New Forums Press.

Cuseo J. (2004). The student information sheet. *On Course Newsletter* (June). Monkton, MD.

David, L. (2015, June 20). *"Constructivism," in learning theories.* Retrieved from https://www.learning-theories.com/constructivism.html

Dean, C. B., Hubbell, E. R., Pitler, H., & Stone, B. (2012). *Classroom instruction that works: Research-based strategies for increasing student achievement* (2nd ed.) Alexandria, VA: Association for Supervision and Curriculum Development.

Dill, B. T., & Zambrana, R. E. (Eds.) (2009). *Emerging intersections: Race, class, and gender in theory, policy, and practice.* New Brunswick, NJ: Rutgers University Press.

Dovidio, J. F., Eller, A., & Hewstone, M. (2011). Improving intergroup relations through direct, extended and other forms of indirect contact. *Group Processes & Intergroup Relations, 14,* 147–160.

Duckworth, A. (2016). *Grit: The power of passion and perseverance.* London: Vermillion.

Eagly, A. H., & Johnson, B. T. (1990). Gender and leadership style: A meta-analysis. *Psychological Bulletin, 108,* 233–256.

Elbow, P. (1986). *Embracing contraries.* Oxford: Oxford University Press.

"Exploring Diversity" (2019, Fall). *Teaching Tolerance,* Issue 63, p. 16.

Gorski, P. C. (1995-2019). *Key characteristics of a multicultural curriculum.* Critical Multicultural Pavilion: Multicultural Curriculum Reform (An EdChange Project). Retrieved from www.edchange.org/multicultural/curriculum/characteristics.html

Gurin, P., Nagda, B. (R.) A., & Zúñiga, X. (Eds.) (2013). *Dialogue across difference: Practice, theory, and research on intergroup dialogue.* New York, NY: Russell Sage Foundation.

Hattie, J. A. C. (2009). *Visible learning: A synthesis of 800+ meta-analyses on achievement.* London: Routledge.

Hattie, J. (2012). *Visible learning for teachers: Maximizing impact on learning.* New York, NY: Routledge.

Hewstone, M., Rubin, M. & Willis, H. (2002). Intergroup bias. *Annual Review of Psychology, 53*(1), 575–604.

Howard, K. (2006). *Heterogeneity, race, and critical thinking.* Office of Institutional Research and Planning, University of Maryland. Retrieved from https://www.irpa.umd.edu/Publications/Presentations/2005_Heterogeneity_ Race_and_Critical_Thinking.pdf

Jackson, J. C., & Gefland, M. (2019, October 25). The ordinary diaries that bridged cultural divides. *Los Angeles Times,* p. A11. (To be published in *Behavioral Sciences and Policy.*)

Jensen, E. (1998). *Teaching with the brain in mind.* Alexandria, VA: Association for Supervision and Curriculum Development.

Johnson, D. W., & Johnson, R. T. (1989). *Cooperation and competition: Theory and research.* Edina, MN: Interaction Book Company.

Jones, J. (1989) Students' ratings of teacher personality and teaching competence. *Higher Education, 18,* 551–558.

Kagan, S. (1992). *Cooperative learning.* San Juan Capistrano, CA: Resources for Teachers, Inc.

Kagan, S. (1994). *Cooperative learning.* San Clemente, CA: Kagan Publishing.

Kagan, S. (1998). New cooperative learning, multiple intelligences, and inclusion. In J. Putnam (Ed.), *Cooperative learning and strategies for inclusion* (2nd ed.). Baltimore, MD: Paul H. Brookes.

Kagan, S. (2014). Kagan structures, processing, and excellence in college teaching. *Journal on Excellence in College Teaching, 25* (3-4), 119–138.

Kanter, R. M. (1977). Some effects of proportions on group life: Skewed sex ratios and responses to token women. *American Journal of Sociology, 5,* 965–990.

Karp, D. A., & Yoels, W. C. (1976). The college classroom: Some observations on the meanings of student participation. *Sociology and Social Research, 60,* 421–439.

Kurfiss, J. G. (1988). *Critical thinking: theory, research, practice, and possibilities.* ASHE-ERIC, Report No. 2. Washington, D.C.: Association for the Study of Higher Education.

Levitz. R. (1992). Minority student retention. *Recruitment & Retention in Higher Education, 6*(4), 4–5.

Linkov, V. (2014). Tokenism in psychology: Standing on the shoulders of small boys. *Integrative Psychological & Behavioral Science, 48*(2), 143–160.

Lyman, F. T. (1992). Think-pair-share, thinktrix, thinklinks, and weird facts: An interactive system for cooperative thinking. In N. Davidson & T. Worsham (Eds.), *Enhancing thinking through cooperative learning.* (pp. 169–181). New York, NY: Teachers College Press, Columbia University.

Magolda, M. B. B. (1992). *Knowing and reasoning in college.* San Francisco: Jossey-Bass.

Marzano, R., Pickering, D. J., & Pollock, J. (2001). *Classroom instruction that works: Research-based strategies for increasing student achievement.* Alexandria, VA: Association for Supervision and Curriculum Development.

Mercado, C. I. (2001). The learner: Race, ethnicity, and linguistic difference. In V. Richardson (Ed.), *The handbook of research on teaching* (4th ed., pp. 668–694). Washington, DC: American Educational Research Association.

Metz, G., Cuseo, J. B, & Thompson, A. (2019). *Peer-to-peer leadership: Research-based strategies for peer mentors and peer educators.* Dubuque, Iowa: Kendall Hunt.

Meyers, C. (1986). *Teaching student to think critically: A guide for faculty in all disciplines.* San Francisco: Jossey-Bass.

National Council for the Social Studies (NCSS). (1991). *Curriculum guidelines for multicultural education.* Retrieved from http://www.socialstudies.org/positions/multicultural

Neer, M. R. (1987). The development of an instrument to measure classroom apprehension. *Communication Education, 36,* 154–166.

Padrón, Y. N., Waxman, H.C., & Rivera C. (2002). Issues in educating Hispanic students. In S. Stringfield & D. Land (Eds), *Educating at-risk students.* Chicago: The University of Chicago Press.

Parker, W. B. (2006). Public discourses in schools: Purposes, problems, possibilities. *Educational Researcher, 35*(8), 11–18.

Pettigrew, T. F. & Tropp, L. R. (2000). Does intergroup contact reduce prejudice? Recent meta-analytic findings. In S. Oskamp (Ed.), *Reducing prejudice and discrimination* (pp. 93–114). Mahwah, NJ: Lawrence Erlbaum Associates.

Piaget, J. (1978). *Success and understanding.* Cambridge, MA: Harvard University Press.

Posner, H. B., & Markstein, J. A. (1994). Cooperative learning in introductory cell and molecular biology. *Journal of College Science Teaching, 23,* 231–233.

Pratt, D., & George, R. (2005). Transferring friendship: Girls' and boys' friendships in the transition from primary to secondary school. *Children & Society, 19*(1), 16–26.

Pratto, F., Liu, J. H., Levin, S., Sidanius, J., Shih, M., Bachrach, H., & Hegarty, P. (2000). Social dominance orientation and the legitimization of inequality across cultures. *Journal of Cross-Cultural Psychology, 31,* 369–409.

Rendón, L. I. (1994). Validating culturally diverse students: Toward a new model of learning and student development. *Innovative Higher Education, 19*(1), 23–32.

Rendón-Linares, L. I., & Muñoz, S. M. (2011). Revisiting validation theory: Theoretical foundations, applications, and extensions. *Enrollment Management Journal, 5*(2), 12–33.

Robinson, V. (2011). *Student-centered leadership.* San Francisco: Jossey-Bass.

Roediger, H. L., Dudai, Y., & Fitzpatrick, M. (Eds.) (2007). *Science and memory: Concepts.* Oxford: Oxford University Press.

Rogers, C. R. (1975). Can learning encompass both ideas and feelings? *Education, 95,* 103–106.

Rosser, S. V. (1988). Group work in science, engineering, and mathematics: Consequences of ignoring gender and race. *College Teaching, 46*(3), 82–88.

Scharf, A. (2018). *Critical practices for anti-bias education.* Teaching Tolerance: A Project of the Southern Poverty Law Center. Retrieved from https://www.tolerance.org/.../2019-04/TT-Critical-Practices-for-Anti-bias-Education.pdf

Schmid, M. E., Gillian-Daniel, D., Kramer, S., & Kueppers, M. (2016). Promoting student academic achievement through faculty development about inclusive teaching. *Change, 48*(5), 16–25.

Shayer, M. (2003). Not just Piaget; not just Vygotsky, and certainly not Vygotsky as alternative to Piaget. *Learning and Instruction, 13,* 465–485.

Sherif, M., Harvey, D. J., White, B. J., Hood, W. R., & Sherif, C. W. (1961). *The Robbers' cave experiment*. Norman, OK: Institute of Group Relations

Shernoff, D. J., Ruzek, E. A., & Sinha, S. (2016). The influence of the high school classroom environment on learning as mediated by student engagement. *School Psychology International, 38*(2), 201–218.

Sidanius, J., Levin, S., Liu, H., & Pratto, F. (2000). Social dominance orientation, anti- egalitarianism, and the political psychology of gender: An extension and cross-cultural replication. *European Journal of Social Psychology, 30,* 41–67.

Slavin, R. E. (1990). *Cooperative learning: Theory, research, and practice*. Englewood Cliffs, NJ: Prentice-Hall.

Slavin, R. E. (2012). Cooperative learning. In J. A. Banks (Ed.), *Encyclopedia of diversity in education* (Volume 1, pp. 453–456). Thousand Oaks, CA: Sage Publications.

Slavin, R. E., & Madden, N. A. (2001). *Reducing the gap: Success for all and the achievement of African-American and Latino students*. Washington, DC: Office of Educational Research and Improvement.

Smith, D. (1997). How diversity influences learning. *Liberal Education, 83*(2), 42–48.

Smith, D. (2015). *Diversity's promise for higher education: Making it work* (2nd ed.). Baltimore, MD: Johns Hopkins University Press.

Stambor, Z. (2006). How laughing leads to learning: Research suggests that humor produces psychological and physiological benefits that help students learn. *APA Monitor on Psychology, 37*(6), 62. Retrieved from http://www.ronberk.com/docs/media_laughing.pdf

Stephan, W. G., & Stephan, C. W. (2004). Intergroup relations in multicultural education programs. In J. A. Banks & C. A. M. Banks (Eds.), *Handbook of multicultural education* (2nd ed.), pp. 782–798. San Francisco, CA: Jossey-Bass.

Sunstein, C., & Hastie, R. (2015). *Wiser: Getting beyond groupthink to make groups smarter.* Boston, MA: Harvard Business School Publishing.

Thompson, A. & Cuseo, J. B. (2014). *Diversity and the college experience* (2nd ed.). Dubuque, Iowa: Kendall Hunt.

Tinto, V. (1997). Classrooms as communities: Exploring the educational character of student persistence. *Journal of Higher Education, 68*(6), 599–623.

van Engen, M. L., & Willemsen, T. M. (2004). Sex and leadership styles: A meta-analysis of research published in the 1990s. *Psychological Reports, 94,* 3–18.

Vygotsky, L. S. (1978). Internalization of higher cognitive functions. In M. Cole, V. John-Steiner, S. Scribner, & E. Souberman (Eds. & Trans.), *Mind in society: The development of higher psychological processes* (pp. 52–57). Cambridge: Harvard University Press.

Wiener, H. S. (1986). Collaborative learning in the classroom: A guide to evaluation. *College English, 48,* 52–61.

Wilkinson, I. A. G., Parr, J. M., Fung, I. Y. Y., Hattie, J. a. c., & Townsend, M. A. R (2002). Discussion: Modeling and maximizing peer effects in school. *International Journal of Educational Research, 37*(5), 521–535.

Ziv, A. (1988). Teaching and learning with humor: Experiment and replication. *Journal of Experimental Education, 57*(Fall), 5–15.

Reflections and Applications

7.1 Review the sidebar quotes contained in this chapter and select two that you think are particularly meaningful or inspirational. For each quote you selected, provide an explanation of why you chose it.

7.2 Review the strategies for *connecting students with their teacher and building positive student-teacher relationships* on **pp. 118–122**. Select three that you think are most important and intend to put into practice.

7.3. Look over the questions on the Student Information Sheet inlcuded in Appendix A (**p. 169**) and identify those questions that you think would be most appropriate or effective to ask students you're now working with or will be working with in the future.

7.4 What personal story or experience could you share with students to increase their trust in you and help them feel more comfortable about sharing their own stories with you?

7.5 Identify an icebreaker activity you think would be an effective way to "warm up" students to one another and establish an early sense of class community? (For possible options, see **pp. 123–124**)

7.6 If you were to intentionally form small learning teams composed of diverse students, what types or forms of student diversity do you think would be: (a) present in your classroom, and (b) most important to include in the groups you form?

7.7 Review the seven key procedural features of *cooperative learning* and the strategies suggested for implementing that are provided in Appendix B (**p. 173**). Identify a strategy associated with these features that you would think would be most appropriate and effective for the students you are now working with or will be working with in the future.

Culturally Inclusive Assessment: Evaluating Student Learning with Equity & Validity

Chapter Purpose and Preview

This chapter identifies a wide array of practices for evaluating and grading student performance both fairly and accurately. These assessment practices discussed in this chapter also increase students' motivation to learn and strengthen the quality of feedback students receive about their academic performance, serving to elevate the educational achievement of all students and the achievement of minority students in particular.

"An obvious question to pose when developing assessment instruments is, 'To what extent does this assessment promote quality and diversity simultaneously?'"

—Ginsberg & Wlodkowski, *Diversity & Motivation*

Principles of Effective and Culturally Inclusive Assessment

Listed below are principles central to the equitable and valid assessment of student learning and academic achievement. Some of these principles may be implemented more easily in certain subject areas than others, but most are applicable across the curriculum and at any level of education.

Student assessment should include outcomes relating to holistic ("whole person") development. Performance on standardized tests is an important and heavily emphasized measure of student learning, but it doesn't measure all ways in which students have learned and developed. Other relevant indicators of learning include such student outcomes as:

"Those schools with strong achievement may be in the most need for school climate overhaul because they may be focused on output and are not developing the student as a whole."

—Terrance Mootz, assistant superintendent, Cicero Illinois (quoted in DeWitt, 2018)

- ▶ Development of *lifelong learning* skills (e.g., learning how to learn, how to think deeply, and how to acquire and communicate knowledge)
- ▶ Development of *interpersonal* skills (e.g., enhancing social intelligence, intercultural communication skills, and leadership qualities)
- ▶ *Emotional* Development (e.g., understanding, managing, and expressing emotions effectively)
- ▶ *Ethical* Development (e.g., clarifying personal values, developing personal character and civic responsibility)
- ▶ *Physical* Development (e.g., acquiring and applying knowledge about one's body to minimize disease, maximize wellness, and achieve peak performance)
- ▶ *Identity* Development (e.g., developing a positive self-concept, self-efficacy, and a sense of personal direction or purpose).

"The multicultural curriculum should help student develop the skills necessary for effective interpersonal, interethnic, and intercultural group interactions."

—National Council for the Social Sciences

These different dimensions of development are interrelated. They do not operate independently, but intersect and interact with each other to affect student learning, development and personal well-being (Love & Love, 1995). For example, students' social and emotional well-being enhances their sense of self-efficacy (Bandura, 1997), and when students participate in educational programs that promote social emotional learning, they demonstrate greater gains in academic achievement (Durlak et al., 2011).

Research also indicates that when students engage in physical exercise through outdoor play, it not only reduces their risk of childhood obesity, it also enhances their social and emotional well-being (Wells & Evans, 2003) and elevates their level of academic achievement (Gable, Krull, & Chang, 2012). Children living in poverty are less able to go outside and play at home, which means that the increasingly common practice of canceling recess to increase class time and student performance on standardized tests may, ironically, have particularly detrimental effects on the academic achievement of low-income students (DeWitt, 2018).

Effective assessment of student learning should include assessment of changes in students' attitudes, behaviors, and cognition (ways of thinking). By definition, learning is a process of *change* (Ambrose et al., 2010). This change can take place in any of three key domains, sometimes referred to as the "ABCs" of student learning outcomes, namely:

> A = *Affective*—learning outcomes that involve change in students' *attitudes*, *perspectives*, or *viewpoints* (e.g., changes in their motivation to learn or attitude toward diversity)
>
> B = *Behavioral*—learning outcomes that involve change in students' *actions* (e.g., their frequency of interaction with members of diverse groups) and *habits* (e.g., improvement in their study skills or strategies)
>
> C = *Cognitive*—learning outcomes related to change in students' *knowledge* and *thinking* skills (e.g., their gaining more historical knowledge and ability to think critically).

A *variety* of assessment methods should be used to evaluate student learning. Effective assessment is diversified assessment; it avoids overreliance on a single method (Kornhaber, 2012). Using multiple, diverse methods of evaluation allows for cross-validation of student learning, which reduces the risk that the assessment outcome is unduly influenced or biased by the particular method used (Chapman & King, 2005). Research indicates that there is considerable variation among students in terms of their preference for, and comfort with, different methods of evaluation (Lowman, 1995; McKeachie, 1986). Timed classroom-based tests may be one student's meat but another student's poison. For students whom test-taking is not their preferred or strongest suit, evaluating their academic achievement with additional assessment methods supplies them with other, more personally compatible and equitable opportunities to demonstrate what they have learned. When teachers vary or rotate assessment methods, they increase the likelihood that all students will at least have occasional opportunities to demonstrate their

> "Talk with parents about what good learning looks like … Create a social-emotional learning team that includes a school counselor, teachers, administrator, nurse, parents, and students."
>
> —Peter DeWitt, in *School Climate: Leading with Collective Efficacy*

knowledge and skills in a format that matches their strongest suit (Sedlacek, 1993; Suskie, 2000).

Diversifying student assessment methods is consistent with the principles of Differentiated Instruction (Scharf, 2018) and Universal Design for Learning (UDL)—a cognitive neuroscience-based model developed at the Harvard Graduate School of Education that has been intentionally designed to accommodate students different differences in approaches to learning. This model calls for a curriculum that allows students multiple ways to acquire knowledge and express (demonstrate) the knowledge they acquire (Rose & Meyer, 2002). These multiple methods supply a more sensitive measure of the learning and engagement of minority students, enabling them to demonstrate academic competence and excellence in ways not captured by traditional indicators. As diversity scholar Daryl Smith points out, "If excellence means excelling on multiple-choice tests or raising one's hand first in class, then only a few will be deemed interested or excellent" (2015, p. 240).

> **Consider this ...**
>
> Using different evaluation methods creates a more comprehensive and balanced system of student assessment that has greater (a) *validity*—by counterbalancing the weaknesses of one method with the strengths of another, and (b) *equity*—by accommodating different skill sets that different students bring to the learning process.

One way in which teachers can diversify their assessment methods is by drawing them from the following categories:

- ▶ *product* assessments—e.g., written essays, stories, poems, research reports, or projects.
- ▶ *performance* assessments—e.g. tests, oral presentations, oral examinations, debates, science demonstrations, media presentations, or through artistic expression (visual arts, drama, or music) and
- ▶ *process* assessments—e.g. student interviews, journals, or portfolios (Ginsberg & Wlodkowski, 2009).

Teachers can also diversify assessment by basing their exams on information drawn from a *variety of informational sources* (teacher presentations, class discussions, assigned readings, etc.), and by assessing student work that's completed *inside* the classroom (e.g., quizzes or exams) and *outside* the classroom (e.g., take-home tests, assignments, or projects).

Students should have the opportunity to demonstrate their knowledge through *different communication modalities* (e.g., writing, speaking, and multi-media presentations). Just as students may differ in their preferences for acquiring knowledge, they may differ in their preferred way of expressing or demonstrating knowledge they've acquired. Thus, whenever possible, teachers should supply students with different avenues through which they can communicate and demonstrate what they have learned. An English teacher who was identified as "outstanding" by both her students and fellow teachers, routinely gave her students assignments in which they were to write two essays on a key topic. On the third assignment, students were allowed to choose from

"Principals and teachers who want to be leaders of student learning should consider using multiple forms of assessment."

—*Leadership for Student Success: A Partnership of the Laboratory for Student Success and the Institute of Leadership Development*

"Students generally need a range of opportunities and approaches to demonstrate what they know."

—Margery Ginsberg & Raymond Wlodkowski, in *Diversity and Motivation*

"Teachers should use multiple culturally sensitive techniques to assess cognitive and social skills."

—James A. Banks, *Cultural Diversity and Education*

among five or six other methods of evaluation. Among the options she offered to students were: (a) a third written essay, (b) a creative writing piece, (c) a dramatic act to be performed in front of class (alone or as part of a team project), or (d) an original video that students presented in class that could be created individually or in teams. Students were also allowed to suggest other methods for demonstrating their knowledge which, pending her approval, they could use (Wilson, 1987).

Assessment should include a balanced blend of methods that generate both *quantitative* **and** *qualitative* **evidence of student achievement.** *Quantitative* assessment involves collecting data on student learning in numerical form that's summarized statistically (e.g., average test scores on multiple-choice exams). *Qualitative* assessment involves collecting non-numerical ("human") data on student learning in non-numerical forms, such as students' spoken words, written words, or observable behaviors, which are summarized in the form of recurrent themes or patterns (e.g., thematic patterns that appear across students' written work on essay assignments or the ideas they deliver orally during group presentations and class discussions).

A major advantage of quantitative assessment is that the data collected on student performance can be efficiently and objectively scored by machine, requiring less teacher time to grade and providing students with faster feed-back. A disadvantage of quantitative data is that they provide little information on the thought process students used to arrive at their answers. The major disadvantage of qualitative assessment is that it relies on data that are more time-consuming and labor-intensive for teachers to grade; however, since the data are expressed in students' own words, richer information is generated about the thought processes that students used to arrive at their correct answers or led them astray.

Quantitative and qualitative evaluation methods should be viewed as *complementary*, not competing approaches to student assessment. When both are used, they provide a "mixed method" approach to assessment that is more comprehensive and cross-validating—because the disadvantages of one method are counterbalanced by the advantages of the other. Both methods may also be *integrated* into the same assessment item. For example, on a multiple-choice test question, qualitative data may be collected by asking students to accompany their selection with a short written statement about why they made that choice. These written responses can supply teachers with qualitative information on the nature of the thought process that led students to their thought product—the particular bubble they filled in on their answer sheet. The importance of teachers' gaining access to students' thought processes is underscored by educational researcher, John Hatie (2012a)

> [Effective] teachers have high levels of empathy, and know how to "see learning through the eyes of the students" and show students that they understand how they are thinking and how then their thinking can be enhanced. This requires that teachers pay special attention to the way in which students define, describe, and interpret phenomena and problem-solving situations, so that they can begin to understand these experiences from the unique perspectives of students (p. 100).

Teacher-constructed tests should call for for students' *recognition* knowledge and *recall* of knowledge. Different cognitive skills are used by students when they answer test questions that ask them to express and answer in their own words (e.g., an essay question) and test questions that ask them to select an answer from answers supplied for them in their own words (e.g., a multiple-choice question). The former requires students to *recall* correct information and the latter asks them to *recognize* it.: Neither of these types of questions is more valid or "authentic" than the other, and both engage students in higher-order thinking, but in different ways. Multiple-choice questions place more emphasis on analysis and thinking discriminatively; essay questions place more emphasis on synthesis and thinking integratively. At all levels of schooling, and in life beyond school, there will be times when students need to use cognitive skills that involve generating and synthesizing information on their own (e.g., orally or in writing), and times when they need to analyze information and make discriminating choices among options available to them (e.g., by reading or viewing). Thus, exposing students to test questions that require use of both of these cognitive skills is a good assessment practice. In addition to developing a wider range of thinking skills, this assessment practice also helps students prepare for the different types of tests they will encounter at higher levels of education and on certification exams required for entry into professional occupations (e.g., nursing, teaching, and law).

Thus, teacher-constructed exams should include a balance of blend of questions calling for knowledge recall (e.g., essay or short-answer questions) and questions calling for knowledge recognition (e.g., multiple-choice questions or true-false questions—which are essentially multiple-choice with two choice options). Different sections of the exam could be devoted to each of these types of testing formats, or the formats may be combined into the same test question. As previously noted, on multiple-choice and true-false questions, students could be asked to explain or justify their choices in writing, such as they would on an essay or short-answer question Or, students may earn bonus credit on multiple-choice questions and true-false questions for not only for choosing the correct answer, but also explaining (in writing) why it was correct (Zinsser, 1988). Students could also be awarded partial credit for making an incorrect choice if they provide a reasonable explanation why they thought it was correct. Allowing students the opportunity to offer an explanation for an answer they chose, particularly on test questions that may be more subjective in nature, acknowledges that there may be different ways to interpret a fact or a truth, which can help students move beyond oversimplified "dualistic" (right or wrong) thinking (Butler, 1993). This may be especially appreciated by students from diverse cultural backgrounds "whose experiences, behaviors, beliefs, and values may challenge an instructor's ways of understanding" (Ginsberg & Wlodkowski, 2009, p. 273).

Assessment should include assignments that encourage students to work *independently* (individually) and *interdependently* (in groups or teams). Developing students' capacity for independence and interdependence have been identified by postsecondary scholars as key student development outcomes (Chickering, 1969; Chickering & Reisser, 1993). Because students

"Teachers' feedback to students should attend to the content of their understanding in addition to the correctness of their answers."

—Vivian Robinson, in *Student-Centered Teaching*

are more likely to develop skills that they are evaluated on, or held accountable for doing, assessing students on their ability to work individually and collectively can foster student development of these competencies. This practice also makes assessment more inclusive by accommodating students from cultures that may differ with respect to valuing value individualism or interdependence.

On group projects, students should be assessed on the basis of both their *individual* and *collective* performance. Student surveys indicate that high-achieving students report high levels of dissatisfaction with group projects for which all members of the group receive the same grade, because they feel the individual effort they expended, and the personal contribution they made to the group's final product, exceeds the efforts and contributions of their less motivated teammates (Fiechtner & Davis, 1991). These findings strongly suggest that teachers avoid using the common and convenient practice of assigning a blanket "group grade" to all members of a learning team. Instead, *individual accountability* needs to be built into the process of evaluating group work. One way to do so is to ensure that the contributions of individual members are clearly identifiable (and assessable) by having each member assume responsibility for contributing a distinctive piece to the group's final product—e.g., a portion of textbook content, a section of a unit covered in class, or particular cultural perspective. To ensure that students also demonstrate *collective accountability*, they should also be assessed on how well they connect or integrate their personal contributions with the contributions of their teammates.

The Importance of Using Multiple and *Frequent Assessments*

Evaluating student achievement on a few high-stakes tests is a poor assessment practice because it relies on a small sample size to draw a general inferences about how much students have learned or achieved. Each separate assessment of student learning represents *one* estimate of student learning, which may be an underestimate or overestimate—referred to in statistics as an "error of measurement" (Dodge, 2003). Such measurement errors vary randomly across different assessments conducted at different times. Thus, the most effective way to decrease the magnitude of measurement errors is to increase the number of assessments, which serves to average out these random errors of underestimation and overestimation, resulting in a more accurate (valid) overall assessment of student achievement (Gage & Berliner, 1984; Gronlund, 1985).

In addition, if multiple assessments are used, students experience more frequent assessment which has the following educational benefits.

▶ Frequent assessment encourages students to "stay on top of things," providing them with an incentive to study consistently throughout the term, rather than procrastinating and letting their work pile up. This benefit of frequent assessment is supported by research showing that students who take weekly quizzes in advance of a major exam earn higher scores on the exam than students who just study for the exam without taking the weekly quizzes beforehand (Landrum, 2007).

▶ Frequent assessment enables students to focus on and learn a limited amount of material at a time, giving them more opportunity to learn the material deeply. Tests that cover large amounts of information are more likely to result in students using "surface learning" strategies (e.g., memorization) because the sheer quantity of material they're trying to digest leaves them with less time to learn it deeply (Ginsberg & Wlodkowski, 2009; Wieman, 2007).

▶ Frequent assessment helps students successfully complete larger assignments that require work to be done over an extended period of time. On large, long-term assignments, students could be asked to submit partial, sequential "installments" that the teacher assesses at interim points throughout the term. For example, for a research report or project due at the end of the term, students might submit separate installments of their work in the following sequence of stages: (a) topic identification after two weeks; (b) annotated bibliography by four weeks; (c) outline by eight weeks; (d) first draft by the tenth week; (d) second draft by the twelfth; and (e) final draft at the end of the term.

By submitting work in multiple installments, having those work installments assessed and receiving ongoing receiving frequent feedback the teacher, students are more likely to stay on track and make steady progress. Frequent installments also serve to minimize procrastination and task avoidance because the task seems less overwhelming when it's attacked in smaller, more manageable steps. Supporting this point are studies show that writing tasks are less likely to be avoided and "writer's block" less likely to be experienced when writing is completed in small steps with specific deadlines set for completing each step (Kellogg, 1994; Rennie & Brewer, 1987). Having students submit frequent installments of their written work is also an effective instructional strategy for detecting plagiarism and "ghost writing."

▶ Frequent assessment results in students being assessed earlier in the term and receiving *early feedback*, thus enabling them to make adjustments in their learning habits and strategies to improve their subsequent performance. Students are also likely to be motivated to attend to early teacher feedback because it comes soon enough in the term for them to take action on it to improve their final grade.

Lastly, early assessment benefits teachers because it enables them to proactively identify and address individual differences in students' class-entry skills and level of preparation (Education Commission of the States, 1995).

Using Assessment Practices that Increase Students' *Intrinsic Motivation* to Learn

Motivation to learn may be either (a) *extrinsic*—driven by external factors, such as getting good grades and pleasing parents, or (b) *intrinsic*—driven by internal factors, such as intellectual curiosity and the joy of learning or mastering interesting cognitive tasks. Studies show that when students motivation to learn is intrinsic, they learn more deeply (Deci & Flaste, 1995; Pink, 2009). In contrast, when student motivation is driven by extrinsic rewards, it's more likely to result in "shallow learning of surface features and completion of work regardless of the standard and for the sake of praise or similar rewards" (Hattie, 2012a, p. 42). The following assessment practices are recommended for increasing students' intrinsic motivation to learn material on which they will be evaluated and graded.

Design test questions that relate to current events and are relevant to their personal lives (e.g., home life, peer relations, or future plans). Students become more intrinsically motivated to prepare for tests covering content that has real-world relevance, relates to their life experiences, or fits within "their frame of reference" (Wlodkowski, 2008). When assessment is situated in a context that is meaningful to students, it becomes more "authentic" (and culturally relevant).

Invite students to construct and submit test questions to include on exams. This practice can increase students' level of engagement in the test-preparation process, and in so doing, increase their sense of ownership or control of the performance-evaluation process—which increases intrinsic motivation to engage in the performance task and reduces performance anxiety (Thompson, 1981). In addition, this practice sends a message of high expectations to students by suggesting to them that their teacher respects their ideas and ability to ask relevant questions. To incentivize student submission of test questions, points could be awarded to students who construct questions and additional awarded to students whose questions are judged by the teacher to be worthy of inclusion on the exam.

When assigning projects or papers, supply students with a topic menu from which they may choose a subject that most interests them. Studies consistently show that when people are given choices and opportunities to make their own decisions about what they will do, it increases their sense of self-determination and their intrinsic motivation to do what they've chosen to do (Deci & Flaste, 1995). Consequently, giving students choices and decision-making opportunities about the academic tasks they are to perform, their intrinsic motivation to perform those tasks is likely to increase, and they are more likely to view their engagement as being self-determined, rather than being controlled or compelled by someone else (e.g., their teacher).

When students are given an assignment, accompany it with a rationale for why it's being assigned. Taking just a moment of time to explain the

> "Assessment that is culturally responsive illuminates the connection between knowledge as others have defined it and meaning that is relevant to individual experiences and belief systems."
>
> —Ginsberg & Wlodkowski, *Diversity & Motivation*

purpose of an assignment and its benefits can decrease the likelihood that students will perceive it as academic "busy work" and increase the level of effort they invest in it. Research consistently shows that students' academic motivation and academic performance increase significantly when they perceive class assignments to be personally relevant (Hulleman & Harackiewicz, 2009; Hyungshim, 2008). This has been found to be particularly true of students from underrepresented groups (Winkelmes, 2013).

Devise assignments that ask students to apply course concepts to current events occurring at school or in the local community. For instance, students could be given assignments that ask them to locate current events in the popular media (e.g., by perusing the local or national news) and relate those events to topics covered in class (e.g., by creating a collage or scrapbook composed of class-relevant newspaper articles, pictures, and cartoons). Students might also be asked to review the classified section of the local newspaper to find an ad for a position that interests them. They can then write a letter of application for the position in which they describe knowledge, skills, and attributes they are learning or developing at school that would make them a desirable candidate. (Prior to the assignment, local employers might be invited to class to discuss what they look for in a well-written letter of application.)

After completing assignments, have students reflect on their and assess what they learned. This practice may be efficiently implemented by including a short final step that asks students to write a brief reflection on (a) what they thought was the major objective or intended learning outcome of the assignment, (b) whether they experienced the assignment's intended outcome, and (c) if they learned or took away something else from the assignment other than its intended outcome—which is an important one to ask because students can experience unanticipated learning outcomes—referred to by educational researchers as "collateral learning" or "incidental learning."

Create assignments that encourage students to make connections between different class topics or instructional units. For example, after covering a unit on diversity, students could be given an assignment that asks them to connect ideas discussed in the diversity unit with ideas previously covered in units on history or geography. Prompting students to make cross-unit connections engages them in the cognitive processes of integration and synthesis, both of which are valuable higher-order thinking skills (Anderson & Krathwohl, 2001; Bloom, Hastings, & Madaus, 1971). The human brain is naturally wired to seek patterns and make connections (Caine & Caine, 1991, 1994; Jensen, 2008). In fact, when learning takes place in the brain, actual physical (neurological) connections are formed between brain cells (Zull, 2011). Thus, assignments that ask students to make connections between concepts promote "brain-based" or "brain-compatible" learning (Jensen, 2008).

> "The closer assessment procedures come to allowing learners to demonstrate what they have learned in the areas where they will eventually use that learning, the greater will be their motivation to do well."
>
> —Ginsberg & Wlodkowski, *Diversity & Motivation*

Consider this ...
Assessments that encourage students to make conceptual connections between different concepts build stronger neurological connections in the brain, making learning more meaningful and memorable.

Using Assessment Practices that Increase the Likelihood Students Will Succeed and Demonstrate Academic Excellence

As suggested by the common expression, "I know it when I see it," students are more likely to exhibit excellence if they know what it looks like. Showing students concrete examples of outstanding work provides them with models to aspire to and perhaps surpass. The following strategies may be used to help students actually "see" what excellence looks like and inspire them to achieve it.

Provide students with examples or illustrations of excellent (grade "A") work achieved by previous students. Teachers could save different forms of outstanding work demonstrated by students in classes they have taught in the past (e.g., outstanding student essays, presentations, or projects) and share them with current students as models worthy of emulation. The exemplar of excellence could be the total work of a single student (e.g., an outstanding research paper written by that student), or exemplars of different components of a total work product submitted by different students, each of which illustrates excellence with respect to that particular component. For example, the class could be shown selected portions of a research paper submitted by different students that illustrate excellence with respect to: (a) a well-written introduction and thesis statement, (b) effective paragraph construction and transitions, (c) strong conceptual arguments and research documentation, and (d) a powerful summary and conclusion.

Providing students with visible exemplars of outstanding work can help them them get a clearer understanding of what excellence looks like and stimulate their motivation to achieve it. At the very least, this should reduce the likelihood that teachers will hear student complaints like the following: "I'm not really sure how my essay answers can be improved to give her what she wants" (Erickson & Strommer, 1991, p. 49).

Before having students begin work on an assignment, equip them with a *checklist of criteria* or *scoring rubric* that will be used to evaluate their work product. The criteria that a teacher use to assess and grade students' performance shouldn't be concealed from students or sprung on them after the fact. As DeWitt (2018) notes: "It all begins with learning intentions and success criteria. This can be controversial for teachers because [sharing] success criteria means showing students what success looks like before they complete a learning task in the classroom. This should not be so controversial. Imagine sending a child into a soccer game without his or her ever having watched a soccer match on television or in real life" (p. 89).

Sharing performance-evaluation criteria with students ahead of time enables them to self-assess the quality of their work and self-correct their mistakes during the learning process. Supporting the effectiveness of this practice are the results of meta-analyses of numerous research studies indicating that

> "Evidence that other students—students just like them—have done excellent work is a strong motivator."
>
> —Robert E. Scott & Dorothy Echols Tobe, *Communicating High Expectations*

> "Teachers must develop a scoring rubric for any assignment and show the rubric to the students so that they know what the teacher values. Such formative feedback can reinforce the 'big ideas' and the important understandings, and help to make their investment of energy worthwhile."
>
> —John Hattie, *Visible Learning for Teachers: Maximizing Impact on Learning*

instructional practices which promote the development self-directed, "assessment-capable learners" have a very large effect on student learning (Hattie, 2009, 2012b).

The following checklist of criteria could be shared with students who have been assigned a research paper so they may self-assess and self-direct their work before submitting it.

- *Organization*. Does my paper include:
  - ___ an introduction with a clear thesis statement?
  - ___ well-defined section headings?
  - ___ clear transitions between paragraphs?
  - ___ a conclusion that relates to to the thesis statement?

- *Documentation*. Does my paper include:
  - ___ a variety of references rather than reliance on limited and similar sources?
  - ___ use of some primary sources rather than to exclusive reliance on secondary references (e.g. textbooks)?
  - ___ a blend of historical sources and current publications?

- *Presentation*. Is my paper presented in a format that is consistent with the guidelines I received about:
  - ___ page margins?
  - ___ line spacing?
  - ___ paper length?
  - ___ how references are to be cited in the body of the paper?
  - ___ how references are to be cited in the works-cited section at the end of the paper?

Teachers could create checklists of evaluation criteria like this for any assignment and share it with students in advance so they may self-assess the quality of their work while they are working and improve the quality of their final work product before submitting it for teacher evaluation and grading.

A variation of this strategy would be to supply students with a checklist of assessment criteria beginning work on an assignment and have them use it to evaluate work products of varying quality submitted by students from previous classes. This practice can sharpen students' awareness of the factors that differentiate excellent, average, and subpar work, and help them keep these factors in mind while completing their own work. Supporting this practice is supplied by research indicating that the quality of students' written work improves significantly if they are first given the opportunity to review examples of excellent and poor writing and identify criteria they will use to evaluate the quality of their own writing (White, 1985).

Improving Student Achievement on Classroom Tests by Clarifying Learning and Performance Expectations

Students performance on classroom exams should accurately reflect what students have learned or achieved and not be compromised by inadequate instruction, unclear test instructions, or poor test construction. The following practices, maximize the likelihood that student performance classroom tests are not contaminated by factors relating to the quality of instruction received by students prior to the test or the quality of the test itself.

In advance of an exam, students should be provided with as much relevant information as possible about the test's *format*. When students are less uncertain about the nature of an upcoming test: (a) the more effectively they can prepare be for the test, (b) the less anxiety they experience during the test, and (c) the more likely their test results are a valid indicator of what they have learned. To reduce students' uncertainty about a forthcoming exam, the following information could (and should) be shared with students prior to the exam:

- ▶ the amount of time they will have to complete the exam
- ▶ the number and nature of questions (e.g., how many test questions and how many of them will be essay, multiple-choice, or true-false questions);
- ▶ the point value that different types of test questions will carry (e.g., if the test will consist of multiple-choice and essay questions, what percentage of the total test grade will be determined by each of these types of questions),
- ▶ the materials that students should bring, and are allowed to bring, to the exam (e.g., calculators, but not cell phones).

To ensure that students are clear about what they are to study and learn, provide them with *specific learning objectives* prior to the exam. If students are simply told that the test will "cover material covered in class and in your assigned reading," they are basically being told that "everything is important." Not all material covered in class or in their assigned readings is equally important and warrants equal study time. Because students are not subject matter experts, they're not always able to identify concepts that require the most attention and deepest learning. Supplying students with specific learning objectives helps them focus their attention and study time on the most important concepts they're expected to master, thus they spend the brunt of their study time learning what is central and critical, and less time memorizing what is peripheral or trivial.

Teachers who take the time to construct specific learning objectives not only help students by supplying them with an effective study guide, they also helps themselves by (a) prioritizing what they want their students to learn, and (b) designing exams that have *content validity*—exams that ensure alignment between content assessed and content taught (Anastasi & Urbina, 1997).

> "The only instructional sin greater than teaching trivial information is to test and grade students about such knowledge."
>
> —Stanford Ericksen, *The Essence of Good Teaching*

Supplying students with specific learning objectives before exams should not be misconstrued as "giving away" test answers or "teaching to the test." Students can be directed to critical concepts and instructed how they are expected to demonstrate their knowledge of these concepts without being shown the exact questions that will appear on the exam. For example, a specific learning objective could state that students will be expected to *evaluate* cultural bias in the reporting of historical incidents, or students will be expected to *apply* the concept of privilege to a current event. Neither of these specific learning objectives reveals to students the exact test question that will be used to assess their mastery of the objective. Students do know, however, that these are concepts on which they should spend study time and think deeply about because they will be tested on them.

Whether or not teachers "teach to the test," students will "study to the test"—they will study what they think (or guess) will be on the exam (Frederiksen, 1984; Gamson, 1993). Learning objectives minimize the guessing game and reduce the risk that students will spend their study time studying "the wrong things."

Specific learning objectives should not only inform students about what they are expected to know but also *how* they will be expected to show they know it. Learning objectives can be phrased in a way that alerts students to how they will be tested on the concept targeted by the objective. For instance, if student learning of a concept is to be tested with a multiple-choice or true-false question, the learning objective for that concept should contain the verb "recognize"—because that's how students will be expected to demonstrate their knowledge of the concept—by recognizing the correct answer among answers provided for them (rather than producing the answer on their own). In contrast, if student knowledge of the concept is to be tested with a short-answer or essay question, which will require them to recall or generate the answer on their own, the learning objective should contain a verb like "cite," "provide," or "supply." These action verbs alert students to what action they will be expected to do on the exam to demonstrate their knowledge of the concept—by producing the correct answer on their own, rather than selecting it from answers provided for them. Teachers may want to use recognition test questions (e.g., multiple-choice or true-false) for subject matter they think students should just be familiar with; for concepts they think students should actively rehearse, be able recall on their own, and express in their own words, recall test questions may be better suited (e.g., short answers or essay).

Because multiple-choice and true-false questions ask students to recognize the correct answer among answers provided for them, a learning objective which indicates the concept will be tested in this way signals to students that they can study it by carefully examining information in their class notes and textbook about it and knowing it well enough to be able to recognize accurate information relating to it. This is an effective study strategy for students to use because they are studying the concept in a way that aligns with how they will be tested on it—by reading about it on the exam and recognizing correct information relating to it. On the other hand, recall test questions (e.g., short-answer questions and essay questions) do not require answer recognition, but answer *production*—students must produce information on their own. If they were to study

▶ Specific learning objectives *increase motivation to study* because students see a clear connection between what they are studying and what they will be tested on. Nothing may be more disheartening and demotivating for students than to study hard for a test and discover later (during the test) that they studied "the wrong things." Research shows that when students (and humans in general) do not perceive a connection between the effort they expend and the results they achieve, it lowers their self-efficacy (Bandura, 1997) and can create a sense of "learned helplessness" (Seligman, 1998).

▶ Specific learning objectives enable students to *self-monitor* their learning and identify concepts they have not mastered—*before* they are tested on those concepts. Said in another way, learning objectives enable students to engage in proactive self-diagnosis, helping them detect gaps in their learning and pinpoint sources of confusion before they adversely affect their test score and class grade.

▶ Specific learning objectives *reduce test anxiety.* Research indicates that when people's task-performance expectations match the performance task, people experience less performance anxiety (Tracey & Sherry, 1984). Specific learning objectives increase the match between students' expectations of how they will be expected to perform and the actual performance task (the test), thus reducing test anxiety. (Reducing students' test anxiety should also reduce the need for teachers to respond to the perennial, test-anxious student question: "Will this be on the test?")

▶ Providing students with specific learning objectives promotes *teacher-student rapport.* Teachers who take the time and make the effort to supply students with study guides in the form of specific learning objectives are more likely to be perceived as being transparent and helpful—as opposed to playing a guessing game or game of "keep away"—withholding information about the test and then "ambushing" students on the test with "trick questions." The importance of teacher transparency for promoting teacher rapport with the class is underscored by the results of a major survey that asked students to list teacher behaviors that inhibit positive teacher-student relationships. Among the top-ten inhibitors reported by students were teachers who: (a) "are not specific about what the test will cover," (b) "create trick questions," and (c) "give tests that don't correspond to lectures" (Ludweig, 1993).

for an essay test question by just looking over their class notes and reviewing their reading highlights, they would be using a study strategy that does not match what they will be expected to do on the test itself—which is to recall the answer and produce it on their own. Learning objectives that alert to students to information they will be expected to recall produce on their own signals to them that this material needs to be studied with strategies that involve rehearsal and memory *retrieval*—such as reciting the information without looking at it.

Highly motivated and capable students may underachieve on exams because they studied the wrong things, or because they studied the right things in the wrong way. Whether students will demonstrate their knowledge of material they studied on exams they studied depends on whether they studied it in a way that aligns with the way they're tested on it (Karpicke & Roediger, 2008). Effective learning objectives ensure this alignment by informing students not only about *what* concepts they are expected to know for the test, but also *how* they will be tested on those concepts.

In addition to helping students prepare for exams, specific learning objectives have a number of other educational benefits, such as those included in **Figure 8.1**.

TABLE OF SPECIFICATIONS

Figure 8.1

Content Area	Thinking Process		
	Application	Evaluation	Synthesis
Bias			
Privilege			
Discrimination			

Learning objectives should be constructed that prompt that students to engage in higher-order thinking. The thought processes that students are required to use on tests and assignments influences the thought processes they will use when studying and preparing for tests and assignments. If teachers want students to engage in higher-order thinking (e.g., analysis, evaluation, synthesis), students are more likely to engage in those important cognitive skills if teachers actually require them to use those skills on tests and assignment. As John Hattie (2012a) notes, "Students are very good at ignoring what you say ('I value connections, deep ideas, your thoughts') and seeing what you value (corrections to the grammar, comments on referencing, correctness, or absence of facts)" (p. 88).

Research indicates that higher-order thought processes, such as critical and creative thinking, are suppressed when they must be performed under time pressure (Hart, 1983; Hertel & Brozovich, 2010). If students spend their study time studying facts, it's unlikely they will suddenly be able to engage in the higher-order thinking skill of integrating and synthesizing those facts during a timed exam. If students are supplied with specific learning objectives before exams that call for them engage in higher-order thinking during their study time, it gives them the time and incentive to develop those skills and apply them at test time (Marton & Saljo, 1976).

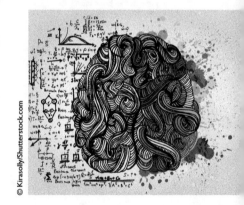

© Kirasolly/Shutterstock.com

Teachers can specify particular content (concepts) on which students are expected to engage in higher-order thinking by creating a "table of specifications" (Chase, 1999), also known as a content-by-process matrix, which crosshatches concepts to be tested with specific higher-order thinking processes that students are expected to apply to those concepts. (**See Figure 8.1**.) By ensuring that entries appear in each cell of the matrix, teachers ensure that their exams are targeting key concepts and encouraging students to engage in higher-order thinking with respect to those concepts.

It does take time to construct and supply students with specific learning objectives, but what it costs teachers in time is likely to be far outweighed by the benefits gained in student learning and teacher-student rapport. This favorable cost/benefit ratio is captured in the following reflections of an instructor who implemented the practice of constructing study guides with specific learning objectives:

I decided to try using more detailed study guides. These guides would be questions from which exam questions would be drawn, thus ensuring that the students paid attention. Making these decisions required substantial effort but deepened my understanding of my objectives. I often gave questions that asked for more careful analysis, synthesis, and critical thinking than I had been able to use previously. Even so, grades quickly rose. What I had come to gradually was an outcome-based course design (Nelson, 2010, pp. 184–185).

Using the Results of Classroom Tests to Enhance Student Learning and Teaching Effectiveness

Teacher-constructed tests are more than just a tool for evaluating students and assigning them grades. Classroom tests serve two other key evaluative purposes: (a) *summative* evaluation—to "sum up" and *prove* that students are learning, and (b) *formative* evaluation—to "shape up" and *improve* teaching effectiveness. Research on high-performing schools reveals that one of their distinguishing practices is using students' test results to improve their instructional programs (Heck, Marcoulides, & Lang, 1991).

> "When the cook tastes the soup, it is formative [evaluation]; when the guests tastes the soup, it is summative [evaluation]."
>
> —Robert Stake, Professor Emeritus of Education, University of Illinois

Class performance patterns should be used as feedback to improve the quality of teaching and the quality of teacher-constructed tests. One way in which teachers can use students' test results to improve both the effectiveness of their teaching and the validity of their testing is by conducting an *item analysis* of the class's test performance. Item analysis involves computing the percentage of students in class that answer each test item correctly and then analyzing this information to pinpoint specific test items on which the largest percentage of students performed poorly. Students' poor performance on certain test questions may result from reasons other than their failure to master the concept tested by the question—such as students not receiving adequate instruction on the concept prior to the test, or the question being awkwardly worded.

It may also be possible that the question was culturally biased, leading to different interpretations by students from different cultural groups. For example, consider the following math problem that was once presented to a class of students from different socioeconomic backgrounds: "It costs $1.50 to travel each way on the city bus. A transit system 'fast pass' costs $65 a month. Which is the more economical way to get to work: the daily fare or the fast pass?" Students from higher-income suburban families immediately interpreted the question to mean that the individual in the problem was commuting to work five days per week at a rate of $3 per day. However, lower-income, inner-city students didn't always interpret it this way and were more likely to seek further clarification by asking questions like: "How many jobs are we talking about?" and "Is it a part-time job?" (Ladson-Billings, 1995a, 1995b). This example suggests that item analysis be conducted for different subgroups of students to assess whether a disproportionate number of students from certain cultural groups performed poorly on particular items. This information may then be used to improve the equity of future exams.

After conducting item analysis, test scores and test grades could be readjusted if students lost points lost on ambiguously worded or culturally biased questions. On future tests, these test questions could be rewritten. If item-analysis reveals that were other test items on which a large number of students in class performed poorly, these concepts items could be re-taught at a slower pace, or with greater scaffolding, to improve students' learning of them. As Vivian Robinson (2011) points out in *Student-Centered Leadership*: "Questions must always be asked about the causes of student progress or lack of it and the skill and effort being put into crafting the conditions that are needed for improvement. If those efforts are of high-quality, then over time the outcome will improve" (p. 90).

Another way in which teachers can obtain feedback that may be used to improve the quality of their test construction and students' test preparation is to ask students about the test after they receive their results. For example, students could be asked:

▶ Were there questions or concepts included on the exam that you didn't expect to see?

▶ Which questions or parts of the exam did you find most challenging? Most confusing?

▶ How much time did you spend preparing for this test?

▶ Did you receive the grade you expected? Why?

▶ Based on the amount of time and effort you put into preparing for this test, do you think the grade you received was an accurate reflection of how much you learned?

▶ Now that you have experienced the test and seen your test results, would you have studied for it differently? If yes, in what way(s)?

These questions can be used as a springboard to launch students into an honest discussion of the quality of their test preparation and the quality of the test itself. Teachers can then use student feedback generated from this discussion to improve the clarity and validity of their subsequent exams. Seeking out and responding to student feedback is a good teaching practice in general, and because it respect the input of all students, it can be a particularly effective way to provide personal validation to students from minority cultural groups (Ginsberg & Wlodkowski, 2009).

Students should be allowed opportunities to *retake exams or re-submit assignments* to *improve* the quality of their work and class grade. Supporting this recommendation is research indicating that when students are given the opportunity to repeat and improve their performance on tests or assignments, they typically make significant gains in learning and academic achievement (Bloom, 1984; Wormeli, 2006). Effective learners learn from their mistakes and use them as feedback to strengthen their subsequent performance. Providing opportunities for students to review, revise, and improve their work is consistent with the "mastery learning" model of education. This model posits that initial differences among students in their

> "The key to linking diversity to effectiveness is not only regularly collecting and analyzing detailed data on students ... but by *disaggregating* the data by race, ethnicity, gender, and economic class."
>
> —Daryl G. Smith, professor emerita of education and psychology, Claremont Graduate University

level of achievement on tests and other measures of learning do not reflect differences in their ability or potential to learn. Instead, these initial differences in achievement reflect the fact that students need different amounts of time, practice, and feedback before they are able to master certain concepts.

Advocates of the mastery learning model don't deny that individual differences exist among students in natural (innate) abilities and talents. However, they view these differences as differences in the *rate* or *speed* at which individual students are able to learn particular concepts or skills (Bloom, 1968, 1978; Levine, 1985). Differences in students' initial level of achievement often reflect differences in their prior cultural experiences and learning opportunities. If students who initially display lower levels of achievement are given additional time and opportunity to learn the material and are motivated to learn it, they will eventually achieve a level of mastery comparable to students who performed well from the start.

Naturally, if teachers allow students to re-learn material, retake tests, and resubmit assignments, an upward shift in class grades is likely to follow. Such an an elevation of grades should be viewed as a welcomed development if the purpose of education is to maximize the level of academic achievement of all students, and particularly disadvantaged students whose gap in achievement stems from their less-privileged backgrounds. When students are willing to put in the extra time and effort to correct their mistakes and improve their performance, teachers should neither feel guilty about, nor criticized for, "lowering academic standards" or "dumbing down the curriculum." For teachers who still fear that giving students an extra opportunity to improve their academic performance will lead to "grade inflation," some of that fear can be mitigated by averaging students' first and second scores rather than replacing their lower first score with their higher second score.

Teachers should consider using a "forgiving" grading system that allows students to drop their lowest test score. This practice acknowledges and accommodates the reality that student performance on a particular day may have been compromised by illness, stress, or other interfering issues. Such a

"We need to distinguish between bad inflation resulting from unjustifiably high grades and good grade inflation [resulting] from more effective pedagogy and consequently improved achievement."

—Craig Nelson, Professor Emeritus of Biology, Indiana University; President, International Society for the Scholarship of Teaching and Learning

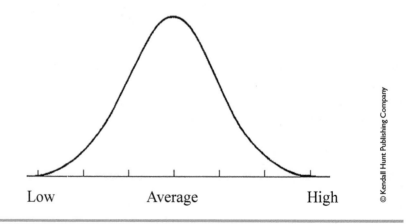

Figure 8.2

The Normal or Bell-Shaped Curve

Low   Average   High

© Kendall Hunt Publishing Company

forgiving grading system sends a message to students that their teacher is sensitive to their life circumstances and personal challenges outside the classroom. This message is likely to be especially appreciated by underprivileged students who may be experiencing particularly challenging life circumstances.

Dropping a student's lowest grade might be more appropriately applied to smaller tests or quizzes than to major exams and assignments. Used in this manner, the practice is less likely to be viewed as diluting academic rigor or lowering academic standards.

To maximize the learning and academic achievement of all students, teachers should use a grading system that is *criterion-referenced* rather than norm-referenced. A student's grade should reflect how much or how well that student has learned. A *criterion*-referenced grading system bases a student's grade on a set, performance-based standard or criterion (e.g., percentage of questions the student answered correctly). In contrast, *norm*-referenced grading bases a student's grade on how well the student performs (ranks) in relation to other students. Students who score higher than most of their classmates receive a high grade; students who score in the middle of the pack receive an average grade; and students who score lowest (relative to their peers) receive a low grade. This grading scheme is designed a "normal" distribution (bell-shaped curve) of grades, as illustrated in **Figure 8.2**.

> "Grade students against learning objectives, not against other students."
>
> —*Critical Practices for Anti-bias Education*, Southern Poverty Law Center

The common belief that student grades should be distributed in this bell-shaped fashion shouldn't take precedence over student-evaluation methods that maximize the learning of all students and shift the curve to the right. If teachers are explicitly expected or tacitly encouraged to produce a bell-shaped distribution of grades, they will consciously or unconsciously engage in teaching and testing practices that ensure it happens, even if these practices do not improve the learning of all students and reduce achievement gaps.

Practices Ensuring a "normal curve" distribution of grades is also clearly inconsistent with the idea of holding high expectations for all students, which is an idea supported by a formidable body of research (Rosenthal & Jacobs, 1968; Dusek & Gail, 1983; Rubie-Davies, 2014). Grading on a curve is also inconsistent with the principles of mastery learning and growth mindset. As Hattie (2012a) points out: "Mastery goals arise when students aim to develop their competence and they consider ability to be something that can be developed by increasing effort. Performance goals arise when students aim to demonstrate their competence, particularly by outperforming peers, and they consider ability to be fixed, and not malleable or able to be changed" (p. 43).

Moreover, curve grading can lead to student tracking and creating unequal educational opportunities. As Burris (2014) warns: "Ranking students based on their perceived intellectual abilities can result in different access to academic curriculum and the opportunity to learn" (p. 3). Curve grading is a competitive grading scheme that essentially pits students against one another. Research in social psychology reveals that when people compete for limited resources with from unfamiliar or disliked racial and ethnic groups, negative attitudes toward members of these groups are intensified (Burgess & Sales, 1977; Swap, 1977; Worchel & Austin, 1986). Thus, a curve grading scheme is more likely to impair rather than improve interethnic and interracial harmony (Aronson & Patnoe, 1997; Johnson & Johnson, 1987). In contrast, grading according to absolute standards has been found to reduce invidious social comparisons between students and facilitates collaboration among students (Boyer, 1987).

There is another benefit of grading according to absolute: It supplies teachers with assessment data that can be used to improve the quality of classroom instruction and test construction. As Erickson and Strommer (1991) point out:

> Grading according to [absolute] standards is more likely to point up problems and lead to improvements in teaching and test-taking practices. If several students do poorly on an exam, the low grades usually prompt some serious soul searching. Was instruction adequate? Was the exam poorly constructed? Or did students simply not study enough? We can correct such problems, but only if we detect them. Grading on a curve too often hides ineffective teaching, poor testing, and inadequate learning. So long as we give a reasonable number of A's and B's and not too many D's or F's, no one makes a fuss (pp. 154–55).

Grading practices that elevate student learning should always trump practices designed to ensure student grades get distributed in the form of a "normal curve." Effective teachers do not devise assessment practices to intentionally spread out and conveniently sort out students into grade categories; they design assessment practices that maximize the learning of all students and minimize achievement gaps between students of different cultural groups.

Consider this ...

Effective, culturally inclusive assessment emanates from an educational philosophy that the purpose of education is not to "spread out" students into grade categories and "weed out" weaker students from the best and brightest, but to "max out" the learning and educational attainment of all students.

Promoting Learning by Providing Students with Effective Feedback

"People can't learn without feedback. It's not teaching that causes learning. Attempts by the learner to perform cause learning, dependent upon the quality of feedback and opportunity to use it."

—Grant Wiggins, *Feedback: How Learning Occurs*

In a review of over 800 meta-analyses of 50,000 research findings and almost 240 million students, it was found that one of the distinguishing characteristics of high-impact teachers was their focus on providing students with effective and timely feedback (Hattie, 2009). When students receive teacher feedback that they can use to improve their academic performance (as opposed to just assigning test scores and class grades), it increases their motivation to learn (Hattie & Timperley, 2006) and their sense of self-efficacy (Zimmerman & Kitsantas, 2005).

Box 8.2 Effective Teacher *Feedback*: Seven Central Features

1. **Personalized:** delivered in a *personally validating manner* that recognizes the student's individuality, addresses the student by name, and is customized to the student's particular needs.

2. **Positive:** includes recognition of the student's *strengths* and *progress*, and conveys optimism that the student can improve in areas which need improvement.

3. **Proactive:** delivered at *early, formative stages* of the learning process, allowing time for the student to improve performance before falling too far behind.

4. **Prompt:** delivered *soon after* the student completes the learning task.

5. **Precise:** focuses *specifically* on what the student needs to do to correct mistakes and strengthen subsequent performance.

6. **Persuasive:** provides the student with a compelling reason *why* the feedback should be attended to and acted upon.

7. **Practical:** supplies the student with improvement strategies that are *actionable* and *manageable* to implement.

As previously mentioned, advocates of mastery learning argue that differences in students' performance levels do not reflect differences in their ability or potential to learn, but represent differences in the rate or speed at which students master particular concepts or skills. When students receive timely and effective teacher feedback that enables them to learn from their mistakes, it reduces the time it takes for them to master concepts they're expected to learn (Guskey, 2009).

Feedback is most effective for promoting student learning when its delivery is: (1) prompt, (2) proactive, (3) precise, (4) practical, (5) persuasive, (6) personalized, and (7) positive. These "Seven Ps" of effective feedback are defined in **Box 8.2.**

Provided below is a more detailed description and rationale for these principles along with specific practices that teachers can use to put the principles into practice.

1. *Personalized* Feedback

Studies show that when most teachers deliver feedback, it's addressed to the whole class and individual students often do not pay close attention to it because they think it doesn't apply to them personally (Carless, 2006). Students are also more likely to attend to feedback and be responsive to it when it's customized to their personal performance. Studies show that students do not respond well to feedback that's too impersonal (Higgins, Hartley, & Skelton, 2001). Instead, they're more receptive to feedback and respond to it non-defensively when it's delivered in a personalized manner. Teachers can deliver personalized feedback to students through such practices as: (a) addressing the student by name when delivering the feedback, (b) signing his or her name at the end of written feedback to simulate a personal letter, and (c) including a postscript to the feedback that expresses interest in some "non-academic" aspect of the student's life (e.g., a short note expressing interest in how a student's athletic endeavors are going or how an ailing family member is feeling).

When time constraints or class size prohibit the teacher from writing a personal note to all students on a returned test or assignment, a personal note may be written to a subset of students (for example, students with last names from A–M). On the next assignment or exam, personal notes may be written to a different subset of students (students with last names N–Z). This rotational practice ensures that every student in class receives personalized feedback from the teacher on a periodic basis.

2. *Positive* Feedback

Research shows that students with low self-esteem receive negative feedback, they tend to overgeneralize and become demoralized by it (Halvorson, 2010). Corrective feedback is less likely to be viewed less negatively and less likely to lower students' sense of self-esteem or self-efficacy if it is accompanied by positive comments about the student's work.

Providing detailed feedback on students' tests and assignments is time-consuming, particularly in large-sized classes, so it's natural for teachers to focus their limited time on feedback about what students need to correct or improve, rather than on what they're doing well or what they have improved. To guard against this "criticism trap," teachers may use one or more of the following practices to ensure that students receive at least a modicum of positive feedback on their tests and assignments.

When calling attention to aspects of student work that need improvement, teachers should also call attention to what the student did well. Feedback can be delivered in a way that's positive yet still challenges the student to do better by delivering it in the following sequence: "warm (compliment)—cool (challenge)—warm (compliment)." The teacher starts with a positive statement about what the student did well (e.g., "You did a good job of supporting your ideas with accurate, detailed information"). This is followed by a challenging but supportive feedback about what the student needs to improve (e.g., "How your ideas are organized needs some improvement"). Then the feedback sequence ends with a positive statement that again reinforces what the student is doing well and expresses confidence that the student can use the feedback provided to make the improvement needed (e.g., "Keep up your good work of providing solid support for your ideas; I'm sure you can improve your organization by just giving more thought to my suggestion about grouping ideas into different categories and arranging those categories into separate sections").

Point out strengths in students' work that may not relate directly to the grading criteria. For instance, student effort may not be a grading criterion, but if a student is exhibiting behavior indicative of motivation and engagement, that positive behavior might be included along with the teacher's performance-based feedback (e.g., "I appreciate your attentiveness and involvement in class"). In studies of K–12 teachers who generate significant gains in student achievement, verbally reinforcing student effort is one practice these teachers have in common (Dean et al., 2012; Marzano, Pickering, & Pollock, 2001). Effort-reinforcing feedback benefits all students, and it's especially effective way to provide minority students with personal validation (Rendón & Garza, 1996).

Acknowledge the ways in which the student's work has improved, even if the student's work still needs further improvement. When students make gains in their individual performance relative to their previous level of performance, this is a positive learning outcome and an indicator of teaching effectiveness. As Robinson (2011) argues:

> Because the most powerful predictor of a child's current achievement is his or her prior achievement, "value added" rather than absolute measures of achievement are required to make judgments about a teacher's contribution to student learning. The bottom line for leaders and teachers is the difference they make to student learning not the students' absolute level of achievement (p. 89).

Thus, even if a student's performance has not yet reached an absolute level of competence, any relative improvement in the student's performance should be noted by the teacher and conveyed to the student. For instance, the student could be told: "You still have a way to go with respect to _____, but here's how you have improved: _____." Research indicates that this type of self-referenced feedback—feedback about current performance relative to previous performance, has greater impact on a student's sense of self-efficacy than feedback that compares the student's performance with other students (Chan, as cited in Hattie, 2012a). This benefit of self-referenced feedback has significant implications for promoting student learning because self-efficacy and academic achievement are strongly related (Margolis & McCabe, 2003).

Praise students for their effort and strategies rather than their ability. Praising students for how "smart" or "intelligent" they are sends them the message that their success is related to some fixed trait or immutable characteristic. In contrast, focusing praise on students' effort and use of effective learning habits or strategies sends them the message that their success is not due to something they "have" but from something they do. When teachers focus their feedback on students' work ethic and learning strategies, they are more likely to develop a "growth mindset"—the belief that intelligence is grown or developed rather than a "fixed mindset"—the belief that intelligence is a fixed (unalterable) trait that you have or you don't (Dweck, 2006). Teachers should avoid feedback that promotes a fixed mindset students who develop such a mindset view test results only in terms of grade earned and as an indication of their intellectual ability, rather use teacher feedback to improve their future learning and promote intellectual growth (Dweck, 2007). Halvorson (2010) points out another downside to focusing teacher praise on students' intelligence:

> Say to a child who does well on an exam, "Nice job, Tommy! You are so smart!" and what will Tommy think the next time he doesn't do so well?

Praise for hard-work, persistence, use of good strategies, and determination, on the other hand, reinforces the idea that these are the key ingredients for success and makes the recipient more resilient in the face of difficulty (p. 230).

Compared to many countries that view effort as the primary driver of student learning and academic achievement, America places more emphasis on intellectual ability and academic aptitude (Drew, 1996). This is reflected in tests that America has developed to measure intellectual attributes (e.g., IQ and SAT). It is noteworthy that the original IQ test was developed by a French psychologist, Alfred Binet. Public school officials in France commissioned him to find a way to identify school children who were at risk of falling behind their peers. Once these students were identified, the the school system's plan was to provide them with compensatory educational opportunities that would close their achievement gap. Later, the French version of the IQ test was adopted in America, but was viewed as a measure of innate ability (Nicolas et al., 2013).

When intelligence tests and other measures of intellectual performance are viewed by educators as indicators of fixed, innate ability, it leads to the development of a fixed mindset among students and lower-scoring students' sense of self-efficacy. Furthermore, since students' scores on standardized tests are heavily influenced by family income level and prior educational opportunities, test results can perpetuate beliefs about the intellectual "inferiority" or "deficiencies" of lower-scoring groups of students (Smith, 2015). Such disparaging beliefs have a long history, tracing back to the 1860s, when Englishman Sir Francis Galton misinterpreted Charles Darwin's theory of natural selection to erroneously conclude that white, middle-class Englishmen were more evolved and had genetically higher levels of intelligence than the English working class and ethnic groups that had been colonized by the British Empire (Rust & Golombok, 2009).

Teachers can play a pivotal role in preventing the perpetuation of false interpretations about standardized tests being measures of innate intellectual *ability*, which leads to a "fixed mindset," by countering these beliefs with classroom-based tests and student-feedback practices that value student effort and effective learning habits and strategies, which promote "growth mindset," academic achievement, and educational equity.

3. *Proactive* Feedback

For feedback to be effective, students must receive it early enough in the learning process to be able to apply it to their subsequent work and improve their final performance (Sadler, 2008). When feedback is delivered proactively, it allows ample time and opportunity for students to remedy shortcomings before they result in grades, lower self-efficacy, and damaged self-esteem. Research suggests that most students view assessment in terms of "performance goals"—that tests and assignments are measures of their performance competence and their goal is to prove to others that they are competent (Dweck, 1999). When performance goal-oriented students aren't successful, they are more likely to attribute their poor performance to low ability (rather than to low effort or ineffective strategies), feel ashamed or dejected about

> "Some recent philosophers seem to ... affirm the intelligence of an individual is a fixed quantity, a quantity that cannot be augmented. We must protest and react against this brutal pessimism; we will try to demonstrate that it is founded on nothing."
>
> —Alfred Binet, originator of the IQ test, 1909

> "Teachers need to stop overemphasizing ability and start to emphasize increased effort and progress (steep learning curves are the right for all students regardless of where they start)."
>
> —John Hattie, *Visible Learning for Teachers: Maximizing Impact on Learning*

their lack of success, and if their poor performance occurs early in the learning process, they are not likely to persist until they achieve competence. In contrast to "performance" goal-oriented students, other students approach their assessments with a "mastery" goal-orientation. These students see assessments as learning opportunities. They don't view initial mistakes as personal failures; instead, if they aren't initially successful at academic tasks, they continue to persist until they gain greater competence and they experience pride or pleasure when they overcome mistakes during the learning process (Dweck, 2006).

Because research indicates that most students have performance goals rather than mastery goals, teachers may need to be intentional about developing a mastery-goal mindset. They can do this by designing early, manageable assignments after which students receive proactive feedback on how to improve their performance, are given opportunities to make improvements (with teacher guidance if necessary), and are rewarded for the improvements they make. Such early performance-improvement experiences help students develop a mastery goal-orientation, which helps them persist on learning tasks until they achieve competency or proficiency.

4. *Prompt* Feedback

When students receive feedback soon after engaging in a learning task, it increases their motivation to attend to it and make use of it (Malone, 1981; Eggen & Kauchak, 2004). Prompt feedback has also been found to promote retention of knowledge and skills acquired during the learning task (Dihoff, Brosvic, & Epstein, 2003; Epstein, Epstein, & Brosvic, 2001). Although teachers may not be able to immediately supply students with detailed feedback after every assessment, they still can provide students with prompt and informative feedback by making answer keys available and posting problem solutions soon after students complete classroom tests and assignments.

5. *Precise* Feedback

When teachers provide feedback that to students that identifies *specific* aspects of their work needing improvement, they are more likely to take action on the feedback provided because they know precisely what they must do. Supporting this assertion is research conducted at Harvard which found that improvement in students' writing was directly related to the *specificity* of action strategies included in the feedback they received from instructors following their writing assignments (Buskey, cited in Light, 1992).

In contrast, students are less likely to respond constructively to feedback that insufficient information about what they did wrong and how to do better (Higgins, Hartley, & Skelton, 2001). Although the majority of teachers believe the feedback they provide students is detailed enough to help them improve their future work, research indicates that less than half of students feel the same way (Carless, 2006). Students certainly have a right to report that teachers fail to give them precise feedback if the only feedback they receive is a blanket grade (Brophy, 2004) or if they receive generic teacher comments like: "Your paper needs to be better organized." A general comment like as this can be transformed into more specific feedback if the teacher were to take it one step further and elaborate on it by saying: "Your paper's organization needs improvement. You can do that by beefing up your introduction, including a thesis statement, and tying your conclusion back to your thesis statement."

Specific feedback also informs students where they stand in class. Research suggests that people seek and value three types of feedback: (a) appreciation—e.g., "tell me how good I am," (b) coaching—e.g., "here's a better way to do it," and (c) evaluative—"here's where you stand" (Stone & Heen, 2015). One distinguishing characteristic of successful students is that they engage in *self-monitoring*, which includes regularly checking and being of how well they are learning and progressing academically (Gettinger & Seibert, 2002; Pintrich, 1995). Teachers can promote the development of self-monitoring by encouraging students, (or instructing them) to add the points they earn on each completed test and assignment to their cumulative total and calculate their overall class grade as the term progresses.

6. *Persuasive* Feedback

Students are more likely to make efforts to improve when receiving feedback which conveys the message that their teacher has *high expectations* for improvement. Reinforcing this conclusion is a study conducted by Yeager et al. (2013) in which seventh graders at a racially diverse middle school wrote essays about a personal hero. Teachers graded the essays as they normally would, accompanied by usual comments like "unclear," "needs an example," etc. Then the researchers randomly attached a sticky note to the teachers' graded essays before returning them to the students. Half the students received a feedback-only sticky note that simply said, "I'm giving you these comments so that you'll have feedback on your paper." The other half received a high-expectation note saying, "I'm giving you these comments because I have very high expectations and I know you can reach them." None of the students were aware that they were involved in a study, so they all thought that their teachers had written the sticky notes. When the students were offered an opportunity to revise their essays and improve their work, the results were striking. Among white students, 87 percent of those who received the high-expectation teacher message turned in new essays, compared to 62 percent of those who received the feedback-only note. Among African American students, the effect was even greater: 72 percent who received the high-expectation teacher note turned in a revised essay, compared to only 17 percent who received the feedback-only note. Furthermore, students submitted who revised essays improved the quality of their work that earned earned higher scores on their second work product—from both their teachers and from outside graders who were hired for the study.

In addition to being motivated more by feedback that conveys high expectations for improvement, students are likely to be more motivated by "non-controlling" feedback that avoids use of coercive language (e.g., you "must" or you "have to"). Instead of a teacher saying "You must improve your spelling," a less-controlling and more motivating message would be: "I've noticed your spelling has not been improving. Do you have any idea why not, or what might be done to improve it?" (Reeve, 1995).

Another way, teachers may be able to supply students with corrective feedback that is more motivating (and less threatening) is by refraining from using the color red to correct student mistakes. No definitive research evidence supports this suggestion; however, it is reasonable to conclude that people associate the color red with apprehension ("red flag"; "red alert") or humiliation ("red-faced"). Thus, it's likely that students will feel less personally threatened by corrective feedback delivered to them in a color other than red. Socially intelligent and culturally sensitive teachers do everything possible to minimize the risk that their feedback to students has an adverse effect on their self-esteem or self-confidence.

7. *Practical* Feedback

Feedback is "constructive" when students can "build on it" to improve their work. One straightforward way in which teachers can ensure that students make constructive use of their feedback and take action on it is by *requiring* them to do so. The results of two independent studies support this practice. In both studies, instructors returned exams to students with feedback that referenced textbook pages or class notes where the answer to each test question was found. On test questions the students answered incorrectly, they were required to write a short paragraph identifying the correct answer and explaining why it was correct. When the academic performance of these students was compared with students in other sections of the same course who did not receive the referenced feedback and were not required to correct their errors, the students who received feedback that required them to correct their errors: (a) earned a higher score on the final course exam, (b) liked the course more, and (c) reported greater self-confidence in their ability to learn the course material (Clark, Guskey, & Benninga, 1983; Guskey, Benninga, & Clark, 1984).

A less prescriptive approach than *mandating* students to correct their mistakes is supplying them with strong *incentives* to do so. For example, students could be allowed to redeem some (or most) of their lost points and improve their overall grade by correcting answers they got wrong and resubmitting their work. Or, on writing assignments, students could be allowed to rewrite and resubmit their work (or sections thereof) after modifying it in accordance with corrective feedback they received from their teacher on their first written product.

> **Consider this ...**
> Effective and equitable assessment provides students with feedback that enables them to identify their mistakes, provides them with opportunities to correct their mistakes, and motivates them to continually improve their performance.

Internet Resources

Culturally Inclusive Assessment Strategies:
https://learninginnovation.duke.edu/blog/2018/11/inclusive-assessment/

Fair & Equitable Assessment Practices:
http://www.queensu.ca/teachingandlearning/modules/assessments/23_s3_01_intro_section.html

Mastery Learning & Grading:
https://www.ted.com/talks/sal_khan_let_s_teach_for_mastery_not_test_
scores?language=en
https://www.redesignu.org/sites/default/files/uploads/MMA-%20Building%20
a%20Mastery-Based%20Grading%20Policy%20150802.pdf

Assessing Higher-Order Thinking Skills:
http://www.ascd.org/publications/books/109111/chapters/General_
Principles_for_Assessing_Higher-Order_Thinking.aspx

Providing Students with Effective Performance-Improvement Feedback:
https://www.edutopia.org/blog/tips-providing-students-meaningful-feedback-
marianne-stenger http://www.ascd.org/publications/educational-leadership/
sept12/vol70/num01/Seven-Keys-to-Effective-Feedback.aspx

References

Ambrose, S. A., Lovett, M., Bridges, M . W., DiPietro, M., & Norman, M. K. (2010). *How learning works: Seven research-based principles of smart teaching.* San Francisco: Jossey-Bass.

Anastasi, A., & Urbina, S. (1997). *Psychological testing* (7th ed.). Upper Saddle, NJ: Prentice Hall.

Anderson, L. W., & Krathwohl, D. R. (Eds.) (2001). *A taxonomy for learning, teaching, and assessing: A revision of Bloom's taxonomy of educational objectives.* New York: Addison Wesley Longman.

Aronson, E., & Patnoe, S. (1997). *The jigsaw classroom.* New York: Longman.

Bandura, A. (1997). *Self-efficacy: The exercise of control.* New York: Freeman & Co.

Bloom, B. S. (1968). *Mastery learning. Evaluation Comment, 1*(2). Los Angeles: University of California, Center for the Study of Evaluation of Instructional Programs.

Bloom, B. S. (1978). New views of the learner: Implications for instruction and curriculum. *Educational Leadership, 35*(7), 536–576.

Bloom, B. A. (1984). The 2-sigma problem: The search for methods of group instruction as effective as one-to-one tutoring. *Educational Researcher, 13*(6), 4–16.

Bloom, B. S., Hastings, L. T., & Madaus, G. F. (1971). *Handbook of formative and summative evaluation of student learning.* New York, NY: McGraw Hill.

Boyer, E. L. (1987). *College: The undergraduate experience in America.* New York: Harper & Row.

Brophy, J. (2004). *Motivating students to learn* (2nd ed.). Mahwah, NJ: Erlbaum.

Burgess, J. M. & Sales, S. (1977). Attitudinal effects of "mere exposure": A reevaluation. *Journal of Experimental Social Psychology, 7*, 461–472.

Burris, C. C. (2014). *On the same track: How schools can join the twenty-first century struggle against resegregation.* Boston, MA: Beacon Press.

Butler, J. E. (1993). Transforming the curriculum: Teaching about women of color. In J. A. Banks & C. Banks (Eds.), *Multicultural education: Issues and perspectives.* Needham Heights, MA: Allyn & Bacon.

Caine, R. N., & Caine, G. (1991). *Teaching and the human brain.* Alexandria, Virginia: Association for Supervision and Curriculum Development.

Caine, R. N., & Caine, G.(1994). *Making connections: Teaching and the human brain.* Menlo Park, CA: Addison-Wesley.

Carless, D. (2006). Differing perceptions in the feedback process. *Studies in Higher Education, 31*(2), 219–233.

Chapman, C., & King, R. (2005). *Differentiated assessment strategies: One tool doesn't fit all.* Thousand Oaks: Corwin Press.

Chase, C.I. (1999). *Contemporary assessment for educators.* New York: Longman.

Chickering, A. W. (1969). *Education and identity.* San Francisco: Jossey-Bass.

Chickering, A. W., & Reisser, L. (1993). *Education and identity* (2nd ed.). San Francisco: Jossey-Bass.

Clark, C. R., Guskey, T. R., & Benninga, J. S. (1983). The effectiveness of mastery learning strategies in undergraduate education courses. *Journal of Educational Research, 74,* 210–214.

Davis, B. G., Wood, L., & Wilson, R. C. (1983). *ABCs of teaching with excellence.* Berkeley, CA: University of California.

Dean, C. B., Hubbell, E. R., Pitler, H., & Stone, B. (2012). *Classroom instruction that works: Research-based strategies for increasing student achievement* (2nd ed.) Alexandria, VA: Association for Supervision and Curriculum Development.

Deci, E, L., & Flaste, R. (1995). *Why we do what we do: Understanding self-motivation.* New York: Penguin Group.

DeWitt, P. M. (2018). *School climate: Leading with collective efficacy.* Thousand Oaks: Sage.

Dihoff, R. E., Brosvic, G. M., & Epstein, M. L. (2003). The role of feedback during academic testing: The delay retention effect revisited. *Psychological Reports, 53,* 533–548

Dodge, Y. (Ed.) (2003) *The Oxford Dictionary of Statistical Terms.* New York: Oxford University Press.

Drew, D. (1996). *Aptitude revisited: Rethinking math and science education in America's next century.* Baltimore, MD: Johns Hopkins University Press.

Durlak, J. A., Weissberg, R. P., Dymnicki, A. B., Taylor, R. D., & Schellinger, K. B. (2011). The impact of enhancing students' social and emotional learning: A meta-analysis of school-based universal interventions. *Child Development, 82*(1), 405–432.

Dusek, J. B., & Gail, J. (1983). The bases of teacher expectations: A meta-analysis. *Journal of Educational Psychology, 75*(3), 327–346.

Dweck, C. S. (1999). *Self-theories: Their role in motivation, personality, and development.* Philadelphia: Psychology Press

Dweck, C. S. (2006). *Mindset: The new psychology of success.* New York: Random House.

Dweck, C. S. (2007). The perils and promises of praise. *Educational Leadership, 65*(2), 34–39.

Education Commission of the States (1995). *Making quality count in undergraduate education.* Denver, CO: ECS Distribution Center.

Eggen, P., & Kauchak, D. (2012). *Educational psychology: Windows on classrooms* (9th ed.) Upper Saddle River, NJ: Pearson.

Epstein, M. L., Epstein, B. B., & Brosvic, G. M. (2001). Immediate feedback during academic testing. *Psychological Reports, 88,* 889–895.

Erickson, B. L., & Strommer, D. W. (1991). *Teaching college freshmen.* San Francisco: Jossey-Bass.

Fiechtner, S. B., & Davis, E. A. (1992). Why some groups fail: A survey of students' experiences with learning groups. In A. S. Goodsell, M. Maher, & V. Tinto (Eds.), *Collaborative learning: A sourcebook for higher education* (pp. 59–67). The National Center on Postsecondary Teaching, Learning, and Assessment, The Pennsylvania State University.

Frederiksen, N. (1984). The real test bias: Influences of testing on teaching and learning. *American Psychologist, 39*(3), 193–202.

Gable, S., Krull, J. L., & Chang, Y. (2012). Boys' and girls' weight status and math performance from kindergarten entry through fifth grade: A mediated analysis. *Child Development, 83*(5), 1822–1839.

Gage, H., & Berliner, D. (1984). *Educational psychology* (3rd ed.). Boston: Houghton Mifflin.

Gamson, Z. (1993). Deep learning, surface learning. *AAHE Bulletin, 45*(8), pp. 11–13.

Gettinger, M., & Seibert, J.K. (2002). Best practices in increasing academic learning time. In A. Thomas (Ed.), *Best practices in school psychology: Volume I* (4– ed., pp. 773–787). Bethesda, MD: National Association of School Psychologists.

Ginsberg, M. B., & Wlodkowski, R. J. (2009). *Diversity and motivation: Culturally responsive teaching in college.* San Francisco: Jossey-Bass.

Gronlund, N. E. (1985). *Measurement and evaluation in teaching* (5th ed.), New York: Macmillan.

Guskey, T. R. (2009). Mastery learning. In T. L. Good (Ed.), *21st century education: A reference handbook* (Vol. I, pp. 194–202). Thousand Oaks, CA: Sage.

Guskey, T. R., Benninga, J. S., & Clark, C. R. (1984). Mastery learning and students' attributions at the college level. *Research in Higher Education, 20,* 491–498.

Halvorson, H. G. (2010). *Succeed: How we can reach our goals.* New York: Plume.

Hart, L. A. (1983). *Human brain and human learning.* White Plains, NY: Longman.

Hattie, J. (2009). *Visible learning: A synthesis of 800+ meta-analyses on achievement.* London: Routledge.

Hattie, J. (2012a). *Visible learning for teachers: Maximizing the impact on learning.* London New York: Routledge.

Hattie, J. (2012b, September). *Know thy impact: Educational leadership. Feedback for learning, 70*(1), 18–23.

Hattie, J. A. C., & Timperley, H. (2006). The power of feedback. *Review of Educational Research, 77*(1), 81–112.

Heck, R. H., Marcoulides, G. A., & Lang, P. (1991). Principal instructional leadership and school achievement: The application of discriminant techniques. *School Effectiveness and School Improvement, 2*(2), 115–135.

Hertel, P. T., & Brozovich, F. (2010). Cognitive habits and memory distortions in anxiety and depression. *Current Directions in Psychological Science, 19*(3):155–160.

Higgins, R., Hartley, P., & Skelton, A. (2001). Getting the message cross: The problem of communicating assessment feedback. *Teaching in Higher Education, 6*(2), 269–274.

Hulleman, C. S., & Harackiewicz, J. M. (2009). Making education relevant: Increasing interest and performance in high school science classes. *Science, 326,* 1410–1412.

Hyungshim, J. (2008). Supporting students' motivation, engagement and learning during an uninteresting activity. *Journal of Educational Psychology, 100* (No. 4), 798–811.

Jensen, E. (2008). *Brain-based learning.* Thousand Oaks, CA: Corwin Press.

Johnson, D. W., & Johnson, R. T. (1987). *The three C's of reducing prejudice and discrimination.* In S. Oskamp & S. Spacapan (Eds.), Interpersonal processes: Claremont symposium on applied social psychology (pp. 239-268). Newbury Park, CA: Sage.

Karpicke, J. D., & Roediger, H. L. (2008). The critical importance of retrieval for learning. *Science, 15*(219), Issue 5865, 966–968.

Kellogg, R. T. (1994). *The psychology of writing.* New York: Oxford University Press.

Kornhaber, M. L. (2012). Standardized testing and standards. In J. A. Banks (Ed.), *Encyclopedia of diversity in education* (volume 4, pp. 2073–2076). Thousand Oaks, CA: Sage.

Ladson-Billings, G. (1995a). But that's just good teaching! The case for culturally relevant pedagogy. *Theory into Practice, 43,* 159–165. doi:10.1080/ 00405849509543675

Ladson-Billings, G. (1995b). Toward a theory of culturally relevant pedagogy. *American Educational Research Journal, 32,* 465–491. doi:10.3102/00028312032003465

Landrum, R. (2007). Introductory psychology student performance: Weekly quizzes followed by a cumulative final exam. *Teaching of Psychology, 34,* 177–180.

Levine, D. U. (1985). *Improving student achievement through mastery learning programs.* San Francisco: Jossey-Bass.

Light, R. L. (1992). *The Harvard assessment seminars, second report.* Cambridge, MA: Harvard University Press.

Love, P., & Love, A. G. (1995). *Enhancing student learning: Intellectual, social, and emotional integration*. ASHE-ERIC Higher Education Report No. 4. Washington, DC: The George Washington University. Graduate School of Education and Human Development.

Lowman, J. (1995). *Mastering the techniques of teaching* (2nd ed.). San Francisco: Jossey-Bass.

Ludweig, L. M. (1993). Student perceptions of instructor behaviors. *The Teaching Professor, 7*(4), p. 1.

Malone, T. (1981). Toward a theory of intrinsically motivating instruction. *Cognitive Science, 4,* 333–369.

Margolis & McCabe, (2003). Self-efficacy: A key to improving the motivation of struggling learners. *The Clearing House, 77*(6), 241–249 .

Marton, F., & Saljo, R. (1976). On qualitative differences in learning: Outcome and process. *British Journal of Educational Psychology, 46*(1), 4–11.

Marzano, R., Pickering, D. J., & Pollock, J. (2001). *Classroom instruction that works: Research-based strategies for increasing student achievement*. Alexandria, VA: Association for Supervision and Curriculum Development.

McKeachie, W. J. (1986). *Teaching tips* (8th ed.). Lexington, MA: D.C. Heath.

Nelson, C. (2010). Dysfunctional illusions of rigor: Lessons from the scholarship of teaching and learning. In L. B. Nilson & J. E. Miller (Eds.), *To improve the academy: Resources for faculty, instructional, and organizational development, 28* (177–192). San Francisco: Jossey-Bass.

Nicolas, S., Andrieu, B., Croizet, J-C., Sanaitioso, R. B., & Burman, J. T. (2013). Sick? Or slow? On the origins of intelligence as a psychological object. *Intelligence, 41*(5), 699–711.

Pink, (2009). *Drive: The surprising truth about what motivates us*. New York: Riverhead Books.

Pintrich, P. R. (Ed.) (1995). *Understanding self-regulated learning*. New Directions for Teaching and Learning, no. 63. San Francisco: Jossey-Bass.

Reeve, J. (1995). *Motivating others: Nurturing inner motivational resources*. Boston: Allyn and Bacon.

Rendón, L. I., & Garza, H. (1996). Closing the gap between two- and four-year institutions. In L. I. Rendón & R. O. Hope (Eds.), *Educating a new majority: Transforming America's educational system for diversity* (pp. 289–308). San Francisco: Jossey-Bass.

Rennie, D., & Brewer, L. (1987). A grounded theory of thesis blocking. *Teaching of Psychology, 14*(1), 10–16.

Robinson, V. (2011). *Student-centered leadership*. San Francisco: Jossey-Bass.

Rose, D. H., & Meyer, A. (2002). *Teaching every student in the digital age: Universal design for learning*. Alexandria, VA: ACSD.

Rosenthal, R., & Jacobs, L. (1968). *Pygmalion in the classroom*. New York: Holt, Rinehart, and Winston.

Rubie-Davies, C. M. (2014). *Becoming a high expectation teacher: Raising the bar*. New York, NY: Routledge.

Rust, J., & Golombok, S. (2009). *Modern psychometrics: The science of psychological assessment* (3rd ed). London: Routlege.

Sadler, D. R. (2008). Beyond feedback: Developing student capability in complex appraisal. *Assessment and Evaluation in Higher Education, 35*(5), 535–550.

Scharf, A. (2018). *Critical practices for anti-bias education*. Teaching Tolerance: A Project of the Southern Poverty Law Center. Retrieved from https://www.tolerance.org/.../2019-04/TT-Critical-Practices-for-Anti-bias-Education.pdf

Sedlacek, W. E. (1993). Employing noncognitive variables in admissions and retention in higher education. In *Achieving diversity: Issues in the recruitment and retention of underrepresented racial/ethnic students in higher education* (pp. 33–39). Alexandria, CA National Association of College Admission Counselors.

Seligman, M. E. P. (1998). *Learned optimism*. New York: Pocket Books (Simon & Schuster).

Smith, D. G. (2015). *Diversity's promise for higher education: Making it work* (2nd ed.). Baltimore: Johns Hopkins University Press.

Stone, D., & Heen, S. (2015). *Thanks for the feedback: The science and art of receiving feedback well*. New York, NY: Penguin Books.

Suskie, L. (2000). Fair assessment practices: Giving students equitable opportunities to demonstrate learning. *AAHE Bulletin, 52*(9), 7–9.

Swap, W. C. (1977). Intergroup attraction and repeated exposure to rewards and punishers. *Personality and Social Psychology Bulletin, 3,* 248–251.

Thompson, R. F. (1981). Peer grading: some promising advantages for composition research and the classroom. *Research in the Teaching of English, 15*(2), 172–174.

Tracey, T., & Sherry, P. (1984). College student distress as a function of person-environment fit. *Journal of College Student Personnel, 25*(5), 436–442.

Wells, N. M., & Evans, G. W. (2003). Nearby nature: A buffer of life stress among rural children. *Environment and Behavior, 35*(3), 311–330.

White, E. M. (1985). *Teaching and assessing writing*. San Francisco: Jossey-Bass.

Wieman, C. E. (2007). Why not try a scientific approach to science education? *Change, 39*(5), 9–15.

Wilson, R. C. (1987). Toward excellence in teaching. In L. M. Aleamoni (Ed.), *Techniques for evaluating and improving instruction* (pp. 9–24). New Direction for Teaching and Learning, No. 31. San Francisco: Jossey-Bass.

Winkelmes, M. A. (2013). Transparency in teaching: Faculty share data and improve students' learning. *Liberal Education, 99*(2), 48–55.

Wlodkowski, R. J. (2008). *Enhancing adult motivation to learn: A comprehensive guide for teaching all adults* (3rd ed.). San Francisco: Wiley.

Worchel, S., & Austin, W. G. (Eds.) (1986). *Psychology of intergroup relations*. Chicago: Nelson-Hall.

Wormeli, R. (2006). *Fair isn't always equal: Assessing & grading in the differentiated classroom*. Portsmouth, NH: Stenhouse.

Yeager, S. C., Purdie-Vaughns, V., Garcia, J., Apfel, N., Brzustoski, P., Master, A., Hessert, W. T., Williams, M. E., & Cohen, G. L. (2013, August 12). Breaking the cycle of mistrust: Wise interventions to provide critical feedback across the racial divide. *Journal of Experimental Psychology: General*. Advance online publication. doi: 10.1037/a0033906

Zimmerman, B. J., & Kitsantas, A. (2005). Homework practices and academic achievement: The mediating role of self-efficacy and perceived responsibility beliefs. *Contemporary Educational Psychology, 30,* 397–417.

Zinsser, W. (1988). *Writing to learn*. New York: HarperCollins.

Zull, J. E. (2011). *From brain to mind: Using neuroscience to guide change in education*. Sterling, CVA: Stylus.

Reflections and Applications

8.1 Review the sidebar quotes contained in this chapter and select two that you think are particularly meaningful or inspirational. For each quote you selected, provide an explanation of why you chose it.

8.2 Review the strategies for *culturally inclusive assessment* on **pp. 139–144**. Select three you think are most important and intend to put into practice.

8.3 Student learning may be assessed in terms of gain or positive change in any of three key domains, sometimes referred to as the "ABCs" of student learning outcomes:

   A = *Affective*—learning outcomes that involve positive change in students' *attitudes, perspectives,* or *viewpoints*

   B = *Behavioral*—learning outcomes that involve positive change in students' *actions* and student *habits*

   C = *Cognitive*—learning outcomes related to positive change in student *knowledge* and *thinking* skills

   Identify one specific student outcome you think would be most important to assess in each of these three domains and explain why you chose it.

8.4 Using different methods to evaluate student achievement results in a more comprehensive and balanced system of assessment that has greater *validity*—by counterbalancing the strengths and weaknesses of the different methods, and greater *equity*—by accommodating different skill sets that students from diverse cultures bring to the learning process.

   Identify three different methods for evaluating student learning you would rely on to diversify your assessment system and explain why you chose each of these methods.

8.5 Teachers should help students prepare for exams in ways that ensure they focus on learning critical concepts, rather than leaving them to their own devices and risking that study "the wrong things." At the same time, teachers need to provide this student support or scaffolding without "lowering academic standards" or "teaching to the test." What strategy would you use to strike this balance and why do you think it would provide students with effective scaffolding without compromising academic rigor?

8.6 Would you feel comfortable implementing either or both of the following assessment practices?
   a) Allowing students to retake exams or re-submit assignments to improve their class grade. Why or why not?
   b) Allowing students to drop the lowest test or quiz score they earned during the term. Why or why not?

8.7 Do you think teachers should use assessment practices that ensure some "spread" or distribution of students grades to avoid charges of "grade inflation?" If yes, why? If no, why not?

8.8 Student learning is enhanced by teacher feedback characterized that includes the seven features listed below. For each of these features of effective feedback, identify a specific strategy or practice you would use to deliver it.
   • *Personalized*: delivered in a *personally validating* manner, which recognizes the student's individuality, addresses the student by name, and is customized to the student's particular needs.

- *Positive*: includes recognition of the student's *strengths* and *progress*, and conveys optimism that the student can and will improve in areas needing improvement.
- *Proactive*: delivered at *early, formative stages* of the learning process, allowing time for the student to improve performance before falling too far behind.
- *Prompt*: delivered *soon after* the student engages in the learning task.
- *Precise*: focuses *specifically* on what the student needs to do to correct mistakes and strengthen subsequent performance.
- *Persuasive*: provides the student with a compelling reason *why* the feedback should be attended to and acted up on.
- *Practical*: supplies the student with improvement strategies that are *actionable* and *manageable* to implement.

Appendix A

Student Information Sheet
Questions Teachers May Use to Get to Know Their Students

The questions listed below are designed to help teachers make personal connections with their students. Not all of these questions need to be used, nor are they all equally relevant or appropriate for students at all ages and levels of education. The list is intended to serve as pool of potential questions from which teachers may select and adapt to the particular student population they serve.

Before asking students to answer these questions, they should be informed that the reason why they're being asked these questions is to help the teacher get to know them as individuals and better connect the class material to their personal experiences, interests, and goals. Students should also be told that if there is any question they feel uncomfortable answering, they have "the right to remain silent" and leave it blank.

Personal Background Information

1. Name you prefer to be called?
2. E-mail address and phone number (optional)?
3. Where are you currently living?
4. Have any of your family members attended college? Graduated from college?
5. Have you attended any other schools? (If yes, where and when?)
6. If you have held jobs or had volunteer experience work, what were they?
7. Will you be working while you're attending school? If so, how many hours per week?
8. Will you have family responsibilities this term?
9. Who or what has had the greatest influence on your life? In what way?
10. What do you think has been the most significant event in your life thus far?
11. If there is something about your life or life circumstances that you wish you could change, what would it be?

Future Plans

1. When you imagine or fantasize about your future, what usually comes to mind?
2. What does being "successful" mean to you?

3. What do you think is the most significant event you will experience or most important decision you will make in the near future?
4. Do you plan to go to college? Any particular college(s) you would like to attend?
5. What careers interest you, or what type of work do you think you would do well?

Personal Strengths, Talents, & Distinctive Qualities

1. What seems to come easily or naturally to you?
2. What would you say is your greatest talent or personal strength?
3. On what types of learning tasks or activities have you experienced the most success?
4. In what subjects do you tend to earn the highest grades?
5. If others come to you for help, advice, or assistance, what is it usually for and why do you think they come to you?
6. What three words best describe you?
7. What would your best friend(s) say is your most likable quality, trait, or characteristic?
8. What would you say has been your greatest achievement or accomplishment in life thus far?
9. Have you received any awards or other forms of recognition? If yes, what for?

Personal Interests

1. What sorts of things do you look forward to, or get really excited about doing?
2. What tends to capture your attention and hold it for long periods of time?
3. What do you really enjoy doing and do as often as possible?
4. When time seems to "fly by," what are you usually doing?
5. When you are with your friends, what do you like to talk about or do together?
6. Do you prefer to learn by listening, reading, doing, viewing, or by some other means?
7. What has been your *most* enjoyable and *least* enjoyable school experience?
8. What are your favorite hobbies or pastimes?
9. If you had a day, week, or year to go anywhere you wanted to go, and do anything you wanted to do, where would you go and what would you do?
10. What's your favorite movie and/or TV program?
11. What's your favorite type of music or favorite musical artist(s)?
12. Is there anyone dead or alive, real or imaginary, whom you've never met but would like to meet and have a conversation with? Why?

Personal Values

1. What matters most to you? What do you really care about or think is very important?
2. If you were to single out something you really stand for or believe in, what would it be?
3. What would you say are your highest priorities in life?
4. If your home contained everything you own, and it caught fire, but you had time to rush in and retrieve one item, what would it be?
5. When you do something that gives you the feeling you're doing the "right thing" or makes you feel good about yourself, what does it tend to be?
6. What about yourself are you most proud of, or take most pride in doing?
7. When you have free time, how do you usually spend it?
8. When your mind drifts, or you begin to daydream, where does it tend to go?
9. When you have extra spending money, what do you usually spend it on?
10. Is there a motto, quote, song, symbol, or bumper sticker that represents something you really stand for or believe in?
11. If there were one thing in the world you could change, improve, or make a difference in, what would it be?
12. Do you have any heroes, or anyone you admire, look up to, or feel has set an example worth following? If yes, who and why?
13. How do you define happiness? What would it take for you to be happy?
14. What does living a "good life" mean to you?
15. Would you rather be thought of as: (a) smart, (b) wealthy, (c) creative, or (d) caring? Why?

* Is there anything else about yourself that you think would be interesting or useful for me to know?

Class & School Attitudes

1. Right now, how do you feel about being in this class—positive, negative, neutral? (Why?)
2. Do you anticipate encountering any challenges or obstacles that might interfere with your success in this class?
3. What or who do you think will be your most valuable resources and sources of support for helping you succeed in this class and school in general?

* Are there other feelings you have about this class or school that you would like to share?

Cooperative Learning
Seven Central Features

Cooperative learning (CL) is a form of collaborative learning that includes a set of structured procedures that are intentionally designed to convert *group* work into *team*work. In short, CL involves the use of small, *intentionally selected* groups of students who work *interdependently* on a well-defined learning task, have *equal opportunity* to contribute to the completion of the task, and are held *individually accountable* for their contributions. The role of the instructor during CL is to serve as an unobtrusive *facilitator*, *coach*, or *consultant* to the learning groups (Cooper, 2003).

More specifically, CL attempts to strengthen the effectiveness of small-group work by infusing it with the following seven procedural features (Cuseo, 2002):

1. Intentional Group Formation
2. Intentional Team Building
3. Explicit Attention is Paid to Developing Students' Social Intelligence and Collaborative Skills
4. Positive Interdependence among Group Members (Collective Responsibility)
5. Individual Accountability (Personal Responsibility)
6. Teacher Serves as Roving Facilitator and Consultant to the Learning Groups
7. Opportunities are Created for Inter-Group Interaction and Integration of Ideas across Different Learning Groups

These seven features are further described below, along with strategies for implementing each of them.

1. *Intentional* Group Formation

Learning groups may be formed on a *random* basis (e.g., students count off numbers consecutively from 1 to 4 and form groups with other students who have the same number) or groups may be formed on an *intentional* basis, whereby teammates are selected according to some predetermined criteria. In contrast to traditional approaches to small-group formation, in which students typically choose their own group members or groups are randomly formed by the instructor, CL begins with the intentional selection of group members on the basis of certain criteria that are expected to magnify the positive effects of small-group learning.

For example, teams may be deliberately formed to maximize student exposure to diverse perspectives by grouping students of different: (a) gender, (b) racial, ethnic, or geographical background, or (c) level of prior academic achievement (e.g., their performance on previous classroom tests). The particular criterion used to form groups, and the decision about whether to place students in heterogeneous or homogeneous groups with respect to this criterion, depends on the teacher's educational objective. However, a core principle of CL is that group formation should not be left to chance; instead, an intentional decision is made about the group's composition to create an optimal social-learning environment.

2. Intentional *Team Building*

Small-group learning often involves both cognitive and social risk-taking; students are more likely to take these risks in an interpersonal climate characterized by group cohesiveness, mutual trust, and emotional security. When a group members have a sense of team identity and group solidarity, they're more likely to work in a collaborative and productive fashion. The following team-building practices may be used to create this sense of collective identity and solidarity.

▶ Before launching into the learning task, group members are given informal interaction time to develop social cohesiveness. For example, they:
(a) participate in icebreaker (warm-up) activities when they first form their group (e.g., learning each other's names and sharing information about themselves), or (b) partake in an activity designed to establish a team identity (e.g., come up with a distinctive team name, symbol, mascot, cheer, or handshake). Such team-building exercises help create an *esprit de corps* among group members, which allows them to feel comfortable engaging in subsequent group work that will them to express their personal viewpoints, disagree with each other civilly, and reach consensus in an open (non-defensive) fashion.

▶ Group members consistently use *team language* when working together (e.g., consciously using words like "we" and "our" versus "me" or "mine").

▶ The same group of students work together across successive class periods.

In contrast to traditional small-group discussions or "buzz groups," which usually bring students together sporadically for a relatively short period of time (e.g., a single class period or portion thereof), CL groups may be asked to meet regularly over an extended period of time (e.g., every class period for five weeks or more). Such continuity of contact provides incubation time for interpersonal bonds to form among group members and opportunity from them to congeal into a tightly knit social-support group.

3. Explicit Attention is Paid to Developing Students' Social Intelligence and Collaborative Skills

In addition to cognitive learning outcomes, a major intended outcome of CL is the intentional development of students' interpersonal communication and human relations skills. To achieve this outcome, the following practices are recommended.

▶ Rather than leaving students entirely to their own devices and hoping they will learn to collaborate effectively through trial and error, provide students with explicit instruction on effective skills for communicating and relating to others prior to, and in preparation for, participating small-group work. Such instruction could focus on equipping students with skills for:
  (a) listening actively,
  (b) encouraging and supporting other group members,
  (c) disagreeing civilly,
  (d) resolving conflict, and
  (e) building consensus.

▶ Intentionally recognize and publicly reinforce effective interpersonal behavior displayed by group members.

   During group work, teachers should be on the lookout to praise effective interpersonal communication and collaboration behaviors exhibited by students in their learning groups. In addition to reinforcing the student's exemplary behavior, this practice also calls public attention to it, allowing it to serve as a model for other students to emulate.

▶ Encourage students to reflect on and evaluate the group's social dynamics.

   Students' social intelligence can be developed by having them engage in reflective thought about, and assessment of, their social interactions. Students could reflect on and assess how effectively their group implemented the social skills they were taught prior to embarking on their group work. Students may also reflect on how the group's social dynamics affected them personally. For example, students could assess their level of comfort with respect to: (a) sharing their thoughts with other group members, (b) questioning their teammates, and (c) expressing views that differed from those of other group members.

4. Interdependence among Group Members (Collective Responsibility)

When people interact in an interdependent fashion, they share common goals, engage in collective effort, and as a result of their collective effort, experience mutual benefits. Arguably, positive interdependence is the quintessential feature of cooperative learning; it's what effectively transforms group work ("talking heads") into bona fide teamwork. The following instructional strategies may be used to promote positive interdependence among students working in small groups.

▶ Have groups create a, jointly-constructed work product.

In contrast to small-group discussions, in which students engage in general discussion of a topic or issue, CL groups are expected to generate a *specific work product* that serves a concrete manifestation of the group's *collective effort*. For example, the CL group may complete a common, final product that takes the form of a worksheet, a list or chart of specific ideas, or a PowerPoint slide that can be presented to the instructor or to the class. When a group works toward a common, concrete goal, its members are more likely to stay "on task" and moving toward the group's end goal—the creation of a unified product that captures the team's collective and concerted effort.

▶ Each group member assumes a complementary, interdependent role with respect to development of the group's final product.

When different individuals in the group have a *specific and indispensable role* to play in achieving the group's goal, it increases all members' sense of personal responsibility and commitment to the group. The following interdependent roles may be assigned to, or adopted by, group members to foster positive interdependence.

1) *Functional* roles—each member performs a particular functional duty for the group, such as:
   (a) manager—keeps the group on task and ensures that all its members make contributions
   (b) recorder—keeps a written record of the group's ideas
   (c) spokesperson—orally reports the group's ideas to the instructor or other groups
   (d) processor—monitors the social interaction or interpersonal dynamics of the group process (e.g., whether individuals listen actively and disagree constructively)
   (e) research runner—accesses and retrieves information for the group
   (f) accuracy coach—attends to procedural details and troubleshoots errors.

2) *Resource* roles—each member takes responsibility for providing one key piece of information that will be incorporated into the group's final product (e.g., information from one chapter of the textbook or one unit of classroom instruction).

3) *Cognitive* roles—each member contributes one component or dimension of higher-order thinking to the group's final product (e.g., application, analysis, synthesis, or evaluation).

4) *Perspective* roles—each member contributes an important perspective or viewpoint (e.g., ethical, historical, economic, or global).

Specialized roles such as these serve to ensure that each group member has a well-defined and well-differentiated responsibility to fulfill throughout the work task. A further advantage of such role specialization is that the quality of each member's contribution to the final product can be readily identified and assessed, thus enabling the teacher to hold students individually accountable when assigning grades.

▶ Teammates must first rely on each other before seeking help from the instructor.

This practice for promoting interdependence may be implemented through use of the following strategies:

a) Questions that individual students ask the teacher are redirected back to the students' team so that teammates get in the habit of first relying on each other before turning to their instructor.

b) Teams are required to seek help from other teams before seeking help from the teacher.

c) When a team benefits from the teacher's help, it passes on the help they received to another team needing similar help.

d) Group members respond as team rather than individually. For example: (a) if a group member has a question for the instructor, all group members raise their hands; (b) if the instructor asks a question of the group, all members respond in unison; (c) when the group finishes its work, all members sign their names on the completed work product.

▶ Promoting positive interdependence by providing individual incentives and rewards. to work interdependently

Teachers can reinforce students' interdependent behavior by (a) awarding extra (bonus) points that count toward each student's course grade if all members of the group perform at a high level (e.g., each group member achieves a score of at least 90%), or (b) having the total points that students receive for group work equal the sum of their individual scores plus the scores of their teammates (Slavin, 1990).

5. Ensuring *Individual Accountability* (Personal Responsibility)

Research in social psychology has documented a phenomenon called "social loafing"—individuals exert less effort to achieve a goal when working in a group than when working alone—because their work effort and work quality cannot be as easily identified in a group setting (Karau & Williams, 1993). To combat social loafing and ensure individual accountability in student learning groups, the following procedures may be employed.

▶ Prior to engaging in a small-group task (e.g., small-group discussion), students first work individually to collect ideas they will contribute to the group and put them in writing. These written products are then turned in to the teacher to serve as evidence that each student made an effortful attempt to contribute to the group's work product.

▶ Each member of the group keeps an ongoing record of the specific contributions made to the team (e.g., by recording those personal contributions in a journal or learning log).

▶ The teacher uses *random response sampling*—a procedure in which a member of the group is randomly selected to report the team's response or provide a summary of the group's ideas.

▶ The groups turn in their work product with all members initialing their individual contribution(s) to it.

▶ Following completion of the group task, students engage in:

    a) *self-evaluation*—all members assess the quality of their individual effort or contribution to the group, and

    b) *peer evaluation*—all members assess the effort or contribution of each teammate (peer evaluation).

▶ Students receive individual grades for group work, not a group grade.

Individual accountability is enhanced when students do not receive the same, undifferentiated, group grade. As discussed in chapter 7, high-achieving students often report disliking group work (e.g., group projects) in which all group members receive the same grade because their individual effort and contribution to the group's final product often exceeds the efforts and contributions of their less motivated teammates—who receive exactly the same grade.

6. Teacher Serves as a Roving Facilitator and Consultant to the Learning Groups

In CL, the teacher doesn't become a spectator or passive bystander, but takes on the role of a coach while students work in groups, periodically checking in with them and interacting with them in a more personal and dialogic fashion than would be possible when teaching the whole class. The teacher serves as a group-learning facilitator and consultant, circulating actively among the learning groups, and engaging in such behaviors such as:

▶ clarifying task expectations,

▶ reinforcing positive instances of cooperative behavior,

▶ catalyzing dialogue among group members,

▶ offering encouragement to groups that may be struggling, and

▶ issuing timely questions designed to promote reflection, elaboration, and higher-order thinking.

By taking an active role with students while they engage in work in small-group work, teachers not only facilitate the group-learning process, they also gain access to students' thought processes, learning strategies, and ways of they relate to others.

7. Creating Opportunities for Intergroup Interaction and Integration of Ideas across Different Learning Groups

Although there may be many occasions where small-group work is an end in itself and cross-group interaction is unnecessary, there are benefits associated with having students access integrate ideas generated across groups. Promoting communication between different learning groups and synthesizing their separate work products has three key benefits:

a) It brings a sense of *closure* to the learning experience.
b) It generates *synergy* across groups.
c) It creates a sense of class *community* by connecting the experiences of small, separated subgroups into a large, unified "group of groups."

The following practices may be used to facilitate intergroup interaction and integration of their ideas.

▶ After completing their work in small groups, one student from each group assumes the role of "plenary reporter" whose job is to share the group's main ideas with the entire class. The teacher records the main ideas reported from each group, validates their efforts, and identifies both commonalities and differences that emerge across groups.

▶ Following small-group work, a "roving reporter" from each team visits other groups to share her team's ideas. Remaining members of her team stay together and play the role of "listener-synthesizer"— whose job is to actively listen to ideas presented by successive roving reporters from other groups and integrate those ideas with ideas generated by their own group (Kagan, 1992).

▶ After completing the small-group task, each learning team rotates clockwise and merges with another small group to share and synthesize their separate work. This share-and-synthesize process continues until each small group has had a paired interaction with every other small group, after which each small group creates a final product that integrates its own ideas with the ideas obtained through their successive exchanges with other groups.

These above-three procedures enable learning group to access and connect their ideas with the ideas of other groups, and in so doing, generate intergroup synergy and a stronger sense of class community.

Glossary

Ableism: prejudice displayed toward people who are disabled or handicapped (physically, mentally, or emotionally).

Achievement Gap: differences in average academic performance between ethnic and racial groups.

Affirmative Action: laws enacted to promote equal opportunity for employment, education, and athletic participation among groups whose opportunities have been limited by past or current discrimination.

Ageism: prejudice or discrimination toward certain age groups, particularly the elderly.

American Dream: a fundamental value held by the United States that all its citizens should have the freedom and opportunity to achieve prosperity and gain upward social mobility through hard work, regardless of their socioeconomic, national, racial, or ethnic origins.

American Indian or Alaska Native: people whose lineage may be traced to humans who were the original inhabitants of North and South America (including Central America), and who continue to maintain their tribal affiliation or attachment.

Anti-bias Curriculum: an educational process designed to promote understanding and fair treatment of groups of different race, ethnicity, social class, gender, etc.

Anti-racist Curriculum: an educational process that engages both educators and students in the detection and dismantling of structural racial discrimination in the classroom, school, and community.

Anti-Semitism: prejudice or discrimination directed at Jews and other people who practice the religion of Judaism.

Apartheid: an institutionalized system of "legal racism" supported by a nation's government. (Apartheid derives from a word in the Afrikaans language, meaning "apartness.")

Asian: people whose lineage may be traced to humans who were the original inhabitants of the Far East, Southeast Asia, or the Indian subcontinent, including: Cambodia, China, India, Japan, Korea, Malaysia, Pakistan, the Philippine Islands, Thailand, and Vietnam.

Backward Design: a lesson-planning process that begins with the end (learning outcome) in mind and works backward from the intended outcome to determine what subject matter and instructional method would best achieve that outcome.

Bias: predisposition toward judging something or someone (positively or negatively) before the facts are known.

Classism: prejudice or discrimination based on social class, particularly toward people of lower socioeconomic status.

Cognitive Dissonance: a state of cognitive (mental) disequilibrium or imbalance that disrupts habitual ways of thinking by forcing the mind to deal with conflicting perspectives simultaneously.

Collaborative Learning: a form of group learning in which students go beyond simply sharing and generating ideas to reaching consensus or making a unified group decision about the ideas they generate.

Collateral Learning: what students learn or take away from a lesson beyond the lesson's intended learning outcome.

Colorism: a form of racism among people of the same racial or ethnic groups that involves bias against other members of their group with darker skin color.

Comparative Cultural Perspective: a reference point that positions us to see more clearly how our particular cultural background has shaped who we are.

Cooperative Learning: a structured form of collaborative learning in which members of a learning team take on specific tasks or roles that they perform individually, thus ensuring individual accountability; yet the roles are interdependent, requiring group members to rely on one another to achieve a common goal (e.g., a unified work product), thus ensuring collective responsibility.

Critical Multiculturalism: an educational process in which students analyze power relationships and inequalities across different cultural groups.

Critical Race Theory (CRT): a perspective that views **race** as not being biologically based, but as a socially constructed concept originally constructed by whites to provide them with advantages or privileges denied to people of color, which continue to disadvantage people of color today.

Criterion-referenced Grading: a grading system that involves determining a student's grade on the basis of a set, performance-based standard or criterion (e.g., percentage of questions the student answers correctly).

Cultural Appropriation: a process in which a dominant culture incorporates into its culture something taken from a cultural group that has been systematically oppressed by the dominant group.

Glossary   **211**

Cultural Pluralism: a society in which smaller cultural groups maintain their unique cultural identities, and their customs and practices are accepted by the larger, dominant culture.

Culturally Inclusive Assessment: using different forms of assessment in ways that effectively accommodate and equitably evaluate students from diverse cultural backgrounds.

Culturally Relevant Teaching (a.k.a. Culturally Responsive Pedagogy): using instructional methods that are relevant and responsive to students from different cultural backgrounds.

Culture: a distinctive pattern of behaviors, beliefs, and values learned by a group of people who share the same social heritage, traditions and ways of living (e.g., their language, fashion, food, art, music, and spiritual beliefs).

Deep Learning: a learning process in which students actively *transform* information they receive into knowledge they "construct" by building it onto what they already know.

Differentiated Instruction: teaching that involves use of a variety of instructional strategies, providing students with different ways to learn and demonstrate what they have learned.

Discrimination: unequal and unfair treatment of a person or group of people motivated by bias or prejudice.

Disenfranchised Group: a social group that has been deprived of rights or privileges.

Divergent Thinking: expansive thinking takes off in different directions, rather than converging on one (and only one) correct answer.

Diversity: the variety of differences among people that make up humanity (the human species).

Diversity Education: an educational process that empowers students to evaluate ideas in terms of their cultural validity and potential bias, and actively engages students in learning experiences that foster interaction with different cultural groups.

Domestic Diversity: cultural differences that exist within the same nation.

Educational Attainment: the highest level of education achieved by a person or group of people.

Empathy: sensitivity to the emotions and feelings of others.

Equality: treating everyone the same.

Equity: treating everyone fairly.

Essentializing: tendency to automatically assume that a specific member of a cultural group possesses the same characteristics generally (or stereotypically) associated with that person's cultural group.

Ethnic Group (Ethnicity): a group of people sharing the same cultural characteristics that have been learned through shared social experiences.

Ethnocentrism: viewing one's own culture or ethnic group as "normal" or "superior" and other cultures as "deficient" or "inferior."

Extrinsic Motivation: motivation driven by external factors (e.g., getting good grades and pleasing parents).

Familiarity Principle: tendency for people to perceive what's familiar as being "good" or better than what's unfamiliar.

Fixed Mindset: belief that a person has a fixed or set amount of intelligence, which cannot be changed or grown.

Formative Evaluation: using the results of assessment to improve the effectiveness of teaching and learning.

Generation 1.5: children of immigrants who have received part of their education in another country and another part in the United States.

Genocide: mass murdering of a particular ethnic or racial group motivated by prejudice.

Groupthink: tendency for like-minded members of the same group not to challenge one another's ideas, resulting in the group overlooking flaws or biases in their own thinking and reaching decisions that are inaccurate or incomplete.

Growth Mindset: the belief that intelligence is not fixed or preset, but can be grown or developed.

Hate Crime: an extreme, aggressive act of discrimination toward a group of people motivated by prejudice (e.g., group-targeted vandalism, assault, or genocide).

Hate Group: an organized group whose primary purpose is to incite prejudice, discrimination, or aggression toward other groups of people based on their ethnicity, race, religion, sexual orientation, etc.

Heterosexism: belief that heterosexuality is the only acceptable sexual orientation.

Higher-Order Thinking: mental activity that involves higher or more advanced thought processes than recalling facts or information.

Homophobia: extreme fear or hatred of homosexuals.

Homosocial Reproduction: the tendency for employees who leave an organization to be replaced by employees with similar characteristics (e.g., race and gender).

Human Relations Skills: ability to relate to others in an effective and socially intelligent manner.

Humanity: universal aspects of the human experience that are shared by all people from all cultures.

Identity Politics: basing political viewpoints and alliances primarily or exclusively on how they impact a particular social group (e.g., the group's gender, race, or religion).

Implicit Bias: an unconsciously-held bias about a particular social group.

Inclusive Pedagogy: a student-centered teaching process that motivates and engages learners from all cultural backgrounds by allowing their voices to be heard and giving them equal opportunity to participate in the learning process.

Individuality: differences among individuals who comprise the same social group.

Institutional Racism: racial discrimination rooted in organizational policies and practices that disadvantage certain racial groups (e.g., race-based discrimination in mortgage lending, housing, or bank loans).

Intentional Group Formation: deliberately forming learning groups of students with certain characteristics to enhance the learning process (e.g., groups composed of students from diverse backgrounds to enhance multicultural awareness and appreciation of diverse perspectives).

Intercultural Communication: communication taking place between individuals from different cultures.

Intercultural Competence: the ability to appreciate and learn from human differences and to interact effectively with people from diverse cultural backgrounds.

Interdependence: a form of collaborative group work in which group members rely on one another to achieve a common goal.

International Diversity: cultural differences that exist between different nations.

Interpersonal Communication Skills: ability to listen and speak effectively when interacting with others.

Interpersonal Intelligence (Social Intelligence): ability to understand, empathize, and relate to others.

Intersectionality: when membership in two or more disadvantaged social categories (e.g., race and social class) intersect to exert a combined effect that further disadvantages people holding joint membership in these multiple categories.

Intrinsic Motivation: motivation driven by internal factors (e.g., students' personal interest in the subject matter being taught or excitement about how it is being taught).

"Jim Crow" Laws: formal and informal laws created by whites to segregate blacks after the abolition of slavery.

Jingoism: excessive interest and belief in the superiority of one's own nation (without acknowledging its mistakes or weaknesses), which is often accompanied by an aggressive, self-serving foreign policy that neglects the needs of other nations or the common needs of all nations.

Latina: Hispanic female.

Latino: Hispanic male.

Latinx: a person of Latin American origin or descen, and a gender-neutral way to refer to someone who is either Latina or Latino.

LGBTQ: lesbian, gay, bisexual, transgendered, and questioning.

Mainstream Curriculum: the traditional, Eurocentric, male-centered curriculum that gives little or no attention to the perspectives and contributions of non-dominant social and cultural groups.

Majority Group: a group whose membership accounts for more than one-half of the population.

Mastery Learning: model of education which posits that initial differences in student achievement on tests and other measures of learning do not reflect differences in their ability or potential to learn, but reflect differences in the amount of time, practice, and feedback students need to master the material.

Melting Pot: a metaphor for a society in which different cultures—such as different cultures brought by immigrants to the U.S.—should "melt away" and assimilated into the dominant culture.

Microaggression: subtle hostile messages that are either intentionally or unintentionally aimed at members of a marginalized group (e.g., asking someone who is a Hispanic person living in America: "Where are you really from?").

Minority Group: a group whose membership accounts for less than one-half of the population.

Multicultural: cultural differences that exist within the same society or nation.

Multicultural Curriculum: a curriculum that integrates diverse cultural perspectives into the mainstream curriculum.

Multiculturalism: a perspective that cultural differences in a society should be preserved and appreciated.

Multiple Intelligences: different talents or abilities that humans possess, which include forms of intelligence other than intellectual intelligence (e.g., social and emotional intelligence)

Multiple Perspective-Taking: viewing ideas and issues from multiple angles or vantage points.

Multiracial Family: a family composed of members from different races.

Native Hawaiian or Pacific Islander: people whose lineage may be traced to humans who were the original inhabitants of Hawaii, Guam, Samoa, and other Pacific Islands.

Nativism: a political policy of preserving or advancing the interests of native inhabitants over those of immigrants, and opposition to immigration based on fears that foreigners (particularly from certain foreign nations) will dilute or displace the home nation's traditional cultural norms and values.

Non-Western Cultures: non-European cultures, such as Asian, African, Indian, Latin American, and Middle Eastern.

Norm-referenced Grading: a grading system that bases a student's grade on how well the student performs in relation to other students.

One-minute Paper: a short, informal writing exercise (taking one minute or less to complete) that prompts students to reflect on the day's lesson.

Open-ended Questions: teacher-posed questions that do not call for just one "correct" answer, but which invite a variety of acceptable responses.

Overrepresented Group: a social group whose percentage (proportion) of a specific subpopulation is higher than its percentage of the overall population. For example, the percentage of people of color living below the poverty line in America is higher than the percentage in the overall percentage of Americans living in poverty.

Own-race Bias: tendency for people to be able to detect differences between the faces of individuals from their own race better than individuals from other races.

Personal Validation: the self-affirming feeling that students experience when they are recognized as individuals, sense that they matter to their teacher, and believe their teacher cares about them.

Positionality: the idea that peoples' cultural background or position strongly influences the knowledge they construct, create, and disseminate.

Prejudice: a negative bias (pre-judgment) about another group of people.

Privilege: an unearned advantage granted to a person or group of people that is not granted to others.

Privileged Legacy: an unearned advantage passed on across generations, such as inheriting money or gaining admission to a college because a family member previously attended the college or gave money to the college.

Qualitative Assessment: gathering non-numerical data to assess student learning (e.g., students' spoken or written words)

Quantitative Assessment: assessing student learning with numerical data (e.g., students' scores on multiple-choice tests)

Race: people who have been categorized into a social group based on their physical traits, such as their skin color or facial characteristics.

Racial Profiling: Investigating or arresting an individual for an alleged crime based on the individual's race, ethnicity, or national origin, and without sufficient incriminating evidence.

Racism: belief that one's own racial group is superior to another group and expressing that belief in attitude (prejudice) or action (discrimination).

Redlining: the practice of marking red lines on a map to indicate neighborhoods where banks will not invest or lend money, many of which are neighborhoods inhabited predominantly by African Americans and other minority groups.

Regional Bias: prejudice or discrimination toward people based on the geographical region in which they are born and raised (e.g., Northerners holding biased views of Southerners and vice versa).

Religious Bigotry (a.k.a. Religious Intolerance): denying the right of people to hold religious beliefs or to hold religious beliefs that differ from one's own.

Scapegoating: blaming a person or social group for one's personal frustrations or failures without evidence or reason.

Segregation: an intentional decision made by a social group to separate itself (socially or physically) from another social group.

Selective Listening: selectively "tuning into" conversational topics that relate only to the listener's personal interests or that support the listener's personal viewpoints, and "tuning out" everything else.

Selective Memory: tendency for prejudiced people to remember information that reinforces their bias and forget information that contradicts it.

Selective Perception: tendency for biased (prejudiced) people to see what supports their bias and fail to see what contradicts it.

Self-Similarity Principle: the tendency for people to associate and develop relationships with others whose backgrounds, beliefs, and interests are similar to their own.

Sexism: prejudice or discrimination toward others based on their sex or gender.

Sexual Diversity: differences in how humans experience and express their sexuality, including differences in sexual orientation—what gender (male or female) an individual is sexually attracted to, and sexual identity—what gender an individual identifies with or considers himself/herself to be.

Slavery: forced labor in which people are viewed as property, held against their will, and deprived of the right to wages.

Social Capital: advantages and privileges afforded to people by virtue of who they know (e.g., their personal contacts with employers, college admissions personnel, or "power players" in the legal and political system).

Social Constructivist Theory: a learning theory positing that thinking involves "internal" (mental) representations of conversations which people have with other people. Consequently, if people engage in dialogue with others from diverse backgrounds, it enriches the variety and complexity of their thinking.

Social Identity: the social group(s) an individual identifies with, which, in turn, shape(s) that person's identity.

Social Intelligence (a.k.a. Interpersonal Intelligence): ability to effectively communicate and relate to others.

Socialization: the process through which a person's attitudes, beliefs, etc. are learned through social experiences.

Socially Constructed Knowledge: knowledge built up through interpersonal interaction and dialogue with others.

Society: a group of people organized under the same social system (e.g., same system of government, justice, and education).

Socioeconomic Status: the social class of a group of people based on their level of education, income level, and occupational prestige.

Stereotype Threat: tendency for members of a group to perform more poorly on a task when they encounter negative stereotypes about their group's ability to perform that task.

Stereotyping: viewing all (or virtually all) members of the same social group as having similar personal characteristics.

Stigmatizing: ascribing inferior or unfavorable traits to members of a particular social group.

Subordinate Group: a group with less societal power than the majority or dominant group.

Summative Evaluation: assessment that is intended to "sum up" and prove that student learning has taken place.

Team-Building Exercises: icebreaker activities that are engaged in before group work to "warm up" group members to each other and build a sense of team spirit.

Terrorism: acts of violence committed against civilians motivated by political or religious prejudice.

Think-Pair-Share: a small-group learning procedure in which students first gather their thoughts individually and then join a partner to share their thoughts verbally.

Tokenism: a disingenuous and superficial attempt to appear inclusive or promote equality by including a very small number of people from underrepresented groups.

Underrepresented Group: a group whose representation in a specific subpopulation is lower than its representation in the general (overall) population. For example, the percentage of women in the specific field of engineering is lower than their percentage in the general population.

Universal Design for Learning (UDL): a cognitive neuroscience-based model designed to promote the learning of all students through use of diverse methods of instruction and assessment.

Western Culture (Western Civilization): culture that originated in, or is associated with, Europe.

White: people whose lineage may be traced to humans who were the original inhabitants Europe, the Middle East, or North Africa.

White Genocide (a.k.a. "Replacement Theory"): a racist conspiracy theory contending that white people are being displaced by immigrants and people of color, with the secret assistance of prominent Jews.

White Supremacy: the view that whites are a genetically superior group, should maintain dominance over other racial groups, or live in a whites-only society

Xenophobia: extreme fear or hatred of foreigners, outsiders, or strangers.

Index

Printed in the USA
CPSIA information can be obtained
at www.ICGtesting.com
JSHW050314010823
45716JS00002B/8